BLUE POLITICS:
PORNOGRAPHY AND THE LAW
IN THE AGE OF FEMINISM

In 1985 the Special Committee on Pornography and Prostitution, the Fraser Committee, recommended the criminalization of violent and degrading sexually explicit material on the ground that it harmed women. On two occasions (in 1986 with Bill C-114 and in 1987 with Bill C-54) the Mulroney government proposed a more restrictive approach to the regulation of pornography. Despite the support of various feminist and religious / family-oriented organizations, the government's attempts at law reform failed. Obscenity provisions were neither repealed nor replaced by a law criminalizing pornography. *Blue Politics* looks at the social and political mechanisms that initiated, shaped, and finally defeated the controversial legal proposals of the Conservative government in the 1980s.

Dany Lacombe documents the emergence of a feminist definition of pornography, analyses the impact this definition had on the debate between conservative and civil libertarian organizations, and identifies the emergence of groups who strongly resisted the attempt to reform the law: feminists against censorship and sex radicals. Finally, she examines the way in which institutional practices are shaped by and yet shape the power relations between groups. The emphasis is on the way such power relations are embodied in the policy-making process.

Drawing on Michel Foucault's concept of 'power/knowledge,' Lacombe reveals how the process to criminalize pornography inaugurated a controversial politics that produced collective identities and transformed power relations. She shows law reform as a strategy that both constrains and enables action.

DANY LACOMBE is assistant professor at the School of Criminology, Simon Fraser University.

DANY LACOMBE

Blue Politics: Pornography and the Law in the Age of Feminism

UNIVERSITY OF TORONTO PRESS
Toronto Buffalo London

© University of Toronto Press Incorporated 1994
Toronto Buffalo London
Printed in Canada

ISBN 0-8020-2854-3 (cloth)
ISBN 0-8020-7352-2 (paper)

Printed on acid-free paper

Canadian Cataloguing in Publication Data

Lacombe, Dany
  Blue politics : pornography and the law in the
  age of feminism

  Includes bibliographical references and index.
  ISBN 0-8020-2854-3 (bound)   ISBN 0-8020-7352-2 (pbk.)

  1. Pornography – Political aspects – Canada.
  2. Pornography – Social aspects – Canada.
  3. Obscenity (Law) – Canada.   4. Feminism – Canada.
  I. Title.

HQ471.L34 1994   363.4'7'0971   C93-095570-6

University of Toronto Press acknowledges the financial
assistance to its publishing program of the Canada
Council and the Ontario Arts Council.

Pour Kegan Doyle
et en mémoire de Muriel Lacombe

Contents

Acknowledgments

I want to express my profound gratitude and appreciation to Professors Richard V. Ericson and Michal Bodemann for their intellectual guidance, ongoing support, and friendship. My research also benefited from the intellectual encouragement of Marie-Andrée Bertrand, Pat Carlen, Stanley Cohen, Dawn Currie, Tony Jefferson, Lorna Marsden, Dario Melossi, Clifford Shearing, Carol Smart, and Barbara Herrnstein Smith.

In addition I want to thank a number of institutions that supported me during the completion of this research. The Centre of Criminology and the Department of Sociology at the University of Toronto, the Ontario government, the Solicitor General of Canada, and the Social Sciences and Humanities Research Council of Canada have funded me generously. The staff of the Criminology Library at the University of Toronto has been of great help; I specifically want to offer my gratitude to Jane Gladstone for her generous assistance. In Paris, several institutions were invaluable to me. I thank the Ecole des Hautes Etudes en Sciences Sociales, which gave me permission to study with Professors Pierre Bourdieu and Alain Touraine; le Collège International de Philosophie, which allowed me to study with Chantal Mouffe; le Centre Michel Foucault (per François Ewald), and le Centre de Recherche sur la Sociologie du Droit et les Institutions Pénales, CESDIP-CNRS (per Claude Faugeron). I am especially grateful to the administrative, secretarial, and library staff of CESDIP and the GERN (Groupe Européen de Recherche sur les Normativités) for welcoming and accommodating me so kindly. In addition, it is with great pleasure that I thank the University of Toronto Press. Kathleen Johnson did a wonderful job of editing and improving the book; I thank her very much. I am greatly indebted to Virgil Duff for his continual encouragement, especially at times when I felt quite discouraged with the whole project. His friendship was very valuable.

I could not have completed this book without the moral and intellectual support of friends and colleagues, who in their own ways found time and energy to be there for me. I thank Zaheer Baber, Monica Bristol, Kevin Carriere, Mary Condon, Len Guenther, Despina Iliopoulou, Gail Kellough, Sylvie Labrosse, Tammy Landau, Susan Lewthwaite, Maeve McMahon, and all the eccentric housemates I had at the Borden Street Co-op.

I want to express my profound gratitude to my family: to my sister Linda and my brother Norman for the friendly support they gave me by way of telephone calls, letters, and visits; to my father, Roland, for all his love, respect, and magnanimity; and most of all, to my mother, the late Muriel Lacombe, for her inspirational sense of justice and liberty.

Finally, I want to express my deep appreciation of and admiration for Kegan Doyle, who painstakingly edited this book, scrutinized my arguments, challenged even my most cherished ideas, and, most important, never minded the hardship and always applauded the achievements. I owe him my most heartfelt thanks.

BLUE POLITICS:
PORNOGRAPHY AND THE LAW
IN THE AGE OF FEMINISM

1

Introduction

Blue Politics is about pornography, law reform, and political identities. It explores on the one hand the production of pornography as an object of knowledge and of institutional practices, and on the other the production of new collective identities as they were both deployed in the feminist campaign to reform obscenity legislation in Canada during the 1980s.

Sparked by the development of a feminist critique of pornography – one that linked pornography with harm to women – a new anti-pornography movement organized to criminalize violent and degrading sexual representations, arguing that such representations undermined women's efforts to be treated as equal citizens. The ability of this novel ground for criminalization to mobilize social actors represented a radical change in the politics of pornography. To understand this change, we need to backtrack two hundred years. Until the nineteenth century, discussions or representations of sex that did not confront the authority of either the church or the sovereign could, for the most part, freely circulate. With the emergence of various societies for the reform of morals and the suppression of vice in the later part of the eighteenth century, sex was increasingly constituted as obscene when it offended 'public morality.' This notion, however, was not self-evident; it was constructed and defended by the bourgeoisie, part of whose hegemony was based on its being able to differentiate itself at once from the decadent aristocracy and from the ignorant masses (Foucault, 1980a). Once it asserted itself as a distinct class, the bourgeoisie used this 'public' morality to spread its virtues throughout the social body. Pornography, in this context, was not totally suppressed; rather, it was the privilege of the educated male élite because it was believed to corrupt women, children, and the lower orders. Indeed, the nineteenth-century bourgeoisie feared the dissemination of pornography: the greater availability of written texts and the emergence of a new class of readers brought about by advances in print technologies and educational reforms meant more opportunities for the 'seduction of innocents' (Ross, 1989: 178). The fear that sexual material could 'degrade' and 'corrupt' the morals of those weak readers provided the main justification in England in 1857 for legislating against the 'obscene.'[1] Judge Cockburn, who provided the first legal definition of obscenity eleven years after the proclamation of the 1857 legislation, described obscenity's harmful influence on morality: 'I think the test of obscenity is this, whether the tendency of the matter charged as obscenity is to deprave or corrupt those whose minds are open to such immoral influences, and into whose hands a publication of this sort may fall.'[2] Canadian courts adopted this obscenity test, later known as the *Hicklin* test, which prevailed for almost a century. This test did not lead to consistent and predictable practices (Charles, 1966), and in the second half of the 1950s it became the object of a plethora of criticism. Legal and academic objectors pointed to the subjective, speculative nature of the test; they also pointed to its restrictive aspects, and in particular, to the way in which it limited creative and literary expression. The public criticized the obscenity legislation in more conservative terms. The increased availability and widespread distribution in the post-Second World War years of cheap mass-produced sex-oriented material, material without any pretence of literary merit, created a sense of unease in Canada. Many feared that such material would find its way into the hands of young people, who would learn to imitate the actions depicted, and ultimately would become morally perverted (see Canada, 1952: 134; Charles, 1966). They believed that the subjective nature of the *Hicklin* test was directly responsible for the increased availability of this material; consequently, they called for tightening the law.

Dissatisfaction with the obscenity legislation was voiced until 1959, when the Conservative government enacted the first statutory definition of obscenity, a definition the Supreme Court of Canada declared in 1992 in line with the Charter of Rights and Freedoms:[3] 'For the purpose of the Act, any publication a dominant characteristic of which is the undue exploitation of sex, or of sex and any one or more of the following subjects, namely, crime, horror, cruelty and violence shall be deemed to be obscene.'

This new statutory definition of obscenity did not make the determination of obscenity any easier. In the second half of the 1960s, a period characterized by an intense 'politicization' of sexuality, the attempt to instil a particular practice of manners became highly problematic and produced a confrontation between conservatives and liberals over the value of pornography and sex itself (Williams, 1989). Indeed, the pornography debate of the 1960s revolved around a simple question: were representations of sex socially and morally dangerous or sexually liberating?

At the time it became increasingly clear to many in both the public culture and the scientific community that sexually explicit material was not harmful, and consequently that every citizen had the right to read what she or he wanted. Civil liberties organizations attempted to repeal obscenity legislation; they argued that by imposing a single standard of morality the state limited freedom of expression. The courts responded to this attack by developing 'objective' tests, tests that would provide an indisputable definition of obscenity. The courts made it acceptable to talk about sex as long as the discussion did not constitute 'dirt for dirt's sake,' that is, as long as the discussion (or representation) had a serious purpose and treated sex with sincerity and honesty rather than pandering to the sensualist.[4] The law thus recognized that sex had become a relevant contemporary issue, one that needed to be elucidated, talked about, examined, and made known. In this context, the law asserted its responsibility to ensure a frank, candid, and mature discussion.[5]

Linda Williams (1989) contends, in *Hard Core: Power, Pleasure, and the 'Frenzy of the Visible,'* that the 'problematization' of sex since the 1950s has not taken place in the courts alone. In fact, she argues that the legal attempt to circumscribe the obscene has been supported and undermined by new and conflicting 'truths' about sex, such as those produced by sexology, medical science, and the various groups struggling for sexual liberation. It is in the context of an intensified public debate about the nature of sex that we must locate the emergence of a feminist critique of pornography in the late 1970s.

Feminists replaced sex with sexism as the focus of the pornography debate. They argued that the objectification, degradation, and dehumanization of women inherent in pornography contributed to a climate in which women were systematically oppressed. The feminist analysis of pornography claimed to reveal the inability of existing obscenity legislation to eliminate the harm pornography inflicts on women. The subject-matter of obscenity as defined in the Canadian Criminal Code is sex or sex linked with crime, horror, cruelty, or violence. Feminists found the law's emphasis on sex to be outmoded, a relic of our puritan heritage that could not suppress the circulation of truly degrading depictions of women. Therefore, they fought for the replacement of that obscenity legislation with a law that would get at the harm pornography causes to women's right to equality.

The feminist case against pornography became hegemonic in the 1980s, in the sense that it caused conservative and civil liberties organizations to revise their 1960s positions to such an extent that they discussed pornography in terms of women's oppression. Agreeing with feminists, conservative organizations condemned pornography because of its violent and dehumanizing nature and its harmful effects on women; however, they contended that erotica – the sexually explicit material feminists would not want to censor – was as harmful, because it adversely affected the institutions of family and marriage. Civil libertarians also condemned the degrading representations of women in pornography, but could not support their criminalization because science had not proved that they harmed women.

The feminist anti-pornography discourse and its accompanying call for censorship provoked new strategies of resistance. Many resented the feminist orthodoxy on pornography. To summarize briefly, this orthodoxy is premised on two notions of the social world. From a more radical feminist perspective, society is a patriarchy, a system of gender oppression that is systematic and all-encompassing, exercised universally and transhistorically. Evidence of that oppression is the continuum in history of male violence against women, from incest to wife battering or clitoridectomy, from soft-core porn to rape and sexual murder (Ross, 1989: 186). The universal power men hold over women is said to be grounded in biology: male sexuality relentlessly encroaches on feminine sexuality – a nurturing, loving, caring, and natural sexuality. From a liberal feminist perspective, contemporary society is a liberal democratic structure organized by patriarchal social relations. Patriarchy is a system of gender socialization that discriminates against women. The pervasiveness of sex-role stereotyping in society is seen as responsible for women's second-class status because it perpetuates the notion that women are biologically and socially inferior and better suited for certain 'feminine' activities. The power of men is understood as stemming from sexist attitudes and perceptions produced by sex-role stereotyping. In both contexts pornography appears as one of the most influential instruments in mass culture contributing to the subordination of women. The eradication of pornography is, consequently, a necessary condition for the creation of a totally different society – one in which freedom, choice, and consent would truly flourish.

The most trenchant critique of the feminist anti-pornography discourse originated within the feminist community itself. It was initially articulated by intellectuals and artists who feared the political consequences of censorship, and later by sex radicals and sex workers who opposed the feminists' stereotyping.

In particular, feminists against censorship organized around their identity as socialist feminists and developed a critique of pornography and women's oppression that located such practices in the context of capitalist and patriarchal social relations. They criticized the unitary model of male power/female victimization used by the feminist anti-pornography movement, because it did not adequately address the role of capitalism in the commodification and reproduction of a repressive (heterosexual, monogamous, patriarchal) sexuality. They pointed to the insidious censorship practices of the authorities, directed specifically at the work of artists involved in the production of sexually explicit material challenging (hetero)sexual forms of representation. They argued that such practices epitomized the inherent sexist and capitalist biases of state agencies and cautioned feminists not to empower these agencies by giving them the mandate to protect women. They proposed instead to enhance the democratic rights of women by directly empowering them, providing them with services such as rape crisis centres, facilities for sexually assaulted women, and educational opportunities. Feminists against censorship also requested the enhancement of the democratic rights of sexual minorities and feminist artists involved in the consumption and production of sexually explicit material that confronted patriarchal and capitalist relations. In other words, feminists against censorship argued for the right of sexual minorities and feminists to speak against mainstream pornography by producing and consuming 'alternative' sexual images.

Sex radicals and sex workers, for whom pornography is essential, reacted strongly against the moralistic assumptions and prescriptions of the feminist anti-pornography discourse.[6] Because this discourse denies the pleasure some women experience consuming and producing pornography, sex radicals and sex workers found it repressively correct. Sex radicals challenged the feminist argument against pornography by pointing to the diversity of the genre and the diversity of people's, and especially women's, responses to that genre. Instead of reducing these responses to 'the machinations of the social system' (Rubin, 1984: 306), they sought to understand the 'liberatory possibilities' of pornography (Ross, 1989: 188), the ways in which pornography could be used to subvert the social system.

The resistance within feminism to the anti-pornography discourse provoked a re-evaluation of feminism in general. The fact that many women were willing consumers and producers of pornography, seemingly complicit with the 'male gaze' yet able to deflect and appropriate it, struck a blow to the feminist belief that pornography was about oppression only – the belief, in other words, that those who learned to like pornography were victims of patriarchy or capitalism, or both. The admission that pornography is used diversely and by diverse groups meant that pornographic texts could no longer be interpreted simply as the essential ingredient that made sexism palatable in society at large. Thus the feminist resistance to the anti-pornography movement inaugurated an attempt to rethink pornography in a way that (1) would localize it in its (capitalist and patriarchal) social relations of production; (2) account for the way these social relations create new, although not necessarily oppressive, desires; and (3) pay attention to the complexity of the world of desires.

This brief history of the pornography debate reveals some of the changes that have taken place over time in the construction of pornography as a social problem. Moving from a discussion of pornography's corrupting impact on morality to one about the harm it causes to women, moving from a discussion of pornography's sexually liberating effects on society to one about its subversive and transgressive possibilities, we have witnessed how pornography has been a highly controversial yet highly malleable object of knowledge. We have also seen how changes in the understanding of pornography implied changes in the understanding of sexuality and self.

Despite the lack of consensus in the 1980s as to what about pornography made it a social problem, the Canadian government, feeling pressured to act, attempted to reform the obscenity law several times. In 1985 the Special Committee on Pornography and Prostitution (the

Fraser Committee) recommended the criminalization of violent and degrading sexually explicit material on the basis that it harmed women. Rejecting this approach as too liberal, the Conservative government proposed on two different occasions – in 1986 with Bill C-114 and in 1987 with Bill C-54 – a much more restrictive approach to the regulation of sexual representations. Despite the support of feminist and religious/family-oriented organizations, the government's attempts at law reform failed: obscenity provisions were neither repealed nor replaced by a law criminalizing pornography. However, in 1992, five years after the latest anti-pornography proposal, the Supreme Court of Canada held, in *R.v. Butler*, that legislative efforts at pornography law reform were unnecessary because the existing obscenity provisions of the Criminal Code were precise enough to deal with any problems pornography poses for women. The court developed a new test to determine obscenity that directly institutionalized the feminist argument about the harm pornography inflicts on women. In the light of the Charter of Rights and Freedoms, the court declared that the protection of sexual morality could no longer be the rationale for prohibiting obscenity; what made something obscene was the harm that it inflicted on women in their attempt to be free and equal subjects. What makes sexual representations obscene is not the sex but the violent and degrading nature of the sex, because of the impact such representations have on women's right to equality. This decision, then, brought the feminist campaign to proscribe pornography to an end. Time will tell whether this feminist victory will either reproduce or transform the 'order of things.'

Law Reform and 'the Order of Things'

The public campaign in the 1980s to proscribe pornography provides a fertile ground for a critique of existing accounts of law reform. The social constructionist and Marxist traditions in the social sciences have narrativized law reform as part of the 'dispersal of social control,' as part of the inevitable reproduction of 'the order of things.'[7] Attempts to reform the criminal justice system have failed, these traditions tell us, and, worse still, have led to the increased penetration and expansion of techniques of social control into the whole of the social body (Cohen, 1985: 77). Rather than 'doing good,' law reform legitimates and perpetuates the system without fundamentally modifying it; it simply 're-forms,' 're-orders,' and 're-produces' the structure of domination in society (Ericson, 1987: 26). Stanley Cohen, for example, cautions us against penal reform, arguing that alternatives to the criminal justice system are simply 'add-ons' that result in the 'widening of the net of social control' (1979, 1983, 1985). Ericson and Baranek (1982) conclude their analysis of the accused in the criminal justice system by comparing his position to that of the citizen in relationship to the law: human rights, justice, and 'due process' are all reduced to techniques of power re-producing social control (see also McBarnett, 1981). Fudge and Glasbeek (1992) assert that the Charter of Rights and Freedoms cannot bring 'real' change, because it is a strategy essentially inscribed in the logic of reproduction of late capitalism. The Charter simply perpetuates social and economic inequality. Shearing and Stenning (1984) present Disney World as the quintessence of disciplinary power: the fences, the monorail, the parking, the instructions to the visitors, the employees, and the Disney characters – in sum, all that constitutes Disney's fantastic universe – function to subject, discipline, and normalize the unsuspecting fun-seeker. While it may seem that I have caricatured the abovementioned studies, the conventional wisdom on law reform is actually that simple: 'nothing works.' No matter where or when, it is the same as it ever was – social control.

This view of law reform as a 'technique of disciplinary power' is based on an essentialist reading of the work of Michel Foucault, a reading that must be abandoned. Among the many negative aspects of this reading is the construction of law reform along a unitary and circular logic. 'Social problems' are created by the state to persuade the public to support law reform as the only sensible solution. Agents of the state, working with institutions in the public culture such as the media and the social sciences, engineer social problems capable of promoting public support to reinforce the same constraining social order. Law reform, then, is hopelessly compromised in the logic of social control. Thus the law reform process is described in essentialist terms and reduced to a unitary and all-encompassing logic. In other words, the social problem itself, the social movements concerned with it, the knowledges produced about it, the ideologies constructed around it, and the law to deal with it are all just by-products of the movements of that great monolith, social control. The politics of law reform appears in this perspective as the results of totalizing forces organized around a logic that is independent of social actors (Bourdieu and Wacquant, 1992). Agency is determined, resistance denied.

The conventional wisdom concerning law reform is in fact incapable of accounting for resistance, for the emergence of unconventional subjectivities, values, and beliefs, because it assumes the existence of a single dominant ideology (Abercrombie, Hill, and Turner, 1980). Among other things, this assumption ignores the conflictual nature of social processes. We need to confront this reductive view of the social world with a dynamic view that highlights the *process* by which that world is organized in a more or less coherent manner (Bourdieu, 1977; Collins, 1989; Clifford and Marcus, 1986; Herrnstein Smith, 1988). Analyses of law reform must therefore acknowledge that 'social problems' are contested terrains, embattled places where power, law, and knowledge are ready to be mobilized and organized hegemonically.[8] This means that our analyses of law reform must start from the particularities of conflicts, the contingencies of each 'social problem.' This also means that our analyses must pay attention to the lived realities of those who create problems, and examine how people define themselves and shape their lives in terms of commonsensical values and practices.

A Methodological Note

The essentialism and determinism of law reform studies create a fundamental challenge for further research: that of ridding our representations of the social world of some persistent dualisms. In particular, we must stop thinking of structure and agency as opposed terms; they are in fact mutually constitutive. Giddens, in his theory of 'structuration' (1976; 1979; 1981; 1982; 1984), attempts, albeit only at a theoretical level, to demonstrate the social production of the 'structure.' Structures only exist, he argues, in so far as they are invented and reproduced in the everyday practices of social agents who are themselves constituted by structures. This model of reproduction is far from being rigid; to the contrary, every action that supports the reproduction of a structure is itself an act of production. Agency, therefore, 'may initiate change by altering that structure at the same time as it produces it' (Giddens, 1976: 128). It follows that structure should not be conceived any longer as simply determining action. Rather, it should be conceived as both constraining and enabling (Giddens, 1979: 69–70).

A major shortcoming of Giddens's theory is that it is not empirically grounded. This makes it appear at times that structure is something subject to the wills of knowledgeable human agents (Baber, 1991). While Giddens appears to reinscribe a simple voluntarism, law reform studies partly influenced by his theory represented the construction of social problems as a consensual process without reference to social conflicts within communities; thus they appear to reinscribe a simple determinism (Gusfield, 1981a; Ericson, 1985; 1987; Ericson and Baranek, 1982, 1985; Cohen, 1983; 1985; Giffen and Lambert, 1988). My analysis here tries to avoid determinism and voluntarism by conceptualizing law reform as a mechanism that generates practices, practices that both enable and constrain action (Bourdieu and Wacquant, 1992). Thus it seeks to analyse the productive aspects of law reform – the deployment of collective identities, knowledges, and institutional practices – without having to make reference to a subject that is either fully constituted or always empty throughout the course of history (Foucault, 1980b: 117).

A more useful approach to the social world than Giddens's – one that also conceives structure and agency as mutually generative – is, ironically enough, found in the later work of Michel Foucault. And it is Foucault's work, particularly his genealogical method, that I have drawn upon extensively in understanding the recent politics of pornography.[9] Foucault's genealogy is a form of history conceiving the subject as constituted through practices of normalization and liberation (1988). To analyse this production, genealogy advises us to give up the attempt to formulate a global, systematic, and overarching theory of power; instead genealogy points to the *relational* nature of power:

Power in the substantive sense, *'le' pouvoir*, doesn't exist. What I mean is this. The idea that there is either located at – or emanating from – a given point something which is a 'power' seems to me to be based on a misguided analysis, one which at all events fails to account for a considerable number of phenomena. In reality power means relations, a more-or-less organized, hierarchical, co-ordinated cluster of relations. (Foucault, 1980b: 198, emphasis in original)

Foucault's relational notion of power is useful because it avoids the implication so prevalent in law reform studies that society is a coherent totality we can examine in terms of a dominant structure; rather,

Foucault's concept emphasizes the *productive* nature of power: 'We must cease once and for all to describe the effects of power in negative terms: it "excludes," it "represses," it "censors," it "abstracts," it "masks," it "conceals." In fact, power produces; it produces reality; it produces domains of objects and rituals of truth. The individual and the knowledge that may be gained of him belong to this production' (Foucault, 1979: 194).

Genealogy, then, is a method for investigating the constitution of identities and knowledges on the basis of various rules, strategies, and innovations found in the cultural environment (Foucault, 1988: 51; 1980b). It works by taking seriously the various claims of truth people make regarding the knowledge they have of their world and themselves, while at the same time recognizing such knowledge as directly implicated in relations of power. This method thus implies the inseparability of power and knowledge. There is no truth independent of power relations, no truth without a politics of truth. Foucault implores us to admit

that power and knowledge directly imply one another; that there is no power relation without the correlative constitution of a field of knowledge, nor any knowledge that does not presuppose and constitute at the same time power relations. These 'power-knowledge relations' are to be analyzed, therefore, not on the basis of a subject of knowledge who is or is not free in relation to the power system, but, on the contrary, the subject who knows, the objects to be known and the modalities of knowledge must be regarded as so many effects of these fundamental implications of power-knowledge and their historical transformations (1979: 27–8).

Genealogy thus rejects the traditional view of power as a force originating in a centre, possessed by a class or group of people, used to repress those who would want to take hold of it. Rather than seeking to answer the 'why' of power – that is to say, to search for the origins, conditions, and causes of power – genealogy seeks to describe the 'how' of power by conceptualizing power in terms of a 'political anatomy,' a 'micro-physics,' a body of forces and relations inscribing itself in the body (Ewald, 1975: 1237). In other words, genealogy examines how the production of bodies and souls takes form: not only how they are organized, classified, and categorized, but also how they resist being objectified.[10] Resistance, for Foucault, is an essential component of power relations: 'There are no relations of power without resistance; the latter are all the more real and effective because they are formed right at the point where relations of power are exercised; resistance to power does not have to come from elsewhere to be real, nor is it inexorably frustrated through being in the same place as power; hence, like power, resistance is multiple and can be integrated in global strategies' (Foucault, 1980b: 136). In sum, genealogy asks new questions of the knowledges people claim about themselves and their world: from which power relations do you come from? What kinds of objectifying and subjectifying effects do you produce on the individual?

In this book I will attempt to tease out a genealogy of the politics of pornography law reform by investigating the rise and demise of the anti-pornography proposal of the Conservative government (Bill C-114 and Bill C-54). By genealogy, I mean an analysis of this politics in terms of 'power-knowledge relations' and a conceptualization of the pornography debate as a network of strategies that both constrained and enabled social action. My task will be to concentrate on the knowledges various organizations and institutions produced on pornography, and to understand those knowledges as strategies embedded in historically specific beliefs and institutional practices. I will address a series of conceptual and practical operations through which pornography is constituted in our society as an object of knowledge and a target of institutional practices, as well as a terrain for the production of collective identities.

The first part of *Blue Politics* will investigate the process by which social actors constitute pornography as an object of knowledge. Chapter 2 will document the emergence of a feminist definition of pornography, a definition that directly challenges the previous conservative and civil libertarian 'truth claims' about the nature and effects of pornography by focusing on the degradation of women inherent in pornography. The ideological hold of 'science' and 'rights' on the feminist argument that pornography is an impediment to women's right to equality will be presented. I will then provide a critical assessment of the radical feminist theory of pornography and sexuality – a theory that fuelled the feminist anti-pornography movement.

Chapter 3 will analyse the impact of the feminist discussion of pornography on the debate between conservative and civil libertarian organizations. It will further analyse the emergence of collective identities (feminists against censorship, sex radicals, and sex workers) who strongly resisted the attempt to reform the law. An examination of the way conservative, civil liberties, and feminist and sex radical organizations mobilized scientific and legal discourses to produce diverse knowledges will reveal the significance of those discourses in law reform and the diverse possibilities they raised.

The second part of *Blue Politics* will examine the way in which institutional practices have articulated power/knowledge strategies on pornography. Discussing first the creation of a commission of inquiry (chapter 4) and then the two anti-pornography proposals (chapter 5 and 6), I will investigate the mechanisms that led to the failure of the Conservative government's attempt at law reform. Chapter 4 will analyse specifically the recommendations of the report of the Special Committee on Pornography and Prostitution (Canada, 1985). Of major interest will be the precarious process through which the report developed an argument for criminalizing *only* violent and degrading sexual representations after claiming, with the feminists, that *all* pornography is sexist and thus harms women. My analysis will also demonstrate how the report embodied the balance of opinion on pornography in the society at large, but in a way that was constrained by the committee's membership, legalistic mandate, liberal policy orientation, and consultative procedures.

Chapter 5 will explore the strategies leading to the making of the first anti-pornography bill, Bill C-114. I will ask how, in the light of the strength of the feminist position in the campaign to proscribe pornography, the Conservative government could ignore women's concerns and produce a proposal more draconian than the Fraser Committe report. I will demonstrate how the growing public pressure from pro-censorship forces in society, the policy-making process within the Department of Justice, and the consultative process within the Conservative caucus all contributed to the production of a specifically anti-sex proposal.

Chapter 6 will probe the failure of the government's final effort at law reform, Bill C-54. This chapter will pose the question: how could this failure happen when the Conservative government had a majority in the House of Commons? To answer, I will first show how the government was incapable of striking a compromise between feminists and conservatives; then I will analyse the impact of 'the revolt of the librarians' on the government. Finally, in examining how the recent judgment of the Supreme Court of Canada, *R.v. Butler*, has actually institutionalized the feminist argument that pornography harms women, I will ask whether pornography law reform did ultimately fail.

Blue Politics will conclude with a discussion on the enabling potential of law reform; I will argue that the attempt at law reform was a process through which pornography became a contested terrain, the site for the production of political identities, and the arena for the emergence of competing knowledges. By reflecting on the two main discourses that have framed the politics of pornography law reform – science and law – I will show how 'constraints' can also enable.

As an epilogue, I will ask whether, in the light of the post-modern effort to radically problematize 'objective' notions of aesthetic value, the law will ever be able to distinguish justly between art and obscenity.

Finally, just a note about the title. *Blue Politics* is a deliberately ambiguous formulation. *Blue* refers to a number of elements in the story I am about to tell. Most obviously, perhaps, blue suggests pornography itself, as in 'blue movies.' Blue, however, makes one think of the police, 'the boys in blue,' and 'the thin blue line' of the law. Blue is also the colour of the Progressive Conservative party, which was at the turbulent centre of the porn wars in the 1980s. *Blue Politics* also connotes something quite negative: these politics 'give me the blues.' Indeed, the pornography debates frustrated and exasperated many, both among those for and among those against censorship. Yet, one less obvious meaning of blue points to a more positive connotation of *Blue Politics*. Blue was one of the three colours on the revolutionary tricolour flag – its meaning was liberty, one of the foundational rights of modern democracy. *Blue Politics* thus can be read to mean the politics of liberty – and the pornography debate was and will continue to be, above all, about the meaning of such rights.

Part 1

Pornography as an object of knowledge

2

The Emergence of a Feminist Position on Pornography

From the church's creation of the *Index Librorum Prohibitorum* (1564) to counteract heresy to the conservative attack on sexually explicit material in the 1960s, and from the philanthropic movement to reform literature in the late eighteenth and nineteenth centuries to the public campaign to criminalize pornography in the 1980s, attempts to reform obscenity legislation have been motivated by the fear of a moral falling off. This 'fall' has always been contrasted with a 'golden age,' an age of order, decency, discipline, self-restraint, tradition, and propriety. One of the difficulties with the idea of the 'golden age' is, as the historian Jeffrey Weeks says, 'that the more we search for it, the more we seem to find ourselves locked into an endless maze where the goal is always just around the next corner' (1986: 90). In most cases the reformers are not even certain exactly when the golden age was. But one can be sure that the period longed for also had its heralds of decline and blight (Pearson, 1983).

The interesting point about the 'golden age,' of course, is not its historical 'truth' but its symbolic power. As the influential cultural theorist Raymond Williams states, drawing attention to the 'golden age' is nothing more than 'a well-known habit of using the past, the "good old days," as a stick to beat the present' (1973: 12). The belief in the tranquillity of the past often reveals more about people's fear of, and discontent with, present social changes than about past realities. The late eighteenth- and nineteenth-century philanthropic movements to reform manners were preoccupied with the growth in literacy and the greater availability of popular literature (Kendrick, 1987; Rembar, 1969; Thomas, 1969). On the one hand, they saw the growth of the reading public as an opportunity for inculcating and disseminating bourgeois morality throughout the social body.[1] On the other hand, they feared the bad influence of literature on the newly literate or semi-literate masses. Thus they succeeded in prohibiting literature which they feared might reach 'the others,' whose moral standards were perceived as so vulnerable and easily influenced that if they were not kept under control the nation might crumble.[2]

Since the 1960s the fear of literature has slowly given way, for some, to the fear of pornography. For conservatives, pornography has come to epitomize a general moral decline. It is the symbol of everything that is wrong with post-1960s 'permissiveness.' The cataclysmic changes brought on by the 1960s, however, were fervently welcomed by civil libertarians, who perceived the secularization of sex as a liberation from the tyranny of tradition. Pornography was a means to challenge sexual authoritarianism. They argued for the repeal of obscenity legislation, because it would be one more blow to the conservative hegemony over sexuality.

The emergence of the feminist and gay liberation movements in the 1960s is partly explained by the desire to challenge sexual conservatism. For example, sex had been defined historically for women as an adjunct to their destiny, marriage. But for the women of the 1960s, who were looking for new roles, such a circumscription of sexuality would not do (Ehrenreich, Hess, and Jacobs, 1986; Weeks, 1981; 1986). Consequently, they perceived the fight to repeal obscenity legislation as part of a larger attempt to undermine conservative patriarchal rule over the body. Early feminists, gays, and lesbians embraced pornography as a valuable weapon in the fight for sexual freedom. A decade later, however, some of the achievements of the sexual revolution were highly criticized by the feminist movement. The movement passionately attacked the products of permissiveness: the ubiquity of degrading images of women, the romanticization of sexual violence, and the commercialization of sex. Eventually, for feminists as for conservatives, pornography came to represent everything that went wrong with the sexual revolution.

In this chapter I will examine the emergence of the feminist anti-pornography movement in the late 1970s. I will document and critically assess its theory of pornography – a theory that attempted to make sexism, not sex, the subject of pornography, and provided the movement with its vital energy. I will examine the discourses – scientific and legal – that feminists drew upon to forge their demand for the reform of obscenity legislation. To better appreciate the changes brought about by feminists, I will begin by presenting the two dominant positions on pornography in North America in the 1960s.

The Religious and Moral Rationales for the Prohibition of Obscenity in the 1960s

In the late 1950s many religious conservatives strongly reacted against the increased availability of sexually explicit magazines, the so-called girlie magazines. Conceiving of sex as ignominious, religious conservatives argued that human dignity could be maintained only through the repression of sex. Of course, not all church doctrine took this extremely negative position towards sex. The Reverend Donald Soper, for example, argued in the early 1960s that sex is a Christian practice: 'Sex is part of the raw material of the Kingdom of God. If it is dedicated to that high purpose it is both beautiful and good' (1961: 42). In other words, the church recognized sexual pleasure and the satisfaction of sexual desires as long as these took place in private, within the bonds of marriage, and for the purpose of procreation. According to Harold J. Gardiner, the literary editor of *America*, a national Catholic weekly,

moral teaching on the whole process of sex holds, as a basic and cardinal fact, that complete sexual activity and pleasure is licit and moral only in a naturally completed act in valid marriage. All acts which, of their psychological and physical nature, are designed to be preparatory to the complete act, take their licitness and their morality from the complete act. If, therefore, they are entirely divorced form the complete act, they are distorted, warped, meaningless and hence immoral. It follows, therefore, that any deliberate indulgence in thoughts, words or acts which, of their intrinsic nature, are slanted toward, destined for or preparation for the complete act, and yet performed in circumstances in which the complete act is impossible, have ceased to be a means toward an end and have become ends in themselves. All sin, whether sexual or otherwise, always entails such a confusion, in one way or another, of means and ends. (1975: 161)

Joseph Buckley, in his popular exposition of the role of sex in the life of Christians, is unequivocal about the unity of sex and procreation: 'Why may not man use sexual intercourse and *seek the pleasure attached to it*, contrary to its natural pattern? ... Because man is not the master of this function. Human life is God's domain ... and so, likewise, is the process that leads to human life. A process belongs reductively to the same category as the object to which it leads' (quoted in Gardiner, 1975: 164). From this religious standpoint,[3] pornography is a sin because it produces sexual pleasure and the satisfaction of desire 'with complete indifference to any creative purpose' (Soper, 1961: 42). Conceived as 'an evil thing,' a means that 'promotes lust,' pornography must necessarily be prohibited (Soper, 1961: 43).

The church's rationale for prohibiting pornography was usually based on the spiritual and social impact of sexually explicit material. Pornography, it was argued, 'invariably tends to degrade the lives of those who indulge it' and violates their integrity (Soper, 1961: 43; Keating, 1971). It is un-Christian and immoral, and renders the individual incapable of distinguishing between right and wrong. It is harmful because, in encouraging sexual thoughts, it sidetracks the reader from beneficent and productive roles in the community. Soper contends that '[a] personality which very regularly feeds upon pornography becomes progressively enfeebled and unable to concentrate on, or to wrestle with, more worthy ideas and attitudes' (1961: 45). The decrease in self-respect and human dignity caused by pornography then becomes responsible for the destruction of the moral fabric of nations.

The evidence cited by religious conservatives to demonstrate that pornography corrupts public morality took the form, at times, of affirmations about the causal link between pornography and a panoply of social problems, such as illegitimate birth, divorce, alcohol and drug use, lack of respect for authority, sex crimes, murder, and even increases in venereal disease (Keating, 1971). While statistics were useful in their campaign, their objections were based almost entirely on 'common sense.' As Keating argues, 'To deny the need for control is literally to deny one's senses. Credit the ... public with enough common sense to know that one who wallows in filth is going to get dirty. This is intuitive knowledge. Those who will spend millions of dollars to tell us otherwise must be malicious or misguided or both' (1971: 110). Common sense clearly told the conservatives that exposure to sexually explicit material leads to immoral and asocial conduct; common sense also told them that such material had to be censored.

Although not necessarily Christian, some conservatives opposed sexually explicit material because it offended the collective morality. Moral conservatives like Lord Devlin asserted the necessity of a common morality bonding citizens if a society was to exist:

Without shared ideas on politics, morals, and ethics no society can exist. Each one of us has ideas about what is good and what is evil; they cannot be kept private from the society in which we live. If men and women try to create a society in which there is no fundamental agreement about good and evil they will fail; if having based it on common agreement, the agreement goes, the society will disintegrate. For society is not something that is kept together physically; it is held by the invisible bonds of common thought. If the bonds were too far relaxed the members would drift apart. A common morality is part of the bondage. The bondage is part of the price of society; and mankind, which needs society, must pay its price. (Devlin, 1959: 22–3)

Pornography is dangerous to society because it undermines morality – that is to say, it constitutes a threat to the existence of the community. As an affront to morality, pornography must be legally proscribed. Devlin explains the relationship between law, morality, and the protection of society as follows: 'But the true principle is that the law exists for the protection of society. It does not discharge its function by protecting the individual from injury, annoyance, corruption, and exploitation; the law must protect also the institutions and the community of ideas, political and moral, without which people cannot live together. Society cannot ignore the morality of the individual any more than it can his loyalty; it flourishes on both and without either it dies' (Devlin, 1959: 23). Moral conservatives asserted the link between immoral thoughts and public morality as an uncontested moral fact – as a valid argument for the prohibition of pornography.

The Liberal Rationale for the Repeal of Obscenity Legislation in the 1960s

Give me the liberty to know, to utter, and to argue freely according to conscience, above all liberties. *Milton*

Some liberals challenged the conservative arguments for the prohibition of 'obscene' material by questioning the idea of the common good, others by pointing to the narrowness and rigidity of traditionalist morality (for example, Rist, 1975). Still others questioned the conservative position by asking if 'immorality' in itself was a sufficient ground for criminalization. To the question, 'Is it morally permissible to enforce morality as such?' (Hart, 1963: 4), liberals answer 'no' and invoke John Stuart Mill's seminal essay *On Liberty*:

The only purpose for which power can rightfully be exercised over any member of a civilized community against his will is to prevent harm to others ... His own good either physical or moral is not a sufficient warrant. He cannot rightfully be compelled to do or forbear because it will be better for him to do so, because it will make him happier, because in the opinions of others, to do so would be wise or even right. These are good reasons for remonstrating with him or reasoning with him, or entreating him, but not for compelling him, or visiting him with any evil in case he do otherwise. (1947: 84–5)

In other words, to judge whether a practice is harmful, one need not take into consideration the repercussion of such a practice on the general moral code (Hart, 1963: 50–2). Conservatives like Lord Devlin refuse such an assessment because they make an analogy between vice and treason and assume that both have the same destructive effect on society (Devlin, 1959: 14–15). Hart argues that such an analogy fails because offenses against morality do not jeopardize the whole societal structure. Referring specifically to the effect of homo-. sexuality on society, Hart is unequivocal: 'But we have ample evidence for believing that people will not abandon morality, will not think any better of murder, cruelty, and dishonesty, merely because some private sexual practice which they abominate is not punished by the law' (1963: 51). Consequently, according to the harm principle, not all material that is offensive to public morality need necessarily be harmful.

For liberals, whether or not consuming pornography is harmful is an empirical question that only science can answer (Feinberg, 1973). The report of the Commission on Obscenity and Pornography (United States, 1970), an American commission created in 1967 to investigate the effects of pornography, provided the evidence liberals were looking for. The commission obviously shared the liberal perspective on sexuality and pornography, and adhered to the view that 'interest in sex is normal, healthy, [and] good' (1970: 53). In the report, obscenity legislation is described as a menace to 'one of the most important foundations in our liberties,' freedom of expression (1970: 60). The report contends that the right to free speech is a special entitlement, which can be restricted only if speech causes harm to others. On the basis of extensive scientific research on the effects of 'sexual materials'[4] on individuals, the report claims to have found 'no evidence to date that exposure to explicit sexual materials plays a significant role in the causation of delinquent or criminal behavior among youth or adults' (1970: 59). Pornography is not harmful; on the contrary, the evidence of the report suggests that exposure to sexually explicit material has positive effects. Studies undertaken by the commission indicate that upon viewing sexually explicit material people tend to become sexually aroused, are likely to masturbate, increase the frequency of their sexual activities, and talk more about sex. In the long run, the material leads to satiation. The research also shows that such material 'liberalizes' attitudes: people are more accepting of pre-marital sex, non-procreative sex, and homosexual sex (1970: 169–308). Studies acknowledge the change from a conventional morality to a more permissive one, but they affirm that sexually explicit materials are only one of the many factors responsible for the change. The committee points to the more important effects on sexual morals produced by the spread of effective methods of contraception, changes in the position of women in society, and increases in education and mobility (1970: 61).

The report, a typical document of the time, welcomes the move toward a more tolerant morality as a sign of progress, and concludes on the basis of its extensive research on the effects of pornography that 'federal, state, and local legislation should not seek to interfere with the right of adults who wish to do so to read, obtain, or view explicit sexual materials' (1970: 57).

After scrutinizing the American report, Canadian civil liberties organizations argued that there was no need for section 159 of the Canadian Criminal Code, which prohibited obscenity. They argued that a law must be justified on the basis of a balance between the protection of society and the freedom of the individual. Insisting that pornography is not associated with the commission of criminal offences but is liberating and associated with 'normal and legitimate evolutionary developments' (Fox, 1972: 37), civil libertarians claimed that the legal restriction was thus 'entirely unjustified' (Fox, 1972: 38). Consequently, in the early 1970s they developed a strong argument in favour of amending or repealing the legislation.

The Feminist Anti-pornography Movement

The real problem with pornography lies not in its sexual content, but its abusive nature ... Images of degradation alone can deny human persons their full humanity, create negative anti-women/anti-child/anti-male messages or be exploitative of either sex. Thus, degradation alone can abuse the civil liberties of human persons. (Windsor Coalition against Pornography, letter to Minister of Justice Mark MacGuigan, 1983)

In the late 1970s feminists concerned with pornography made arguments that were very different from those made by civil libertarians and conservatives in the 1960s. Instead of discussing whether sex was immoral or liberating, feminists focused on the way sex was portrayed in most sexually explicit material. They discovered the existence of a 'new' pornography – new because it constituted a drastic change from the depictions of mere nudity of the 1960s. Feminists provided numerous illustrations of the violence and misogynist content of the new pornography:[5]

- one issue of *Hustler* (1978) introduces us to 'Chester the Molester' and his techniques of molestation: lying, kidnapping, assaulting, and raping.

- another *Hustler* issue, 'About Face' (1978), shows a man sticking a gun in a women's mouth and forcing her to suck it, while she appears to enjoy the procedure.

- one issue of *Brutal Trio* (1978) depicts the kidnapping of three generations of women, a grandmother, a mother, and a daughter, who are all beaten up, kicked around, and, after they have passed out, raped.

- in the magazine *Bondage* (1978), women are portrayed as taking pleasure in being tied up, while their vaginas and breasts are surrounded by instruments such as scissors, razors, torches, and hot irons.

For feminists, this 'new' pornography appeared to be less about sex than about sexism (Lederer, 1980).

Feminists discovered this disturbing pornography a few years after uncovering the reality of men's brutality, rape, and wife-battering. The link between pornography and this kind of violence became clear: pornography glorifies and eroticizes sexual violence perpetrated against women. Reflecting on their early involvement in the fight against pornography, feminists with the British Columbia Working Group on Sexual Violence explain the relationship between male violence and pornography: 'Having spent time with the victims of male violence, we took another look and found the sexually explicit pictures were in fact a distorted glorification of the abuse suffered by women we had talked to. We saw images of women bound, gagged, whipped, raped, infantilized, burned, chained, defecated, urinated and ejaculated upon, images which lauded the hatred of women' (1986: 1).

The realization that pornography eroticizes the real violence men perpetrate on women increased feminists' sense of danger, especially because society considers pornography a form of entertainment; most important, it increased their anger at men. This anger led to an attempt at conceptualizing women's oppression in a sexual system of power that organizes the subordination and dependence of women (Brownmiller, 1975; Morgan, 1977; Dworkin, 1979; MacKinnon, 1987; Cole, 1989). For radical feminists, acts of sexual violence against women are instrumental in sustaining the patriarchal system. Pornography is the propaganda of this system, the ideology of male supremacy. In the words of Robin Morgan: 'Pornography is the theory, and rape the practice' (1977: 169).

Conceived as the ideology of male supremacy, pornography's message is clear: women are nothing more than objects. 'We are pussy, beaver, bitch, chick, cunt – named after parts of our bodies or after animals interchangeably,' states Catharine MacKinnon (1987: 199). Pornography robs women of their humanity and dignity; it dehumanizes and degrades women; it suggests that they exist solely for the fulfilment of men's most violent needs and strangest fantasies. Pornography thus is a lie about women and their sexuality. It reduces women, as Andrea Dworkin says, quoting Kate Millett, 'to the one essential: "cunt ... our essence, our offence"' (1979: 201).

In some feminist accounts, pornography is much more than a representation, a fantasy, or a symbol; it is the real thing: 'it is sexual reality' (MacKinnon, 1987: 173), or 'what men like to do to women' (Dworkin, 1984).[6] In other words, pornography is more than hatred of women; it is 'a practice of sexual subordination' for the sexual pleasure of its male producers and consumers (Cole, 1989: 22). Thus pornography is an abusive activity, both real (for the women involved in the production) and ideological (for all women), that ensures the continuation of women's sexual subordination (Cole, 1989; MacKinnon, 1987). Accordingly, 'In, by, through and because of pornography, women are objectified, subordinated, tortured, raped, killed and silenced. In, by, through and because of pornography, our bodies and minds are stolen and sold, as they are in prostitution and rape.'[7] For radical feminists, the link between pornography and women's oppression is unequivocal; pornography's eradication is essential for sexual liberation.

Sexual liberation – women's control over their bodies and their sexuality – was central to the feminist critique of pornography. Because feminists located their critique of pornography in the larger struggle against sexism, they felt the need to distinguish their position against male-defined sexuality from the anti-sex position of conservatives. Thus it was important for feminists to state the existence of 'a clear and present difference' between pornography and erotica (Steinem, 1978). Gloria Steinem's famous distinction became central to the anti-pornography movement. According to Steinem, the pornographic is wrong because it celebrates a power imbalance: 'It is sex being used to reinforce some inequality, or to create one, or to tell us the lie that pain and humiliation (ours or someone else's) are really the same as pleasure. If we are to feel anything, we must identify with conqueror or victim. That means we can only experience pleasure through the adoption of some degree of sadism or masochism' (1978: 54).

Erotica, by contrast, is good because it celebrates pleasure between equals. Steinem claims that erotica is 'a mutually pleasurable, sexual expression between people who have enough power to be there by positive choice. It may or may not strike a sense-memory in the viewer, or be creative enough to make the unknown seem real; but it doesn't require us to identify with a conqueror or a victim. It is truly sensuous and may give us a contagion of pleasure' (Steinem, 1978: 54).

The women's movement in North America responded to the newly defined relationship between pornography and women's subordination by creating feminist anti-pornography organizations all over the continent. The first feminist conference on pornography, organized by Women against Violence in Pornography and Media (WAVPM), was held in San Francisco in 1978. After this conference many anti-pornography groups sprung up. In Canada, for example, we have organizations such as Women against Violence against Women; Canadians against Pornography; Committee against Pornography; the Canadian Coalition against Media Pornography; and various provincial and municipal organizations such as the Working Group on Sexual Violence, from British Columbia, and the Toronto Task Force on Violence against Women and Children.

These organizations were devoted initially to raising women's consciousness about pornography. Their efforts consisted of familiarizing women with the porn industry; touring the porn districts of their respective cities; reading and viewing porn; exposing the commercial exploitation of women; boycotting products advertised in a misogynist context; picketing in front of sex theatres; holding 'Take Back the Night' marches to demonstrate women's commitment to stopping violence perpetrated on women through and by pornography; and exploring the legality of pornographic materials and the possible protection from it offered by the law (National Action Committee on the Status of Women, Memo, May 1983: 14).

By inscribing its critique of pornography in the context of women's oppression, the feminist movement against pornography provided a significant advance over the essentialism of conservative theories and the lack of consideration for structural inequalities of liberal theories. Over time, however, the feminist campaign against pornography became a single-issue movement. It increasingly neglected to address the complexity of the social relations organizing sexism, thus betraying its original premise that pornography is a *product* of sexism. Pornography became, instead, the ultimate *source* of sexism. In the following sections I will examine two processes that help explain this change, the mobilization of the scientific and the legal discourses.

The Language of Causality and the Language of Rights: The Mobilization of Scientific and Legal Discourses

It is our argument that pornography influences the way women see themselves and the way men see and treat women. It thus prevents true equality and the full participation of women in society, and impedes the liberty of women. It causes many kinds of harm, some of them very direct, through the harm it does to women and children forced to participate in the production of pornography, and some less direct, through the effects it has on consumers.

At a tertiary level, there is a more subtle effect, in the cumulative formation of negative and limited attitudes toward women which occurs in a society where pornography is commonplace. (Jillian Ridington, for the National Action Committee on the Status of Women, 1983)

The feminist campaign against pornography argued that pornography violates women's dignity and undermines their right to liberty and equality. In other words, pornography, by inculcating misogynist attitudes in men, is detrimental to women's efforts to be respected as free and equal beings. This argument is based in a reappraisal of the harm principle.

According to the civil libertarian position, the right to liberty and freedom is a negative one. This means that one's freedom must be characterized by an absence of restraint or prohibition as long as it does not infringe on the right to liberty and freedom of others. The imposition of an obligation or a limitation on a person's ability to do what she or he wants (a claim right) is acceptable only when a substantial harm to another has resulted from such freedom. The harm must be substantial, because the creation of an obligation on others is itself an infringement of liberty. According to the Canadian feminist theorist Lorenne M.G. Clark, the historical record suggests that the establishment of negative rights is often followed by their transformation into 'claim' rights. 'The history of social reform is largely the history of first establishing that some previously disenfranchised groups ought to have rights that have already been accorded to others, then removing legal or other social and institutional impediments to their getting what they want, and then fighting further to have these privileges converted into claims' (1983: 47).

The struggle for greater liberty and equality for women therefore necessitates the cost of less liberty and the loss of status for men:

Equality cannot flourish without limiting the privileges some already have in both the private and the public spheres, because the inequalities of the present system were a product of the unequal attribution of rights in the first instance; thus greater equality and liberty for those least advantaged under the present system necessitates placing restrictions on the privilege rights of those who are presently most advantaged. And this must be done by creating obligations either to do or to forbear actions previously permitted, it can be accomplished only at the expense of negative liberty. (Clark, 1983: 50–1)

In order to restrict the liberty of men, in other words, it is necessary to demonstrate that pornography 'creates a clear and substantial risk to others' (Clark, 1983: 54).

Feminists showed that pornography creates 'substantial risk to others' by linking it with three types of harm. First, there is direct harm to women, as with women who have been coerced into the skin trade. A good example of such harm is the experience of Linda Marchiano. Marchiano, better known as 'Linda Lovelace,' the star of the popular movie *Deep Throat*, recounts in her book *Ordeal* (1980) how she was abducted by pornographers and then tortured, forced to, among other things, have sex with a dog, put under constant surveillance, and threatened with death if she attempted to leave Charles Trayner, her producer and forced husband, the king of U.S. porn (Marchiano and McGrady, 1980).

According to anti-pornography feminists, her experience was not exceptional. Most women in the sex trade are victims and abused women. The Canadian feminist Susan Cole claims that most women enter the sex trade because of their experience as sexually abused children. From this experience, they have learned 'that sex takes place within a context of their own vulnerability, at the hands of men whose authority over them is total' (Cole, 1989: 117). The image of a vicious cycle of pornography, sexual abuse, and prostitution epitomizes for feminists the direct harm pornography causes to women.

The second harm resulting from pornography is indirect, because it takes place at the point of consumption. Feminists argue that exposure to pornography encourages and leads to violence against women by 'linking coercion and violence with sexual stimulation' (National Action Committee on the Status of Women (NAC), 1984: 20). It is interesting to note here that the feminist anti-pornography movement has increasingly relied on 'scientific evidence' to sustain the argument that pornography harms women. According to feminists,[8] recent empirical studies on the harms associated with pornography show that in laboratory conditions exposure to material combining sexual stimulation with violence increases the willingness of normal men to act aggressively against women; makes women and men less likely to believe accounts of rape; changes men's attitudes towards women so as to increase men's hostility towards women and men's propensity to rape if one knew that one would not be caught; and in short, encourages men to trivialize, dehumanize, and objectify women.[9] Using this evidence, the feminist movement against pornography concludes that 'exposure to "aggressive pornography"' leads 'in all experiments [to] a desensitization to violence and an increased proclivity to perpetuate violence against women' (NAC, 1984: 20). In other words, science has convincingly demonstrated that pornography harms women. While the feminist anti-pornography movement points to the thoroughness of this scientific research, it endorses the results of science primarily because they confirm what feminists have known all along: 'Victims of sexual and physical abuse often report that the violence against them was precipitated by, or accompanied by, the use of pornography by their violator.'[10]

The third harm the feminist movement associates with pornography is social harm, and it is broader than the others. Pornography harms both women and men by socializing them into straitjacketed gender categories. Pornography is perceived as an educative medium that directly affects the reader. It socializes women into becoming passive and teaches them that to be a victim is a natural component of their attractiveness. According to the National Action Committee on the Status of Women (NAC), 'Women [through pornography] are told that assault and degradation are necessary for their sexual fulfilment.' Men, by contrast, are taught by pornography to deny their capacity for caring: 'Men are shown to be incapable of loving and giving, of sharing sexual joy' (1984: 19). In addition, pornography teaches men the essentials of sexism. The Committee against Pornography states that pornography 'educates boys and men to get sexual excitement from seeing or reading about women being tortured or humiliated. It teaches them to think of women as less than human creatures whose purpose is to provide sexual pleasure for men. This type of education we can do without' (1986).

In other words, whereas pornography encourages women to think of themselves as sexually passive and therefore to accept victimization, it encourages men to be aggressive and to think of women as inferior to them. Pornography becomes a method of socialization that 'is in itself a limitation of the autonomy of women' (Clark, 1983: 55), an infringement on women's rights to equality and freedom.

The social harm of pornography is that, among other things, it inhibits women's efforts to become – and be treated as – equal. It must be eradicated if there is a societal commitment to the notion of sexual equality, a right enshrined in Canadian law. The Canadian Advisory Council on the Status of Women (CACSW) reiterates this point succinctly: 'Pornography not only threatens [women's] physical integrity and safety but also prevents the achievement of their objectives of equality in the workplace, in the home and in social activities. As long as pornography counteracts women's efforts to gain their rightful place in society, it will constitute a serious impediment to their freedom of expression' (1984: 7–8).

Thus, by developing the idea of a social harm, feminists find a new ground on which to criminalize pornography, one based on the harm that pornography inflicts on women's right to equality, rather than on women's right to be free from physical harm. In the event that society refuses to criminalize pornography on the ground that scientific evidence does not conclusively show that pornography is a 'substantial risk to others,' society's commitment to greater equality and freedom for women would provide an alternative ground.

The feminist contention that pornography is 'causally or correlatively' related to violence against women and that it infringes on women's right to equality transformed the feminist anti-pornography movement into a single-issue one. Pornography became the source of sexism; its eradication, through the enactment of anti-pornography legislation, became the promise of equality and freedom. Three factors appear to account for the process that lured the feminist anti-pornography movement to exert pressure for censorship legislation: the politics of science, the politics of interpretation, and the politics of sexuality.

The Politics of Science

Before mobilizing the scientific discourse to buttress their position on pornography, feminists had strongly criticized science for the 'liberal bias' underlying its research on the effects of pornography; in particular, they criticized the research published in 1970 by the American Commission on Obscenity and Pornography (see the articles by Diamond, Bart and Jozsa; and Russell, all in Lederer ed, 1984). The commission's conclusion that pornography is harmless was disputed by feminists on the ground that the research was not objective. Conceived from a male point of view, the research did not focus on the effects of pornography *on women*. To counter what they saw as a biased report, feminists relied essentially on anecdotal evidence from women, as they did generally in the earlier phase of the movement. This evidence was gathered primarily from victims of sexual and physical abuse who found refuge in transition houses and rape crisis centres. The violence these women experienced was said to be causally linked to the consumption of pornography: 'Pornography does not stay in the magazines or films. A friend who was a social worker in Winnipeg tells of a case in which three runaway girls of 12, 14 and 15 were forced to live it. They were picked up by two respectably dressed men who held them captive for a week, subjected them to every variety of sexual abuse, and made movies of their sufferings' (Inglis, 1983: 16).

Another source of anecdotal evidence was provided by the police, who reported that pornographic magazines were often found at the scene of violent crimes against women. This observation was subsequently transformed into a factual account of the link between violence and pornography: '*For years* feminists have been stating that violent pornography has been contributing towards all forms of violence women suffer. This includes wife battering and rape within marriage and outside marriage ... The fact that the child murderer Clifford Olson was found with a suitcase of kiddie porn, some of which he had taken of his victims before he killed them should be enough to put a serious hazard warning on pornography and take it away from the eyes of children' (NAC, 1983b; emphasis in original). However, as soon as scientific evidence corroborated their claim that pornography is linked to violence against women feminists were quick to use it: 'there are at least 60 studies which support the point of view: pornography incites violence towards women' (ibid). With the weapon of scientific verification, the feminist movement sounded more certain than ever: 'We are sure, and can substantiate our claim, that violent and aggressive material with a sexual component – that is, material which would be included in our suggested definition – has contributed to an increase in sexual offenses, violent crimes, and aggressive and anti-social behaviour towards women' (NAC, 1984: 18). Drawing mostly on the works of the social psychologists Donnerstein and Malamuth, the feminist movement finally found clear evidence substantiating their claim that pornography is a 'substantial risk' or harm to others.

Before the mobilization of the scientific discourse, it was difficult for the feminist anti-pornography movement to counteract the civil libertarians' demand for clear-cut proof that pornography is harmful. With the scientific evidence in hand, they believed that the civil libertarians would be forced to reassess their position: 'The civil libertarians have up to now given little credence to the research on this subject; the cause-effect relationship has not in their opinion been adequately demonstrated. The overwhelming evidence of the latest studies, however, should prompt those who truly seek justice to review their stance' (Canadian Advisory Council on the Status of Women, 1984: 6). Science, for feminists, had made it indisputable: pornography harms women by linking violence with sexual stimulation.

There are many problems with the research used by feminists (Fisher, 1985, 1986; Kelley, 1985; Mosher, 1985, 1986; Palys and Lowman, 1984). Fisher summarizes them:

Experiments that demonstrate a pornography-aggression link are structured in a way that is so unlike any natural setting that the results of the research are inapplicable in most 'real world' situations. These problems include the fact that in laboratory research, subjects have only a single, aggressive response open to them; subjects are free to aggress in a punishment-free environment; and the subjects and the stimuli in the laboratory research are both highly atypical. (1986: 166)

Even without going into all the details of laboratory research, it is clear that the male subjects of the experiments are primed to aggress and are given no option other than to aggress by the experimenter; thus it is not surprising that they do so. As Fisher rightly remarks, this aggression provides us with little information, because we do not know how males who have seen violent pornography would react to women if other non-aggressive response alternatives were open to them (1986: 166–7). To date there are no laboratory research experiments incorporating response alternatives other than aggression. Furthermore, in natural settings the fear of punishment or retaliation for sexual aggression might be negligible, but as Fisher affirms, 'it does exist' (1986: 167); whereas in laboratory experiments there is no such risk, because the subjects are given the instruction to aggress, and they know the female victim will not retaliate. Thus we do not know whether violent pornography leads to aggressive attitudes and behaviour in situations where the subjects risk being caught and punished. The absence of non-aggressive response alternatives and of fear of punishment combined with, on the one hand, the fact that the subjects of such experiments are unrepresentative of consumers of pornography and, on the other, the fact that the pornographic material used for such experiments is unrepresentative of the vast majority of sexually explicit material circulating in Canada are serious limitations to the generalizability of laboratory research linking pornography with anti-female attitudes and behaviour.

This scientific research is also problematic because it decontextualizes pornography. Rather than being conceived as a practice, as a representation organized in historical, economic, political, and social contexts, pornography is studied in the laboratory as though it had an essence that was isolable from any real situation in which one might actually produce and consume it. This procedure results in, among other things, the treatment of pornography as *the* problem, whereas theoretically the problem is the social relations that produce pornography and sexism.

The link between pornography and anti-female attitudes and behaviour is definitely plausible, just as plausible as the link between fashion magazines and people's taste in clothes. However, to affirm that a statistical correlation between pornography and anti-female attitudes and behaviour is a valid explanation of the harm pornography causes to women is simply wrong. Such a correlation is premised on the possibility of separating pornography from all other factors influencing anti-female attitudes and behaviour. Modern society is far too complex to justify such an exclusion.

Once again, the question is not whether pornography can or cannot influence attitudes and behaviour. Pornography, like any other representation or spectacle, has an impact on people; but, as Bernard Arcand astutely remarks, in *Le Jaguar et le Tamanoir: vers le degré zéro de la pornographie* (1991), it is just one model of sexuality among multiple and contradictory models that individuals draw upon to make choices and to invent new models for their sexuality (1991: 102–3). In that sense, pornography's effects do not necessarily differ from those of other discourses (Arcand, 1991: 103).

It is instructive to analyse the way in which scientific facts about pornography are mobilized for political action. As the sociologist Joseph Gusfield has shown in his study of drunk driving, *The Culture of Public Problems* (1981), the materials or facts deriving from science are often imperfect, inconsistent, and ambiguous. In the public arena, however, they are 'made' to produce the illusion of certainty, facticity, and authority. Scientists studying the impact of pornography on behaviour and attitudes expressed ambiguities and uncertainties in their reports; however, these were ignored as conclusions were drawn, and the 'facts' of science were disseminated in the public culture (Gusfield, 1981a). Whereas the feminist anti-pornography movement pressured the government to reform the law on the ground that science convincingly demonstrates the harm pornography causes to women, scientists themselves were far more cautious. In fact, the scientists most often quoted by the feminist movement were equivocal about the policy implications of their work:

Can social scientists say with confidence which materials should be controlled and what form of control is desirable? As individuals we are certainly entitled to our opinions about these matters, but as researchers we would be hard pressed to derive a set of rules for regulating pornographic materials on the basis of the empirical inquiries undertaken so far. At best, we are able to specify which types of materials result in given effects (with some of these effects generally accepted as harmful and others more questionably so) and under what conditions the effects are more likely to occur. In general, the research findings presented in the previous chapters probably speak most readily to concerns about the types of harm that follow exposure to pornography raised by feminists – *but with some major qualifications*.
   As we noted earlier, at this point there is not enough evidence from laboratory experiments to conclude that exposure to nonviolent pornography leads to increases in aggression against women under most circumstances. With regard to negative changes in attitudes about women's roles in society, less sensitivity toward rape victims, or tendencies to be less harsh in evaluations of rapists following long-term exposure to pornography *the data are sparse. The data that exist are contradictory*. (Donnerstein, Linz, and Penrod, 1987: 144; emphasis added)

Such contradictions and the reservations of the scientists are ignored by the feminist anti-pornography movement. As Gusfield (1981a) suggests, the reality of a social problem is constructed in the public arena as a call for action rather than as a scientific report. In the case of pornography, the feminist anti-pornography movement created a simple cause-and-effect relation between pornography and harm to women, because such a relation appears clearly identifiable and easy to control. Gusfield argues that this strategy is adopted because 'multi-causality weakens the capacity and purposefulness which make control seem possible' (1981a: 74). The scientific claim that negative attitudes and aggressive behaviour toward women *might* be associated in a laboratory setting with pornography is transformed in the public arena into the *fact* that pornography causes harm to women. This explanation, which appears grounded in knowledge produced by the scientific model, creates a 'factual world of order and certitude' (Gusfield, 1981a: 74); control becomes inevitable.

The Politics of Interpretation

The feminist movement was also able to make pornography the source of women's lack of equality by adopting a reductionist reading of the relationship between text and meaning. In the feminist analysis, pornographic texts mean – and lead to – women's oppression. The source of interpretive authority is the text itself rather than the viewer or reader. Such a view is premised on a traditional understanding of language as transparent, as a direct expression of meaning.

The feminist plea against pornography, *Pornography and the Sex Crisis* (1989), by the Canadian journalist Susan G. Cole, best exemplifies how radical feminists are reductionist in their reading of the relationship between text and meaning. I choose to analyse Cole's reading of pornography because she was one of the most outspoken feminists in the Canadian campaign against pornography. Moreover, Cole's approach is based on the accounts of both Dworkin (1979) and MacKinnon (1987), pioneers of the feminist anti-pornography movement in North America.

Cole argues that current obscenity provisions are faulty because they interpret texts in such a way as to ignore the realities of women's lives. She implies that interpretation, the element of subjectivity in the law, must be done away with if we are to succeed in implementing a feminist legislation against pornography: 'In order for a law to reach the real harm of pornography, it must be concrete. It must consider the activities of people and not the interpretation of pictures. If pornography is considered just a two-dimensional artifact, the legal discourse will focus on philosophical questions concerning personal taste and the meaning of representation, rather than who is getting hurt by whom' (Cole, 1989: 78). To avoid the question of interpretation Cole must adopt an apodictic position on what pornography is and does. She claims that pornography causes the sexual subordination of women; it consists of sexual representations of women in subordinated positions. To avoid interpreting these representations she provides a list of 'specific details regarding what the

products of pornography have to look like in order to be actionable'
(Cole, 1989: 98). Cole does not acknowledge that what something *has
to look like* is always the product of an interpretation. She affirms
that her 'specific details'[11] are concrete and self-evident, and that to
recognize them in a text does not involve interpretation. In other
words, if these 'specific details' were codified in law, they would do
away with the element of subjectivity that characterizes current
obscenity legislation.

The following example will highlight the hopelessness of Cole's
attempt to transcend interpretation. In an exercise in 'decoding,' she
taught her class of grade 12 students how to detect the exploitation
and dehumanization of women in heavy metal rock videos: 'I asked
the students to make a list of all the things the women were doing
in the video (usually not much, except for standing there as objects),
the number of violent acts (many), the gender of the perpetrators
(almost always male) and the gender of the victims (usually female).
The students got the message ... Basing my method on feminist
theories of representation, I was able to show that there were issues
of form rather than just content to be considered' (Cole, 1989: 135–6).
Cole claims that by giving priority to the form over the content of a
text she can avoid the problem of interpretation. But is the form of
a text unmediated? In her method, Cole must identify certain images
or codes as signifying the pornographic genre, and thus she assumes
that there is a one-to-one correspondence between the word or the
image (the signifier 'women not doing much') and its meaning (the
signified 'women being victimized'). This is a fallacy. Saussure, the
father of structuralism, has shown in his *Course in General Linguistics* (1966) that the meaning of a signifier is never fixed but is depend-
ent on its relation of equivalence and difference with other signifiers
in a system of language. The link between the word 'rabbit' (signifier)
and the concept of a little furry animal (signified) is therefore arbitrary. It was not established through some natural connection, but
rather purely through social convention. Consequently, the link can
change and the meaning can be altered: whereas Cole might be more
likely to think of the objectification of women (such as Playboy
bunnies) when she hears the word 'rabbit,' I, as the daughter of a car
dealer, might be more likely to think of the convertible car I long for
but can't afford.

Literary theorists, linguists, semioticians, and anthropologists have
increasingly challenged the view that meaning resides in the signifier,

and have emphasized instead the embeddedness of every utterance in particular social contexts. Perhaps the most influential positions come from the work of Ludwig Wittengstein (1953) and Mikhail Bakhtin (1981), who argue that language must be thought as an ensemble of social games and practices. Following from this argument is the position that language constructs, rather than reflects, the world. The world, then, is a text that does not exist outside of us but is produced by us. The quest for the essential or the true meaning of texts has thus been increasingly forsaken. Instead of searching for a single unified and immutable meaning intrinsic to the text, theorists pay greater attention to the process by which meaning is creatively constructed by readers.[12] The view that meaning is not to be discovered through the working of some immanent essence does not entail the deduction that texts are in practice always relative, indeterminate, and arbitrary. Interpretation is never free, but is always contingent. Meaning thus is always contextually and socially specific (Herrnstein Smith, 1988; Bourdieu, 1977; 1979).

The recourse to context has been of great significance for proponents of the feminist critique of pornography. By contextualizing pornography in social relations that organize the dependency and subordination of women, they made pornography the ultimate expression of sexism. The problem, though, is with the meaning of that context. The context in which pornography takes place in feminist anti-pornography accounts is too rigid. Indeed, context takes on such a totalizing and monolithic form in these accounts that agency ceases to exist.

For example, if we go back to Cole's implicit assumption that the meaning of pornographic codes and images are fixed (as in her example of the decoding of a rock video), we may ask why the meaning she attributes to those codes and images might not be obvious to us all? How can Cole assert that she has access, through her method, to the *real* meaning of pornographic texts? The answer is obvious to her: 'No one likes to believe that they [sic] are being manipulated or victimized' (Cole, 1989: 109). If we read the codes and images differently, if we think, for example, that as heterosexual women we make sexual choices – such as wanting to give one's lover head – and that we indeed consent to certain sexual practices – such as being tied to the bed – we have been manipulated by a sexual system of male dominance and female subordination (Cole, 1989: 110, 124, 126, 131, 143; MacKinnon, 1987: 7, 11, 172, 180–3; Dworkin, 1979). In the context of male power, sexual consent, choice, and preferences are simply liberal illusions.[13] Cole's attitudes are expressed succinctly in her statement that

consent has real meaning only if we accept the liberal terms on sexuality ... If we understand that social and sexual relations are constructed with the interests of male power at stake, if we accept that the socialization process begins at day one and never really lets up, if we understand that what distinguishes humans from any other animal is precisely our malleability and our ability to learn, then consent becomes a buzzword with very little sting. When ideology meets the body, consent no longer exists. (1989: 124)

How, one may ask, is Cole capable of not consenting to male power, to that totalizing sexual system, if, as she claims, 'pornography co-opts all of us' (Cole, 1989: 134)? If pornography, the instrument par excellence of our patriarchal system, determines our sexual identity so as to reproduce male dominance and female subordination, why has it not determined Cole's identity? In short, by conceiving the social context as 'a system that makes sexual abuse inevitable, and an ideology that is certain to keep women down' (Cole, 1989: 131), feminists like Cole cannot account for agency.

Contemporary theories, particularly in anthropology, have made a remarkable contribution to our understanding of contexts by showing how social constraints do not form a unitary structure and do not emanate from above (for example, Rosaldo, 1989). Their analyses suggest instead that the social world is made up of a multiplicity of discourses, which exist only through their continual reproduction and evolution in everyday practices (Bourdieu, 1977; 1979). Such analyses show how meanings and values are constituted through social struggles.

The feminist anti-pornography description of the pornographic text as the most powerful supplier of misogynist interpretive directions must be criticized for its essentialism and inattention to social agency. The challenge contemporary theories pose to the feminist anti-pornography movement lies in the way they contextualize perception in the multiplicity of discursively constituted experiences people have of themselves and the world. This approach will help to identify the assumptions, conventions, and understandings specifying the contours of what can be perceived at any particular conjuncture. If this challenge is not taken up, pornography remains inevitably reduced to a unitary meaning produced by a homogeneous context.

The Politics of Sexuality

The third factor that explains why the feminist anti-pornography movement reduced pornography to female subordination is its view of sexuality, particularly male sexuality, as coercive. We have already seen that feminist analyses of pornography drastically differ from those of conservative and civil libertarian organizations in that feminists emphasize pornography's sexist, rather than sexual, content. This important distinction became blurred in the feminist campaign against pornography. In effect, its tendency to lump together various forms of sexual representations (such as alternative gay and lesbian porn with mainstream heterosexual porn) indicated a difficulty with sex per se. The equation of pornography with sex is problematic, because, among other things, such an equation decontextualizes sex and pornography from the social relations in which they take form and reduces them to a single force or truth: an aggressive male nature and culture desiring to oppress women.

In *Pornography: Men Possessing Women* (1979), Andrea Dworkin asserts the necessity of contextualizing pornography in a sexual system of male domination. However, she claims that male supremacy 'authentically originates in the penis' (1979: 24). Moreover, Dworkin makes the penis the most significant 'symbol of terror' (1979: 15) in human history, because the penis represents men's capacity to verbally assault, threaten, batter, sexually abuse, rape, and murder women (Dworkin, 1979: 15). This capacity of the penis to terrorize and dominate women is fundamental: not only is it the 'outstanding theme and consequence of male history and male culture, [it also] illuminates [man's] essential nature and basic purpose' (Dworkin, 1979: 15–16). In the context of a sexual system founded in the power of the penis, pornography plays a central role:

The pornography itself is objective and real and central to the male sexual system. The valuation of women's sexuality in pornography is objective and real because women are so regarded and so valued. The force depicted in pornography is objective and real because force is so used against women. The debasing of women depicted in pornography and intrinsic to it is objective and real in that women are so debased. The uses of women depicted in pornography are objective and real because women are so used. (Dworkin, 1979: 200-1)

Pornography thus exposes the *truth* of sex: it is a real instance of sex, that is, of male power, and has real consequences for women. Accordingly, male sexuality becomes the political problem facing feminism.

The idea that male sexuality is the problem was also addressed in the work of Catharine MacKinnon, who transformed Dworkin's angry prose into a more analytical account of women's oppression. Conscious of the theoretical dangers of biologism inherent in Dworkin's analysis, MacKinnon adopts a social constructionist position, whereby pornography becomes a 'constitutive practice' of sexuality: 'What matters is the way in which the pornography itself provides what those who consume it want. Pornography *participates* in its audience's eroticism through creating an accessible sexual object, the possession and consumption of which *is* male sexuality, as socially constructed; to be consumed and possessed as which, *is* female sexuality, as socially constructed; pornography is a process that constructs it that way' (1987: 173; emphasis in original). In other words, pornography is a process that constructs both women's and men's sexuality according to what men want. Because what men fundamentally want is the real sexual subordination of women, pornography is real sex: 'Pornography is not a distortion, reflection, projection, expression, fantasy, representation, or symbol either. It is sexual reality' (MacKinnon, 1987: 173). Despite claiming to be social-constructionist, MacKinnon's account is still inscribed in an essentialist view of sexuality, a view, in other words, based on the idea that there is a fundamental antagonism between the sexes that leads inevitably to the subordination of women.

There are striking similarities between the positions of anti-pornography feminists and conservative organizations on both gender relations and sexuality. For example, they see gender relations as determined mostly by biological differences, and they tend to see male sexuality as aggressive. In concluding this chapter, I would like to emphasize the similarity of the contemporary feminist campaign against pornography and sexual exploitation to the religious and moralistic struggles of earlier centuries, struggles that resulted in the consolidation of Victorian morality. I want to suggest that the precarious alliance between feminists and conservatives in the 1980s was not without precedent. Feminists had been involved in these early public campaigns to eradicate sexual exploitation of women. Their efforts brought them into an alliance with the more conservative social-purity movement. Such an alliance resulted in the enactment of controlling and repressive medical, social, psychological, and legal measures that had little correspondence to feminist goals of greater equality. In fact, the outcomes of the morality crusades of the mid-nineteenth century led to the more active surveillance and persecution of those who lived outside monogamous heterosexual marriages. The alliance of nineteenth-century feminists and conservatives was the effect of feminists' adherence to the 'separate sphere' ideology, stressing women's higher morality, purity, and domesticity, coupled with their class bias. The domestic ideology of early feminists assumed that women were essentially moral beings, 'spiritual creatures' in need of protection from the essentially animalistic, vicious men. The obsession with 'male vice' was thus central to the feminist alliance with the social-purity movement (Walkowitz, 1980; 1982). Implicitly, the idea that women needed protection from the violent, insatiable, and unpredictable sexual nature of men turned every woman into a passive victim.

For many women in the Victorian era, sex often meant brutality, the burdens of motherhood, or prostitution. It was difficult, indeed, to assert the pleasures of female sexuality. Some feminists, however, advocated pleasurable sex for women by arguing that male sexuality was not essentially vicious but, rather, constructed. Their position on sexuality was not popular enough to disarticulate the hegemony of the ideology of female victimization and of the need for female protection (Bland, 1983; Walkowitz, 1980; 1982; Taylor, 1981; Burstyn, 1985). It remains to be seen whether the contemporary feminist opposition to the feminist campaign for criminalizing pornography was more successful in undermining the hegemonic association of pornography, sexuality, and danger.

3

Compliance with and Resistance to the Feminist Claim of Harm

The previous chapter showed that the strength of the feminist anti-pornography movement lay in changing the focus of the debate from the immorality of sex to the degradation of women. The movement's attempt to raise consciousness about the sexism and violence alleged-ly inherent in all pornography succeeded in mobilizing many people to campaign against the porn trade, but it also created a strong resis-tance towards law reform. In this chapter I will examine how, in the wake of the feminist anti-pornography movement, four distinct, although not necessarily coherent, positions on pornography emerged, positions that have had a profound effect on blue politics in Canada. They include those of conservative organizations, of civil libertarian organizations, of feminists against censorship, and of sex radicals.

The Conservative Position on Pornography in the 1980s

We have seen in the previous chapter that in the 1960s conservative organizations opposed the publishing of sexually explicit material on the ground that it was an offence to decency and public morality. They argued that by glorifying the separation of sex from procreation, pornography corrupts the mind and potentially damages the moral fabric of society as a whole. In the 1980s, conservative organizations opposed pornography on the same basis; however, their discourse was radically different, and incorporated a model that placed pornography in the context of women's oppression. Witness, for instance, the lan-guage of the United Church of Canada: 'The United Church of Canada forcefully condemns pornography as one form of violence against women in our society. We believe all women are degraded

and violated by its mere existence, and that pornography is a contributing factor in the rape and battering of women ... Our ultimate
dream is justice and dignity for all people and we believe one facet of
justice for women is the eradication of pornography' (1986: 1). For
conservative groups, pornography, the 'evil thing' and 'sinful' means
to 'promote lust' that 'morally depraves and decays' the mind (Soper,
1961), suddenly becomes a form of violence against women, of degradation and dehumanization.

Like anti-pornography feminists, conservative organizations in the
1980s put the issues of justice and human dignity at the centre of
their critique. R.E.A.L. Women of Canada, a conservative anti-femin-
ist group, makes the familiar conservative objection to pornography,
but slips into a language similar to that of feminists; what is wrong
with pornography, R.E.A.L. Women states, is

that much of the questionable material presently available, appears to
divorce sex from the context of a mature, loving relationship. Indeed sex is
most frequently depicted as 'a recreation rather than an expression of love
and affection. *The women and men involved, become mere objects to satisfy
sexual desires, and much of the material would appear to be exploitative
of women depicting them as having value only for sexual purposes.* This
type of material, dehumanizes not only the sex act itself, but also human
beings and society as a whole. The intrinsic dignity, intellect and spirituality
of human persons are ignored and made irrelevant. (1984a: 1; emphasis
added)

The conservative argument that pornography dehumanizes women
and the sex act is similar to the feminist distinction between pornography and erotica. Pornography, for feminists, is an expression of
sexual violence that robs women of their dignity and humanity;
erotica expresses love, mutuality, and fulfilment – things that conservatives value.

While the conservative position still has residual elements of the
old argument, one can see the profound influence of the feminist
anti-pornography discourse. Conservative organizations, for example,
understood the feminist critique of pornography as an attack on the
abuse of human dignity and human rights rather than as an attack on
sex. This critique, they claim, spoke directly to their concerns. Dr
Suzanne Scorsone, head of the Office of Family Life of the Catholic
Archdiocese of Toronto, goes so far as to say that the respect for the

dignity and equality of individuals has always been more central to the conservative opposition to pornography than a concern about sex. For her, the idea that church people are opposed to sex is the product of a biased and ill-informed media. While church people have invariably opposed pornography on moral grounds, their concerns were always more than a simple opposition to the prurient. Indeed, 'the reasoning of the church has always been more or less the reasoning of the feminist groups and human rights groups.'[1]

It is precisely this reasoning – that pornography, by glorifying the sexual subordination of women, assaults women's dignity, humanity, and equality – that, interestingly enough, brought together feminist and conservative organizations into a precarious alliance of anti-pornography, pro-censorship forces. In fact, some of the most active feminist organizations opposing pornography, such as the Toronto Metro Action Committee against Public Violence against Women and Children, the Canadian Coalition against Media Pornography, the Toronto Task Force on Violence against Women and Children, and the Canadian Coalition against Violent Entertainment, worked closely with the churches in the 1980s in the campaign to criminalize pornography. Dr Scorsone, who was a very active member on behalf of the churches in this struggle, asserts that pornography is the issue that reunited the feminist movement – a movement, according to her, strongly divided over the abortion question:

With respect to pornography, I do not find a difference [between church people and feminists], which is why we had as much impact as we did. For perhaps the first time since the beginning of modern militant feminism, you had people who had been opposed to one another because of the abortion issue. Women had become polarized. They would have difficulty saying 'good morning' to each other on the subway; they would dress differently; there were all kinds of social parameters: they were different endogamous groups, if you will. [Then], with pornography, they suddenly found themselves in alliance with one another, and were saying very similar things. And each side looked at the other and said: 'I'm on the side they are, aye!' and gradually people became more comfortable with that. I found that extremely intriguing and very pleasing, because I have been a feminist since I was a child.[2]

This alliance between feminist and conservative organizations was unstable, because conservatives retained their 'traditional' attitude towards sex: that it acquires its true meaning and purpose in the context of the family. (I will return to this point about the alliance later.)

Sex, the Coalition for Family Values argues, is a highly appreciated value among conservatives: 'Our opposition to pornography and to the public exploitation of sex has nothing to do with sex being 'dirty.' To the contrary: it has everything to do with the highest regard for human sexuality and healthy sexual relations in their proper and positive context ... [Sexual relations] must be known in a deeper context of significance if they are to retain their meaning' (Coalition for Family Values, n.d.: 7).

The Reverend Hudson Hilsden, the chair of the Interchurch Committee on Pornography, describes the threat that pornography poses for the conservative appreciation of sexuality: 'All pornography is against the family. There is no such thing as pornographic material supporting the family. It's all extramarital and premarital acts – types of sex generally not supportive of family growth and strength. What all that does is say "if you get pleasure from it it's okay" and we believe that undermines attitudes towards sex and the place of sex in marriage and the family. There's now a desensitization towards this kind of material. People aren't shocked anymore.'[3]

For conservatives, then, sex should be an affair of the traditional family. As long as it expresses marital love, mutuality, and bonding, sex has a purpose and can be celebrated.[4] Pornography is dehumanizing and degrading because it denies sex its purpose and glorifies its abuse. On that basis alone conservative organizations could have opposed pornography; but in the 1980s campaign to criminalize pornography, they opted for a scientific foundation.

The Mobilization of Science: Facts versus Morality

Whereas in the 1960s conservatives appealed to external moral verities as grounds for the prohibition of pornography, in the 1980s, influenced by the feminist movement, they based their appeal on the hard facts of science. Mrs Gwen Landolt, the chair of R.E.A.L. Women of Canada, explains that the conservative opposition to pornography is not about imposing virtue on society any more: 'The point is not that we are prudish. People like to say that. Feminists like to dismiss any one who has a contrary view on soft core pornography. It is not a matter of prudishness, but it is the effect it has on society. And we are saying it is not proper to ignore the scientific evidence on the dangerousness of sexually explicit material.'[5]

Thus anti-pornography feminists and conservatives both mobilized science; but conservatives were willing to push scientific facts further. Drawing on 'new scientific findings based on massive research,' conservative organizations attempted to convince the public that the feminist position on the harm pornography causes to women and society, while substantiated and good in itself, did not take the implications of the relevant scientific research seriously enough. Science, R.E.A.L. Women of Canada argued, unequivocally demonstrates the harm and danger that sexually explicit material inflicts on women and society in general:

Research now available clearly indicates that portrayals of sex (soft core pornography) lead to a desensitization towards anti-social acts such as rape and sexual contact with children. It also changes perceptions and attitudes about the role of the family, marriage and promiscuity. A 1987 study indicates that viewing sexually explicit material causes a loss of respect for and the demeaning of women ... In addition *the viewing of sexually explicit material leads to an addiction for such material and an increased desire for even stronger material.* (R.E.A.L. Women of Canada, n.d.a)

For conservatives, then, the feminist distinction between pornography and erotica is untenable. Indeed, because science has already demonstrated that 'stronger material' (pornography) harms women, as feminists maintain, and now corroborates that 'soft core' material (erotica) causes harm, there is no distinction between pornography and erotica. For conservatives, in other words, the issue of pornography is simple: sexually explicit material harms women, corrupts the individual, breaks up the family, and destroys society – science proves it. The implications of scientific research on pornography for society being so clear,[6] prohibition is the only solution.

Conservatives maintained that all of their moral pronouncements against pornography were currently substantiated by the facts of science. For example, in a leaflet addressed to the Standing Parliamentary Committee on Justice, conservatives argue that scientists have 'discovered profound attitude differences toward sexuality and relationships formed on its basis' (R.E.A.L. Women of Canada, n.d.b: 7). Those exposed to sexually explicit material show a lack of desire to raise a family, approve 'male dominance over females *twenty* times more than did a control group,' and were convinced that sexual pleasure comes without enduring commitment, that sexual repression is a health hazard, that promiscuity is natural, and that children are liabilities.[7] In addition, frequent exposure to sexually explicit material induces a 'greater tendency to accept premarital and extramarital sexual affairs as normal behaviour,' makes acceptable 'the idea of having several partners rather than being faithful to one,' and allows people to 'decrease their capacity to form sound marriage bonds' (Interchurch Committee on Pornography, 1987a).

The fact that conservative organizations recast their moral opposition to sexually explicit material in the language of science shows the hegemony of science in the public culture. The appeal of science lies in its promise to deliver knowledge that is truly objective rather than based on someone's or some group's idea of right and wrong. In the face of increased social, political, and economic changes and conflicts, as well as uncertainty about the future, the facts of science appear to construct a world of truth and order – a savoir that transcends all differences of opinion and can help society maintain a genuine common good. In other words, the aura of indisputability, unequivocality, and certainty surrounding science, particularly in the public culture, gives science pre-eminence over moral reasoning: science produces a moral order that appears almost external to human design (Gusfield, 1981a).

Some conservative organizations clearly perceived the political significance of mobilizing science to produce a position on pornography that could propel people into action. While they embraced scientific evidence for the 'truth' it provides on a subject they knew about all along (thanks to 'common sense'), science's popular appeal was not lost on them. Witness my exchange with Scorsone on the limits of science:

Scorsone: I am a scientist, I am a social anthropologist.

Lacombe: Then you must know the methodological problems with quantitative and qualitative research.

S.: Exactly!

L.: And the difficulty with proving cause-effect relationship, the difficulty to predict, and to –

S.: That's right. In science you cannot prove a thing, you can present relative probabilities of things, you can make something reasonably demonstrable, you can show that something is highly likely in a laboratory setting. But, if somebody with an axe to grind wants to come in and say you have not proven a thing, well, of course not! Only in mathematics can you prove anything and even with chaos theory they are beginning to throw some cold water on that one [laughter]. So can you prove? No! ...

L.: Do you get the sense that in our society today to talk about pornography in terms of morality seems old-fashioned and that one is more likely to move the public by mobilizing science?

S.: Yes, yes ... The problem today is that common sense has been sidelined. You've got to have forty-five thousand studies to prove something. And this is particularly useful to the distributors in this particular area [of pornography] because how the ding dong do you prove that somebody has a lower self-esteem? You know, it is like trying to nail jelly to the wall.

L.: It is interesting what you are saying. The argument of the church people today, then, is not that different from their position on pornography in the 1960s. It is just that in between they have learned to use science.

S.: Yes, exactly.

L.: Why? To be pragmatic?

S.: Yes, and to shift the language. Theology has always done that. Thomas Aquinas took Aristotle and used him to make explicit something that had always been kind of an implicit understanding of the Church and of the faith, *but he used another kind of logical philosophic language to make it explicit in a way that was relevant to his time, and to make it much clearer.* I think the same thing has happened here: *the attitudes, the basic understandings are exactly the same* ... What was simply a common sense perception before, and a theological orientation towards what the nature of sexuality ought to be, all of that came together and has been made explicit in the language of today as opposed to the language of the forties.

L.: In other words, the values are still the same.

S.: The values are still the same, and they have always been both what sexuality is supposed to be about and how you are supposed to treat another human being. It has always been a human rights view.[8]

This extract confirms the importance of mobilizing science in constructing an argument for the prohibition of pornography in the 1980s. As Scorsone explains, science has become the language 'relevant to our time,' and in today's society it is 'common sense' to believe the facts of science, to accept the scientific ways of knowing.

There are times, though, when science contradicts 'common sense,' when science fails, because there is always 'somebody with an axe to grind' who might come along to disprove your facts. When this happens, there is another option, as feminists also knew: to mobilize the law to preserve that ambiguous and cryptic notion, the common good.

The Mobilization of Law to Restore a Conservative Common Good

Like the feminist position, the argument of conservative organizations against pornography combines scientific and legal discourse. For conservative organizations, it is incumbent on the law to protect society and its values, 'the common good,' and thus allow for 'people to achieve their own fulfilment' (Canadian Conference of Catholics Bishop, 1984: 9). Because science has proved pornography to be inherently dehumanizing, conservatives argue that it should be eradicated by law.

By eradicating pornography, the law would reinforce the common good and punish those who work against it (Canadian Conference of Catholic Bishops, 1984: 8–10). The common good, however, is not nearly as common as conservatives would like to imagine. For example, the good life, for them, is guided by a value system in which heterosexuality, the monogamous patriarchal family, and the life of the foetus are all cherished. The alleged universality of this value system necessarily entails the subordination of individual liberty rights to the common good. While conservatives respect certain individual rights, their notion of the common good would automatically suppress, for example, the freedom of sexual orientation and the freedom to control one's body. In other words, the conservative common good does not provide for a truly plural democratic expression of difference and diversity.

Conservative notions of the common good and common sense, and the interests behind them, conflict conspicuously with those of feminists. Yet despite the undemocratic aspect of the conservative position, anti-pornography feminists were willing to join forces with conservatives in the campaign to criminalize pornography.

On 5 February 1984 a symposium on media violence and pornography was held in Toronto. Numerous pro-censorship, feminist, and non-feminist organizations concerned about violence in cultural productions attended the conference. Members of the Federal Bureau of Investigation (FBI) informed their Canadian neighbours about the variety of violent and degrading pornography circulating in the United States that could invade Canada if strict anti-pornography legislation was not enacted. The FBI presented artistic pictures of naked children and young people playing on the beach, and prints of bathing babies that could well have been taken from any family album, alongside images of sexually mutilated babies, thus showing that they were unable to discriminate between images of sexual abuse and images of nudity and consensual sexual activity. They equated sexuality and nudity with pornography. This logic suggests that sexuality, in the broadest sense imaginable, is the problem that must be eradicated in order to control child molesters and rapists. At the symposium, feminists and conservatives implicitly endorsed this sweeping definition of pornography: they implored the public to sign petitions demanding (1) an end to the importation of pornographic materials into Canada, (2) the enactment of censorship laws, and (3) the empowerment of law enforcement agencies involved in the fight against pornography. This anti-pornography, pro-censorship alliance was to become highly significant in the elaboration of a legislation to counteract pornography. I will examine the effect of this alliance when I analyse the institutional responses to the pornography debate.

In sum, this section has shown how the feminist argument that pornography had to be understood in the context of women's oppression had an effect on the conservative movement against pornography. By drawing on the feminist discourse that pornography harms women, conservatives rearticulated their moral pronouncements against the public representation of sexually explicit material. To this end, they mobilized science to produce an unequivocal picture of the harm pornography inflicts on women and on society in general, and resorted to law to challenge a social order that had become less harmonious with their idea of the good life. Unsurprisingly, conservatives sought to join feminists in the anti-pornography movement. Surprisingly, feminists accepted them. Feminists did not succeed in pulling civil libertarian organizations into their movement; however, the strength of the feminist position did force civil libertarians to rethink their position.

The Civil Libertarian Position in the 1980s

In contrast to the 1960s, when they defined pornography in terms of sexual explicitness and its positive impact on sexual liberation, in the 1980s most civil liberties and human rights organizations saw pornography as an affront to women's dignity.[9] They denounced pornography for objectifying, degrading, and exploiting women and children. The Canadian Civil Liberties Association (CCLA), for instance, unambiguously supported the feminist critique of pornography. It had 'no hesitation in joining the National Action Committee on the Status of Women in an unequivocal denunciation of the "new pornography." We refer to those publications and films which appear to celebrate the sexual abuse of women and children. It is hard to fathom how exposure to such material could elicit a reaction more positive than revulsion' (CCLA, 1984: 1). While most civil liberties organizations morally condemned pornography, they could not support the feminist campaign to criminalize it.

Civil liberties organizations agreed in principle with the feminist rationale for criminalizing pornography: anything detrimentally affecting the right to equality should fall within the jurisdiction of the criminal law. For, as Alister Browne of the British Columbia Civil Liberties Association (BCCLA) explains, 'equality is an important social value, and anything which impairs it counts as an important harm to others' (quoted in Russell, 1989: 31). These organizations, however, could not ultimately support the feminist demand for exercising the criminal law against pornography. Science, they argued, does not substantiate the feminist argument that pornography poses a significant threat to women – a threat significant enough to justify restricting freedom of expression. Criticizing the recommendation of the report of the Special Committee on Pornography and Prostitution (Canada, 1985) to criminalize pornography because of its negative consequences on women's right to equality, the BCCLA claims:

Uncontroversially, pornography depicts women as sexual objects. But this is not something which, *in itself*, adversely affects the status of women; that is done only if the depictions produce or reinforce certain attitudes toward women, and those attitudes result in women being treated as second-class citizens. The Committee, however, produces no evidence to show that either of these things is so. Indeed ... the Committee is extremely sceptical about the value of social research that purports to support such views about the effect of pornography. (Browne, 1989: 31, emphasis in original)

In the light of this inconclusiveness, censoring pornography appeared too drastic a measure for them.

One strategy civil liberties organizations used in their opposition to the feminist campaign to criminalize pornography was to mobilize science itself. They found the research showing that men exposed to violent pornography responded more aggressively to women than did those who were not exposed convincing in laboratory settings only. Such findings could not possibly justify criminalizing pornography, even on a feminist ground, because their application was not generalizable to all men, most of whom have never been in laboratory conditions. Civil libertarians also drew on the work of the psychologist Edward Donnerstein, the researcher most often quoted by the anti-pornography movement, and showed that his work does not reveal a substantial link between pornography and violence against women (Borovoy, 1988: 63; see also Victoria Civil Liberties Association, 1987). As for the more plausible link between exposure to pornography and attitudinal changes in men, Alan Borovoy, the general counsel of the Canadian Civil Liberties Association, is not impressed: 'If we could suppress material merely because of its detrimental impact on male attitudes towards women, what about other potentially harmful attitudes? Could we suppress Communist propaganda for undermining our attitudes about the value of preserving democracy? Could we suppress certain feminist material because it might arguably create negative attitudes about the institution of marriage?' (1988: 63).

In sum, civil liberties organizations recognized that pornography, like any other text, influences the reader, but that its effects are not harmful enough to warrant the use of the criminal law. If science could prove that exposure to pornography led to antisocial behaviour, civil libertarians were prepared to advocate its suppression. The evidence, however, was too equivocal.

While civil libertarians pointed to the methodological weaknesses of the studies on pornography premised on the social learning model, they sometimes still uncritically embraced the research premised on the catharsis model. Based on vulgar psychoanalysis, which assumes an essentially antisocial impulse in human nature, this model implies that pornography actually decreases antisocial behaviour. The logic is simple – the more you see, the less you do. Pornography thus plays a useful role, because with it a good number of men, as explained by the Canadian Civil Liberties Association, can 'sublimate their aggressive impulses through harmless fantasy' (1984: 9).

Moreover, in their treatment of pornography as a fantasy, civil libertarians ignored feminist studies of the physical and psychological coercion reported in some pornographic productions. They were oblivious, in other words, to the reality of pornography as a practice, involving real people who produced it and profited by it. Feminists had shown that economic exploitation and sexual oppression in the pornography industry were no fantasy. Had civil libertarians paid more attention to these injustices, they could have discussed with feminists why criminalizing pornography was not the best way to empower women, and they could have discussed the rights and needs of those most vulnerable to exploitation by the porn industry, the porn workers themselves. Such a discussion, however, had to wait for a new player in the pornography debate – feminists against censorship.

The Position of Feminists against Censorship

In the early 1980s, a group of feminists, artists, gays, and lesbians grew dissatisfied with both the feminist campaign to criminalize pornography and the civil libertarian counterposition.[10] I call them feminists against censorship because, in spite of internal differences, this group formed a movement to fight pornography and sexism, on the one hand, and censorship on the other. Many feminists in Canada had learned from experience that law enforcement agencies with the power to censor discriminated against gay, lesbian, and feminist art. They felt that if the campaign to criminalize pornography succeeded, the agencies' power to censor would only be intensified. This is not to say that the movement against censorship was not sympathetic with the goals of the anti-pornography movement. The Ontario Film and Video Appreciation Society (OFAVAS), a feminist and anti-censorship advisory board for filmmakers, journalists, writers, artists, and performers, supported the anti-pornography movement's aim at ending violence against women, but felt that censorship was 'a placebo measure that does nothing about the real problems that discrimination causes, and which, in fact, distracts from giving those problems the attention they deserve and require. Furthermore, the very real danger exists that censorship, perhaps even inadvertently, will serve to silence the very voices that could raise awareness toward social change' (1984a:2).

None the less, this movement criticized civil libertarian arguments about freedom of expression, because such arguments did not examine the structures that oppressed and silenced women and minorities.

To counter anti-pornography feminists and civil libertarians, the movement developed a feminist argument against censorship, an argument less interested in the 'facts' of science than in the social context of pornography and censorship. Moreover, they offered practical solutions that they felt would get at the heart of women's oppression in society, such as pressuring the government for social services to deal with wife-battering, sexual harassment, rape, and other forms of violence against women: services including shelters for battered women, rape crisis centres, child care programs, and educational facilities. Such solutions, they believed, would do more to redress women's unequal status in society than censorship (OFAVAS, 1984a; 1984b).

Feminists against censorship criticized the anti-pornography movement for its implicit bias against sexuality itself. They denounced the determinism and logical incoherence of the argument that pornography reveals men's true sexuality – its latent sadism – and distorts women's nature (Coward, 1982; Wilson, 1982; Burstyn, 1985; Eckersley, 1987). They contended that such a simplistic understanding of pornography foreclosed exploring the mechanisms by which desires, fantasies, and sexual identities emerge. These feminists adopted a view of sexuality as socially constructed and as culturally and historically specific. Drawing on feminist film theories, semiotics, psychoanalysis, and structuralism, they attempted to unravel the mechanisms that make pornography a 'signifying practice' (Kuhn, 1982; Diamond, 1985; Eckersley, 1987). If pornography was not about 'real sex' or 'what men like to do to women,' as the anti-pornography movement assumed, then what made some representations pornographic?

They examined the production of pornographic meaning by using a theory of language that rejects the idea that words or representations have an intrinsic meaning. According to Coward, 'Words do not have a fixed and constant referent (their meaning) which exists out there and which we can embody by using language as a tool' (1982: 11). The production of meaning involves instead a complicated process arising from the structural context in which images or words find themselves. Meanings or significations, Coward says, 'arise from *how various elements are combined*, how the picture is framed, what lighting it is given, what is connoted by dress and expression, *the way these elements are articulated together* ... In other words, just like language, there is no intrinsic meaning in a visual image, the meaning of an image is decided by the way it is articulated, how the various elements are combined together' (Coward, 1982: 11; emphasis in original).

Consequently, this approach is less interested in the apparent content of pornography – for example, nudity or violence – than in the specific devices that make it a genre. According to Coward, pornography is a 'regime of representations of sex' involving three encodings of the female body: the code of fragmentation, the code of submission, and the code of availability. In other words, an image is pornographic only when it is constructed in such a fashion as to take away women's autonomy – women are there to please, their desires are for the male viewers (Coward, 1982; Eckersley, 1987).

Coward's definition allowed for a deconstruction of the distinction between what was traditionally termed 'pornography' and other sexist representations. Thus, for example, Canadian video artist and art teacher Lisa Steele (1985) was able to demonstrate that pornographic codes were not confined to sexually explicit material or the violent material that the anti-pornography movement defined as pornography. Her analysis of various cultural forms, such as product advertising, fashion ads, and films, pointed to the ubiquity of pornographic codes in our society. In the same vein, the feminists Ann Snitow (1979), Beatrice Faust (1980), and Mariana Valverde (1985) compared the construction of women's sexuality and fantasies in the romantic novel and mainstream pornography. Their research showed that in both these genres power and gender differences were eroticized. The feminist Nancy W. Waring (1986) interestingly compared Brian de Palma's film *Body Double*, often referred to as an exemplary pornographic text, with French neurologist Jean Martin Charcot's public theatrical demonstrations of female hysteria at the Salpêtrière Clinic in Paris. Juxtaposing art and science, she showed the pervasiveness and embeddedness of pornographic representations in our culture. In the light of the presence of pornographic devices in genres as different as hard- and soft-core porn, advertisements, popular literature, and science, feminists against censorship criticized the significance the anti-pornography movement gave to sexually explicit images. Such an emphasis was misplaced, they argued, because it suggested that the degree of sexual explicitness was more problematic than sexism (Steele, 1985).

Understanding pornography as a way of seeing, rather than as the truth of sex, these feminists showed the extensive power of sexism in our culture. In a sexist culture, the attempt to criminalize pornography appeared futile to them, because it directed attention only to the tip of the iceberg. A better strategy, they argued, was to make public, through art, the sexism and heterosexism in cultural representations and to challenge this (hetero)sexism by producing alternative, sex-positive images (Diamond, 1985; Burstyn, 1985).

Many feminist artists tried to produce such images throughout the 1980s only to find that their largest audiences were law enforcement agencies and anti-pornography feminists.[11] Feminists against censorship had assumed that if their attempts at challenging the (hetero)sexism of pornography with positive sexual imagery were considered pornographic by the authorities, the anti-pornography movement would realize how repressive and counterproductive censorship is. This was not the case: anti-pornography feminists had little sympathy for their concerns. Cole explains: 'It is possible that our feminist chronicler of sexual fantasy winds up with a lawsuit. What then? Having heard this question repeatedly, I am constantly troubled by the fact that so much caring can go out to the artist while so little goes to the woman who was forced into sex' (1989: 100).

Thus the pornography debate highlighted a moment of tension within the feminist movement, a marked strain that manifested itself in terms of differentiated actions: feminists supporting the criminalization of pornography and feminists dead set against it. But all the while, anti-pornography feminists and feminists against censorship had something essential in common: an assumption about pornography. Pornography was indubitably and unequivocally about woman-hating. This bond had consequences for the politics of pornography in the 1980s, because it automatically marginalized important voices from the debate. The politics of this marginalization will be explored later when I examine the recommendations of the Fraser Committee. Now it is essential to show exactly how, in spite of their ostensibly contradictory positions, anti-pornography feminists and feminists against censorship were actually ideologically similar.

The anti-pornography movement defined pornography as the eroticization of the subordination of women, whereas feminists anti-censorship defined it as a representation eroticizing the subordination of women. In both cases the eroticization in pornography was perceived negatively, as harmful to women: 'woman hating' was pornography's main message. Both movements used the same vocabulary to discuss pornography. For example, in response to the argument that criminalizing violent pornography was futile (because 'pornographic codes' are embedded in most cultural representations), Cole (1989) declared that violent representations of the sexual subordination of women are more 'dangerous' than any other sexist representations and therefore needed to be treated differently. The anti-censorship feminist Mariana Valverde, in *Sex, Power and Pleasure* (1985), anticipated such an argument, but in doing so used the same language: 'Even if violent porn is what angers women most, it is not necessarily the cultural form *most dangerous* to our own emotional and sexual development' (1985: 133, emphasis added). Although anti-pornography feminists and feminists against censorship understood pornography in completely different ways, both used the language of 'danger' to describe it, a language implying that pornography is inherently harmful.

Although the anti-censorship feminist Varda Burstyn, for instance, agrees with the anti-pornography movement that the message of pornography was male dominance, she finds its analysis limited for its failure to understand how 'gender or sexual politics have been mobilized and exploited, in the truest sense of that term, by capitalism' (Burstyn, 1983: 251-2). She proposes a view of pornography that would locate it within the context of patriarchal *and* capitalist social relations. Patriarchy, she argues, sets heterosexist rules for sexuality, whereas capitalism, by marketing these rules in the form of sexual representations, sells a heterosexist ideology. The interaction between capitalism and patriarchy results in 'sexuality [being] increasingly commodified and commodities increasingly sexualized' (Burstyn, 1983: 252). It follows, for her, that the messages of pornography 'are false ideological constructions' that 'sell billions of dollars worth of cosmetics, underwear, high heels, Vic Tanny memberships and *Vogue* magazines. They also create anxiety and energy that is used in dealing with the feeling they provoke, thus actively preventing women from understanding the system which oppresses them and from fighting it' (Burstyn, 1983: 252).

In Burstyn's framework, then, pornography, an instrument of capitalist patriarchy, oppresses both men and women by shaping and constantly reinforcing their sexual anxieties and fetishes. Put simply, pornography distorts and deceives us – a view not so different from that of anti-pornography feminists.

Valverde produces a reading of pornography that is also quite rigid. In her attempt to extract the meaning of pornography, she explains that 'our experience in a sexist society helps in a very important way to determine how we will interpret representations of sex and gender' (1985: 126). While this attempt to contextualize the meaning of a text in sexist social relations is very sensible, Valverde authoritatively professes that

a photo of a woman kneeling down to perform fellatio on a man has a very different social meaning than a picture of a man kneeling to perform cunnilingus on a woman. The first picture implies subordination, while the second merely implies that a man is giving a woman pleasure. The difference in the connotations is not due to anything in the photos themselves, but rather to the 'usual' connotations of women's bodies versus men's bodies. (Valverde, 1985: 126–7)

This reading of oral sex expresses a view of sexism that over-determines all other contexts. Indeed, Valverde's assertion raises the question of what makes the representation of a woman fellating a man one about female subordination: sexism, or the particular context in which this representation finds itself? If it is sexism, as implied here, then it matters little whether the representation of a woman fellating a man is found in sex magazines for men, in feminist magazines, in women's porn, or in sex education magazines. The meaning of the image appears fixed, because it is determined by sexism. Valverde would not agree with this statement;[12] however, her argument above suggests that the 'usual connotations of women's bodies' are fixed in a social system of female subordination and male domination that determines meaning independently of the other contexts in which the representation finds itself and of the other social relations in which the reader finds herself.

The rigidity of this method of reading pornography is shown further in Valverde's discussion of sexual desires. She argues for the development of a feminist sexual ethics grounded in diversity. Yet while saying she would not want to 'shame' a woman for desiring 'to wear high heels and a corset and be tied to her bed by a macho man in cowboy boots' (Valverde, 1985: 201); she does not accept such a fantasy as feminist, because 'the content of [the woman's] desire was produced by sexism' (ibid.). Valverde similarly critiques the practices of advocates of sadomasochism, who claim to use in their sexual games dominant social roles (cop/criminal; teacher/pupil; butch/femme; etc.) to subvert the power structure: 'The fact remains that they are using forms of power which a sexist and exploitative society has produced'

(1985: 175). Patriarchal, exploitative society, for Valverde, produces nothing but the false: false needs, false desires, false consciousness.

In both Valverde's and Burstyn's framework, there is no place to talk positively about sexual pleasure experienced from pornography. The idea that women may enjoy pornographic images and actually identify with them is quickly brushed aside as false consciousness. Consequently, despite their claim that sexuality is socially constructed, their accounts of pornography and sexual desires suggest a normative idea of human sexuality: women might be born free, but everywhere are in chains – or tied to the bed – for they have been manipulated by a totalizing system of oppression. Social construction is manipulation; diversity is distortion; and difference is perversion. What normal sexuality is, however, they fail to explain. They only suggest that it ought to be constructed in opposition to the eroticization of power and be judged by a feminist ethics (Valverde, 1985).

Their argument that society fiendishly manipulates, or constructs in a one-dimensional way, our sexualities and our minds raises the question of how an oppositional position, including the authors' own, could arise in the first place. Oppressive and exploitative social relations certainly shape our identities, but people are always constructed at the intersection of a multiplicity of social relations. Moreover, as suggested by contemporary social theories, the relationship between social agency and structures is mutually generative rather than determined. Analysis indicates that people are constituted by a variety of discourses as they engage in the reproduction and transformation of their everyday practices. Identity in such a model is never determined, but always precariously and provisionally fixed, or, to use Lacan's terminology, 'sutured' at the intersection of many diverse discourses (1966; Mouffe, 1988a). Thus each social agent is inscribed in a multiplicity of social relations, such as those of production, race, gender, sex, nationality, and age. These social relations are articulated in specific contexts to determine positionalities, or 'subject positions,' which are themselves traversed by a multiplicity of discourses: one's identity cannot therefore be reduced to a singularity (Mouffe, 1988a; Smith, 1988).

As Foucault (1980a) has so astutely shown, structural and institutional forces do not function on the mode of repression and negation. Rather than denying people their true nature, these forces constantly produce new knowledges, new practices, new identities, new forms of control, and new forms of resistance. Thus it is possible for us to conceive how capitalism and sexism constrain sexual identities without necessarily distorting them. For example, sexual commodities such as vibrators, leather garments, dildoes, lingerie, ropes, chains, handcuffs, and porn videos are produced under the exploitative economic conditions of capitalism; however, the desire to use them in a consensual manner to explore sexual pleasure and its limits is certainly not oppressive. Actually, as gay and lesbian AIDS activists suggest, these commodities can enhance one's sexuality: the discovery of new pleasures associated with certain commodities can expand the long-time equation of sex with genitals – an equation that has proved fatal for many when the availability of safe contraceptives, abortions on demand, and treatments for AIDS is extremely limited (Kinsman, 1987; interviews, AIDS Committee of Toronto).

Thus despite the apparent differences between the two opposed feminist positions in the pornography debate, there are important affinities in their accounts of pornography and sexuality. Conceived either as the eroticization of the sexual subordination of women or as the representation of this process, sexism is the content of pornography. Sexism, moreover, is presented as a structural force so powerful and encompassing that it determines pornography and our reaction to it. Thus feminists decry the need to establish a feminist ethics to judge representations and desires.

The equation of pornography with 'woman-hating' did not strike everyone within the pornography debate as a universal truth. Throughout the 1980s, in fact, many people, including feminists, afraid or just plain sick of being judged by an austere feminist ethics telling them that what they felt in their bodies was not real, struck out on their own, demanding a true recognition of difference.

The Position of Sex Radicals and Sex Workers

I use the term 'sex radicals' to refer to the increasing number of people who have come to adhere to the approach the historian Jeffrey Weeks calls 'radical pluralism.' Influenced by Foucault's work on sexuality (1980a) and Laclau and Mouffe's work on politics (1985), radical pluralism grounds politics in a pluralist ethics. It provides direction on how to judge conflicts and how to conduct one's life on the basis of liberal democratic principles, accounting for and dispensing a plurality of values and ways of life, rather than a single common good. The aim of radical pluralism, Weeks explains, 'is to provide guidelines for decision making rather than new absolute values. It rejects the temptation of a 'radical morality,' whether one derived from the traditions of feminism or of socialism, two political discourses which lay particular claim to moral insight. Instead it places its emphasis on the merits of choice, and the conditions which limit choices' (1986: 116).

In the realm of sexual politics, this approach draws on the libertarian tradition for its 'sex positive' attitude and aspirations for sexual freedom; but, contrary to this tradition, it rejects any normative notion of sexuality. As the sex radical Gayle Rubin explains, 'A democratic morality should judge sexual acts by the way partners treat one another, the level of mutual consideration, the presence or absence of coercion, and the quantity and quality of the pleasures they provide. Whether sex acts are gay or straight, coupled or in groups, naked or in underwear, commercial or free, with or without video, should not be ethical concerns' (1984: 283).

I have called the people who subscribe to radical pluralism 'sex radicals.' I should mention that the group, which includes advocates of sadomasochism, sex workers, and feminist filmmakers and theorists, did not necessarily use this term to refer to itself. I group them under that label because their resistance to feminist analyses of pornography and sexuality is based on a rejection of any feminist ethics that turns sexual desires, however limited, into false, distorted choices.

The sex radical Amber Hollibaugh describes her first experience of the anti-pornography movement as follows: 'When I heard Andrea Dworkin speak, she named my relationship to porn as a form of being raped. I wanted to say, "Do anything to me but still let me be alive at the end." I had to smash pornography because if I didn't, it would take my life. It was not one more position I should understand and debate as a feminist, but a life and death issue' (in English et al., 1982: 45).

While acknowledging that sexism did, as the feminist anti-pornography movement claimed, have an impact on representations and identities, sex radicals forcefully rejected the argument that their sexual desires, especially for pornography or pornographic scenarios, were false because they arose from a more or less sexist matrix. Hollibaugh responds to the feminist argument: 'That's hogwash. My fantasy life has been *constructed* in a great variety of ways. My sexual desire has been channelled. But what that view takes from me is my right to genuinely feel, in my body, what I want' (41; emphasis in original). In other words, she objects to the denial of the reality of her pleasure. She derides the negativity of the feminist attitude towards pornography and sex: 'You are told that you have a hetero-sexual model for your lesbian sexuality, you have left over penetra-tion fantasies you really should re-examine. There's never been any-thing in that rap about sex that has much joy, pleasure, power or lustiness' (41). In fact, there is little about pleasure in the feminist analysis of pornography and sex because of the tendency of the move-ment to focus on extremely violent sexual images.

The sex radical and lesbian advocate of sadomasochism Gayle Rubin accuses the feminist anti-pornography movement of manipu-lating the public into a moral crusade by choosing images unrepre-sentative of pornography as a whole. The lumping together of sadomasochistic and violent sexual images with non-sexually explicit sexist images, such as those found on billboards, women's magazines, and advertising, enables feminists 'to avoid the empirical question of how much porn really is violent' (in English et al., 1982: 49).[13] In fact, she contends that the mere presence of sadomasochistic pornography is the factor that allows feminists to proceed with a campaign to criminalize representations that are a minority genre. Rubin acknowl-edges the disturbing quality of certain images; however, she criticizes feminists for not realizing that these images are about fantasies: 'What most people do with it is take it home and masturbate. Those people who do s/m are consensually acting out fantasies. The category of people who read and use s/m porn and the category of violent rapists is not the same. We used to talk about how religion and the state and the family create sexism and promote rape. No one talks about any of these institutions any more' (English et al., 1982: 49). Sex radicals reject the link that feminists make between pornography, especially of the violent sort, with real violence by pointing to their own experience with it: they are neither rapists nor murderers.

By asserting their positive relationship to porn and enjoying the aura of transgressivity surrounding their sexuality, sex radicals show that women's reaction to pornography is not simply anger and repul-sion. Pornography carries more than 'woman-hating' messages. The feminists Lisa Duggan, Nan Hunter, and Carole Vance argue that pornography also advocates 'sexual adventure, sex outside of mar-riage, sex for no reason other than pleasure, casual sex, anonymous sex, group sex, voyeuristic sex, illegal sex, public sex. Some of these ideas appeal to women reading or seeing pornography, who may interpret some images as legitimating their own sense of sexual urgency or desire to be sexually aggressive' (1985: 145). The recognition that women respond positively to images created for men's pleasure made it imperative for sex radicals to examine the elements, other than sexism, at work in pornography, and to investigate how women appropriate pornographic images.[14]

Drawing on Freud and Foucault, sex radicals locate pornography in the context of the deployment of various discourses about sex and the self (Benjamin, 1983; Webster, 1981; Snitow, 1983; Waring, 1986; Williams, 1989). Pornography comes to represent all forms of limitations imposed on human beings. Snitow, for instance, contends that pornography,

like a lot of far more respectable twentieth-century art ... is not about personality but about the explosion of the boundaries of the self. It is a fantasy of an extreme state in which all social constraints are overwhelmed by a flood of sexual energy. Think, for example, of all the pornography about servants fucking mistresses, old men fucking young girls, guardians fucking wards. Class, age, custom – all are deliciously sacrificed, dissolved by sex.

Though pornography's critics are right – pornography *is* exploitation – it is exploitation of *everything*. Promiscuity by definition is a breakdown of barriers. Pornography is not only a reflector of social power imbalances and sexual pathologies; it is also all those imbalances run riot, run to excess, sometimes explored *ad absurdum*, exploded. Misogyny is one content of pornography; another content is the universal infant desire for complete, immediate gratification, to rule the world out of the very core of passive helplessness. (1983: 256; emphasis in original)

For sex radicals, then, pornography problematizes sex, selves, and social constraints.

Once sex radicals had shown that pornography was not simply a tool of patriarchal capitalism but a representation questioning sex by incorporating a plurality of practices and discourses that operated across various institutions, they could examine the various powers of pornography. Of major interest to them, especially to those working in film theory, was female pleasure. Assuming that women were not unified beings or one-dimensional dupes but were constructed by a multiplicity of discourses, sex radicals argued that women incorporate contradictions they can mobilize in a 'potentially productive way'

(Mayne, 1985: 92). As the feminist filmmaker Bette Gordon demonstrates in her films, 'women, even in patriarchal culture, are active agents who interpret and utilize cultural symbols on their own behalf' (1984: 196). Far from being the passive receptacle of pornography, the supine object of the male gaze, women respond actively: they appropriate, subvert, and disrupt pornographic codes; they manipulate the male gaze for their pleasure (de Lauretis, 1984; 1987; Williams, 1989; Ellsworth, 1985; Church et al., 1993).

The fact that women read sexist texts à rebours, with a gaze of their own, undermines the argument that women's sexuality is distorted by the dominant male culture. Moreover, it challenges the feminist idea that it is only outside the dominant structures of society that women's sexuality will be able to flourish (Coward, 1982; Williams, 1989; Church et al., 1993). In other words, the idea that women construct pornography by subverting its codes in a productive way problematizes the plea for an alternative feminist pornography or erotica purified from all contaminated social relations. For the feminist filmmaker Gordon, an alternative feminist porn is politically suspect, because it implies 'marginality – the 'other place' outside of culture that women have already been assigned. I don't want to maintain that outsideness' (1984: 194). For other sex radicals, such as Rubin, the idea of an alternative feminist porn is comparable to that of 'sex after the revolution,' an idea 'so removed from anything that we do now that it transcends the flesh itself. It becomes an *absence* of anything that we do now, all of which is contaminated by this earthly, fleshy existence' (in English et al., 1982: 41; emphasis in original).

Because female identities are socially constructed, because they incorporate a variety of historically specific discourses and practices, and because there is no place outside these historical specificities, an attempt to occupy the purified exterior is logically unsound. Moreover, it is politically disastrous; such a move is tantamount to putting women right back where they have been assigned: that most gloriously useless of places, the pedestal.

One group of people who have never been put on pedestals and who know the pains and pleasures of working with mainstream pornography are the sex workers. They reject the feminist idea that all pornography is unhealthy and that an alternative feminist porn is the solution. The stripper Debi Sundahl sums up their attitude: 'We know better than anyone what is healthy and what is not healthy about our work' (1987: 180). But society usually has little time for their opinions. When sex workers have had the opportunity to express themselves in legitimate settings – feminist conferences, books, documentaries – far from organizing the revolution, they have made straightforward rights claims for better working conditions. Describing the poor conditions in which she works, Sundahl asserts that

stripping is traditional women's work as much as waitressing, teaching and secretarial work is. Consequently, it suffers from the same low pay. Considering the high demand for erotic performers and the low supply, and the fact that the service they provide is a rare commodity, most erotic performers are vastly underpaid. The working conditions, overall, are also poor; many theatres are run on a quasi-legitimate financial basis, and are not clean and safe. Often, the basic tools necessary for the job – like adequate sound and light systems, ample dressing room space, and equipment (like washers, dryers and irons) to care for costumes – are not provided. Even though most dancers work more than forty hours a week, no vacation or overtime pay is provided, nor are there any health benefits. Many dancers fear becoming ill because missing one day of work will put their jobs in jeopardy. (1987: 178)

Sex workers propose a strategy for ameliorating the conditions in which they labour. This challenge, far from rejecting pornography, is an attempt to subvert from within the constraining aspects of the skin trade.

That sex workers are asking for empowerment rather than the destruction of their trade, however mainstream it is, suggests that the pornography trade is far less victimizing than the feminist anti-pornography movement suggests. Sex workers have reacted forcefully against the totalizing image that feminists have imposed on them and their profession. They feel that feminists' negative attitude towards pornography and their missionary zeal with respect to its fallen practitioners have impeded them from making concrete improvements in their working conditions. In 1987 the Ontario Public Interest Research Group organized a conference where feminists and sex workers were brought face to face.[15] Sex workers told feminists to stop stereotyping them as victims of economic conditions, family structure, child sexual abuse, forced immigration, or drug addiction. Sex workers opposed this image of their oppression in the skin trade by asserting their decision-making power over their choice of profession, and by claiming pleasure, self-worth, and financial gratification.

In a book of essays by sex workers, Nina Hartley, a self-defined feminist porn star and founder of a women's support group within the porn industry (the Pink Ladies Club) declares:

I find performing in sexually explicit material satisfying on a number of levels. First, it provides a physically and psychically safe environment for me to live out my exhibitionistic fantasies. Secondly, it provides a surprisingly flexible and supportive arena for me to grow in as a *performer*, both sexually and non-sexually. Thirdly, it provides me with erotic material that I like to watch for my own pleasure. Finally, the medium allows me to explore the theme of celebrating a positive female sexuality – a sexuality that has hueretofore been denied us. In choosing my roles and characterizations carefully, I strive to show, always, women who thoroughly enjoy sex and are forceful, self-satisfying and guilt-free without also being neurotic, unhappy or somehow unfulfilled. (1987: 142; emphasis in original)

Sex workers, in short, wanted feminists to understand that despite its constraints the sex trade is emotionally satisfying and even politically enabling. (Moreover, the sex trade has a sense of humour that is disconcerting to the feminist anti-pornography movement. Sex workers organized themselves in a way that clearly indicated how fed up they were with the moralizing attitude of feminists and others – as the acronym COYOTE of the American organization for the rights of prostitutes suggests: Call Off Your Old Tired Ethics.)

Sex workers responded to the attempt to criminalize pornography by organizing. In spite of their failure to convince the feminist anti-pornography movement to re-evaluate its moralistic attitude towards the sex industry, sex workers, however fleetingly, collectively voiced their discontent. Organizing, though, is no easy task. The difficulty is not surprising, considering how the sex industry and its employees are often prey to policing and the law, and how they are generally forced to maintain a low profile. Harassed and trivialized, sex workers have been the least influential of the major players in Canada's blue politics.[16]

Summary

This chapter showed that the concern over pornography in Canada was far from unified and lacked a stable ground. In fact, the public campaign to proscribe pornography was ridden with conflicts. While some argue that the pornography debate of the 1980s was still inscribed in a discourse on censorship and freedom of expression, and that not much has really changed over time, I contend otherwise.[17] The protagonists and antagonists in this dispute, who were not the same as those in the 1960s debate, raised new issues and attributed new meanings to the issues. The initial debate between conservatives and civil libertarians about the immoral or liberating nature of sexually explicit material was displaced by a debate that focused on issues raised by the feminist anti-pornography movement. Sex, the distinguishing feature of pornography in the 1960s, was increasingly superseded by sexism. The degradation, dehumanization, and object-ification of women alleged to be the subject-matter of pornography constituted, according to anti-pornography feminists, an impediment to women's right to equality.

In a strategy of constructing and deconstructing pornography as a harm to women, feminists, conservatives and civil libertarians mobilized the authoritative discourses of science and the law. Feminists and conservatives argued that science unequivocally demonstrated that pornography equals harm. They both resorted to the law to challenge a social order they perceived as less and less harmonious with their ideas of justice.

The anti-pornography movement's call for censorship was opposed by civil libertarians, feminists against censorship, and sex radicals. Their opposition to law reform was framed entirely by the feminist argument that pornography harms women. Civil libertarians agreed with feminists that anything that harms someone's right to equality falls within the jurisdiction of the law; however, they disagreed with the argument that pornography harms women, claiming that the scientific evidence was too equivocal to restrict freedom of expression. In the end, some of them lapsed back into their 1960s argument about the potentially liberatory nature of pornography.

Feminists against censorship and sex radicals responded to the call for censorship differently from civil libertarians. They resisted the equation of pornography and harm by articulating new positions on pornography, sexuality, representation, and freedom of expression. Feminists against censorship organized around their identity as socialist feminists to produce a critique of pornography and women's oppression that located such practices in the context of capitalist and patriarchal social relations. While they condemned pornography for its inherent sexism, they argued that its criminalization would not alleviate women's secondary status in society. They pointed to the class bias and sexist practices of state censorship to convince women that they would be better off fighting for legislation that would directly empower them. Their analysis of pornography, however, was strikingly similar to that of anti-pornography feminists in the way it condemned the genre outright.

Sex radicals, as users and makers of pornography, and sex workers, as pornographic performers, criticized the crusade against mainstream pornography. Opposing feminists' moralistic assumptions and pre-scriptions, sex radicals proclaimed their gratifying experience with pornography. They attempted to develop an understanding of por-nography that would account for women's positive experience of the genre, the diverse uses women and men make of pornography, and the complexity of the world of desires. Sex workers defended them-selves against accusations of false consciousness by saying that they freely chose their work and by pointing to their need to organize the porn trade rather than destroy it.

It now remains to be seen how the government responded to the intense pressure from feminist and conservative forces for censorship, and to the equally intense pressure from civil libertarians, feminists against censorship, sex radicals, and sex workers for freedom of expression.

Part 2

Institutional practices

I have so far demonstrated how, through the process of law reform, particular ways of seeing pornography were constituted. The strategies of naming, of constituting pornography and sex as a problem pointed to the emergence of new collective identities as these were struggling for recognition and attempting to create hegemony. The second part of my study will examine how the 'deployment' of the new and conflictual discursive formations on pornography, sexuality, and self affected institutional practices. While the government of Canada responded to the demand for law reform in its usual fashion – with the creation of a commission of inquiry followed by proposed legislation – the attempt at law reform ultimately failed. In the chapters that follow, I will examine what accounts for that failure and, most important, how the changing power relations of the pornography debate were embodied in the policy-making process and were responsible for the political strategies that were produced. At a theoretical level, such evidence will point to the mutually constitutive nature of 'structure' and 'agency.'

4

The Special Committee on Pornography and Prostitution

In this chapter I will investigate the factors leading to the creation of the Special Committee on Pornography and Prostitution (the Fraser Committee). An examination of the committee's Report (Canada, 1985) and its recommendations concerning pornography will follow. Central to this examination will be an exposition of the paradoxical justification for criminalizing pornography: the Report establishes a feminist rationale based on the harm *any* pornography causes to women's right to equality, but retains the conventional idea that only *extreme* sexually explicit representations are harmful enough to be proscribed.

The Creation of the Fraser Committee

The spread of video technology in the late 1970s is one of several factors that helped propel the 1980s campaign to criminalize pornography. The absence of a classification scheme in Canada to distinguish sexually explicit videos from others led to nasty surprises for some women. According to Susan Clark, a member of the Fraser Committee, 'Women would choose videos and have no clue what they were about, and it was true that women would take a video entitled "Little Red Riding Hood" to find out that it was a very pornographic version ... I think people were amazed and literally shocked to discover what was available. It was a real education, so they were shocked, they did not want to see it in their homes, in their communities, easily available to children.'[1] Many anti-pornography organizations feared that the lack of regulation of video cassettes and video outlets could result in children being exposed to sexually explicit and violent material.

Police organizations amplified the sense that the new technology was dangerous. Project P – 'P' for pornography – a hybrid undertaking of the Metropolitan Toronto police force and the Ontario Provincial Police, is the only law enforcement agency in Canada specializing in pornography. The attorney general and the solicitor general of Ontario created Project P in 1965 to investigate the distribution of sexually explicit magazines in Toronto and the role of organized crime in their production. Satisfied with the result of the investigation, the Ontario government institutionalized Project P, whose mandate has since been to investigate the distribution, manufacture, and importation of obscene materials in Ontario. Thus the government of Ontario mobilized police resources at least ten years before pornography became a central issue in the public culture.

While representatives of Project P claim adamantly that the project's function is limited to enforcing the law, it has taken a very active role in the struggle to reform obscenity legislation. For example, in the early 1980s Project P set up its 'awareness program' to raise consciousness about the 'new' pornography – the type of sexually explicit images feminists claim are more about violence and sexism than about sex. This program involved presenting a smorgasbord of the worst possible depictions of violence and sexuality allegedly available in Canada. Members of Project P claimed that they needed to develop this program because pornography was becoming more violent, and because the public had a right to know. The public, in fact, got to know much more: the obscenity legislation was unenforceable. The police, it seems, needed a more precise law to do a better job at cleaning the smut from the streets.

For example, Dr Suzanne Scorsone was ignorant of the nature of pornography until a member of Project P took her on a tour of the book and video shops on Yonge Street in Toronto. Scorsone recounts her experience:

When I first got involved in this whole affair in the early 1980s, I went around with Project P and Metro Police and the Badgley Commission people. Somebody from Project P took me around Yonge Street and said: 'Here is what is on the shelves and here is what is under the shelves. I could get it in fifteen minutes if I had to.' He said: 'five years ago we could have cleaned the stores out with the obscenity laws but today the courts have ceased to enforce, there is no way we will be doing that if we get negative judgement. If it is unenforceable, it is unenforceable, and this is our problem.' The stuff that he was showing me, some of it involved children, but in a way that the law could not touch ... Some of the stuff was absolutely unreal, and there was nothing that they could do about it because it would have been back in the streets.[2]

With its cries of helplessness, Project P's campaign fuelled the fire of the anti-pornography movement; it amplified the escalating rhetoric of fear and despair and succeeded in mobilizing action to reform the law. But was it the case that the obscenity legislation was unenforceable?

To answer this question, it is necessary to backtrack. An examination of the judicial decisions on obscenity cases since the 1960s suggests the apparent development of an increasingly tolerant attitude towards sex. The way in which judges interpreted the statutory definition of obscenity made it acceptable to portray sex as long as the representation had a serious purpose and treated sex with sincerity and honesty rather than pandering to the sensualist. In other words, the attempt to narrow the legal definition of obscenity, to circumscribe the obscene to an indisputable 'category of social and aesthetic worthlessness,' inadvertently created a valuable context for discussing and representing sex (Williams, 1989: 88). A consequential effect of this classifying strategy was the deployment in the 1960s and 1970s of a variety of sexually explicit texts, texts not declared obscene as long as they had artistic or social worth.

In the early 1980s a trilogy of cases confirmed the existence of tolerant community standards in Canada with respect to sexually explicit material; the interpretation of community standards in these cases shows the increased influence on judges of feminist thinking.[3] The line of cases began with *R. v. Doug Rankine Co.* (1983), wherein it was held that contemporary community standards would tolerate sexually explicit materials as long as they did not 'degrade' or 'dehumanize' one or more of the participants. Judge Borins stated:

Films which consist substantially or partially of scenes which portray violence and cruelty in conjunction with sex, particularly where the performance of indignities degrade[s] and dehumanize[s] the people upon whom they are performed, exceed the level of community tolerance ... [However,] contemporary community standards would tolerate the distribution of films which consist substantially of scenes of people engaged in sexual intercourse ... scenes of group sex, lesbianism, fellatio, cunnilingus and oral sex.[4]

This line of authority, however, was not firmly established. For example, a few months earlier, in a New Brunswick case, the trial judge argued for a more restrictive test of community standards. The level of tolerance was exceeded by magazines which he described as follows: 'The magazines are most explicit and depict sexual conduct, not merely nudity. The conduct shows lesbianism, homosexuality and heterosexuality. Male and female genitalia are explicitly photographed ... There were no pictures depicting sex and "the subject crime, horror, cruelty or violence" as set out in s. 159(8) [of the Criminal Code]. The pictures appear to be of adults consenting to the sexual acts of others.'[5]

This inconsistency in interpreting community standards is found also in cases involving obscene objects. In 1974 a court found lubricants, prosthetics, and devices sold in sex shops to be not only tolerable but in the public interest; three years later another court argued that the same devices offended community standards.[6] Inconsistencies exist also in cases involving live performances. Some courts argued that community standards of tolerance are defied when the performer is nude.[7] Others decided that nudity alone does not overstep the standards,[8] but nudity combined with suggestive touching and postures does.[9] Another court found that a performance involving a nude couple engaged in simulated sexual acts does not exceed community standards.[10] In sum, the judiciary was unable to provide clear and precise community standards. In the light of so much judicial inconsistency, the police's interpretation of obscenity legislation as unenforceable is somewhat justified (Canada, 1985: 111–39).

Because of the lack of judicial unanimity, law enforcement agencies were reluctant to lay obscenity charges for fear of being embarrassed in court. Anti-pornography organizations were furious – one of Project P's projects had most definitely succeeded. Many organizations expressed their anger by inundating their members of Parliament and the minister of justice with letters, petitions, and briefs. Other organizations took a more aggressive approach. In November 1982 a group calling itself the 'Wimmin's Fire Brigade' claimed responsibility for the bombing of three video stores in the Vancouver area – all part of a chain that specialized in adult entertainment. The brigade released a statement condemning sexually violent pornography. While most women's organizations in Canada did not endorse the 'terrorist' actions of the brigade, they sympathized with the group's frustration at not being able to get the police to lay obscenity charges.[11] Meanwhile, retailers and distributors of sexually explicit material and owners of adult entertainment establishments, who found it impossible to get a clear idea of the limits of the law, were expressing their anger at being constantly challenged both in and out of court.

According to a senior counsel at the federal Department of Justice, when the question of display and access of pornographic material was challenged, municipalities and provinces tended to relinquish their responsibility and wait for the federal government to do something. Thus it was in Ottawa that the pressure to act was felt most strongly. Many federal politicians felt the anger of anti-pornography organizations and wanted swift action (McLaren, 1986). In the words of a senior counsel, the issue of pornography 'was subject to a great deal of attention; there was a constant effort to do something about it.'[12] Indeed, in the period between 1977 and the creation of the Fraser Committee in June 1983, Mark MacGuigan, the minister of justice, presented his report on pornography and prostitution. Subsequently, some forty bills against pornography were introduced in Parliament. All but four of those were private members' bills; all were aimed at tightening the law. It is not surprising that the bills fell through, since it is very unusual for a private member's bill to get through the House.[13] The bills introduced by the government also failed. They were usually part of omnibus bills dealing with other pressing issues.[14] In spite of their failure to become law, the presence of these bills indicates the extent to which the anti-porn movement had made itself gradually heard in Ottawa.

Meanwhile, obscenity provisions were being criticized and undermined from another flank; groups against censorship were challenging their severity. Making use of their right to freedom of expression, newly enshrined in the Canadian Charter of Rights and Freedoms, feminists against censorship launched and won several court challenges against the restrictive practices of law enforcement agencies and provincial censor boards. The Ontario Film and Video Appreciation Society (OFAVAS) fought the most important court battle, which was against the Ontario Censor Board. As a way to celebrate the enactment of the Charter, OFAVAS held a press conference to announce its intention to hold a series of adults-only public screenings of films which the Ontario Censor Board had previously demanded be cut. Since the board had to approve the public exhibition of a film or video, OFAVAS submitted the films to the board. The films (Bonnie Klein's *Not a Love Story*, Bruce Elder's experimental film *The Art of Worldly Wisdom*, Michael Snow's *Rameau's Nephew*, and Al Razuti's *Amerika*) had already been screened for selected audiences in Ontario; their distributors were not charged. OFAVAS made it clear in its public announcement that it intended to launch a constitutional test case if the Ontario Censor Board demanded cuts (see MacDowall, 1985). The board issued OFAVAS a one-time, one-location permit only for the screening of Snow's and Elder's films; moreover, the board demanded that cuts be made in *Amerika*. OFAVAS consequently launched an action challenging the power of the Ontario Censor Board. The courts found in favour of the artists. Both the Ontario Divisional Court and the Ontario Court of Appeal declared the powers of the provincial censor board 'unconstitutional,' as they allowed 'for the complete denial or prohibition of freedom of expression.'[15]

This important challenge to the arbitrariness and discriminatory practices of an agency endowed with the power to censor did not stop the calls for a more restrictive regulation of sexually explicit material; on the contrary, it probably made the anti-pornography organizations cry louder and with more urgency. Public campaigns to proscribe pornography escalated in January 1983, when the Canadian Radio-television and Telecommunications Commission (CRTC) granted licences to private companies – the pay-TV channels – that broadcast sexually explicit material. The campaign focused on the intention of the First Choice pay-TV network to broadcast 'Playboy' programs. Pay-TV channels were exempt from the regulation of the CRTC, which operated to uphold the provisions of the Broadcasting Act banning shows that abused a race, religion, or creed. Members of the public, especially women's and church groups, claimed that the lack of regulation would lead to more violence and sex on television. Alarmed anti-pornography forces in several cities organized conferences on the effects of pornography on women. These conferences often brought together feminist and non-feminist pro-censorship organizations, and resulted in the creation of a very strong and vocal lobby group for the immediate reform of obscenity legislation.

The sudden possibility that 'Playboy' would be broadcasting in Canada crystallized the anti-pornography movement's dissatisfaction with the control of obscenity – the law's vagueness, the inconsistencies in the application of the community standards of tolerance, the inability of law enforcement agencies to secure convictions, the law's inability to counter the threat posed by the importation of the worst American pornography. Under intense public pressure in 1983, the Liberal government of Canada created the Fraser Committee; its mandate was to hold cross-country hearings in an effort to achieve a national consensus that would inform policy-making.[16]

The Report of the Fraser Committee

The Fraser Committee, appointed in June 1983 to investigate Canadian views on pornography and prostitution, presented its findings in February 1985 in two large volumes. The report (Canada, 1985) provides useful information on the philosophical, social, scientific, and legal aspects of pornography and prostitution. Here I will concentrate only on the recommendations concerning pornography.

Overall, the report's recommendations reflect the pro-censorship alliance analysed in the previous chapter. They do so, however, in a way that highlights the strength of the feminist position within the alliance. For example, the detrimental effect of pornography on women's right to equality, rather than its immoral content and negative impact on society, is the philosophical rationale for criminalization (Canada, 1985: 95–103). The adoption of this feminist rationale, in fact, resulted in recommendations directly at odds with the request of conservative organizations for total censorship of all depictions of nudity. Total censorship is recommended in only three cases: first, when the material portrays children (people under eighteen years of age) in explicit sexual conduct (recommendation 5); second, when the material was produced in such a way that actual physical harm was caused to any participant ('Pornography Causing Physical Harm,' recommendation 7); third, when the material threatens or undermines fundamental values, such as the right to equality and the right to dignity ('Sexually Violent and Degrading Pornography,' recommendation 7).

While the recommendations embody primarily the anti-pornography pro-censorship position, the report also incorporates the strength of civil libertarians as it makes concessions to their requests. For

example, following the civil libertarian argument that further extend-
ing the reach of the criminal law could lead to unreasonable
encroachments on freedom, the report recommends the classification
of 'lawful pornography'; in other words, sexually explicit material
that is neither violent nor an assault on people's right to equality and
dignity is not prohibited (see 'Display of Visual Pornographic
Material,' recommendations 7, 5, and 45). The objective here is regulation rather than interdiction. Such material should not be subject
to criminal sanction except where it is displayed without proper
warning or if it is made accessible to children (people under eighteen
years of age).

It is clear that the recommendations incorporate the balance of
social forces in society on the issue of pornography. They condense
the pro-censorship alliance in society, but in a way that emphasizes
the strength of the feminist position within the alliance. The Fraser
Committee clearly acknowledges that its approach will not please all
the interests involved:

We appreciate that our proscriptions will not satisfy everyone. Those of
conservative mind will consider us too libertarian in our view that the bulk
of pornography should be regulated rather than banned. Some feminists too
may feel that we have circumscribed the pornography which is to be prohibited too narrowly. Liberals for their part may find our movement outside
the traditional boundaries of harm untenable. It is our belief that, given the
complexities of this area, and the conflict of philosophies to which it gives
rise, our approach represents a rational, fair and realistic balancing of the
interests involved, and a significant advance over the present state of the law.
(Canada, 1985: 260)

Thus the Fraser Committee defends its approach from possible criticism by claiming that it represents a 'rational, fair and realistic'
compromise between all the social forces involved in the debate. A
close reading of the report reveals that it is neither rational, nor fair,
nor particularly realistic. The report, in fact, contains four major
problems. First, the committee affirms the complexity of pornography
as a 'social problem' responsible for the oppression of women, and
states authoritatively that 'the answers to the problems raised by
pornography ... in Canada are not just legal answers' (Canada, 1985:
v); however, it ultimately recommends criminalizing pornography, a
solution that shows it had not fully understood the complexity of

women's oppression. Second, it asserts that only 1 per cent of Canadians consider pornography a major problem (Canada, 1985: 104); however, it recommends that the federal government make the control of the importation of pornography its top priority (recommendation 21). Third, it dismisses on scientific grounds the anti-pornography movement's claim that violent pornography leads to aggression against women, and it dismisses on empirical grounds its claim that pornography's content is increasingly characterized by violence and domination; however, it recommends criminalizing violent and degrading material on the basis that this strategy will ensure greater equality to women (Canada, 1985: 268). Fourth, it justifies the criminalization of pornography to protect and support women's right to equality; however, the legal solutions it proposes empower law enforcement agencies rather than women.[17]

I propose to trace the origin of these incongruities by showing how the Fraser Committee's report incorporated the balance of social forces in society on pornography in a way that was shaped by the committee's membership, legalistic mandate, liberal democratic policy orientation, and consultative procedures.

The Composition of the Fraser Committee

In June 1983, Minister of Justice Mark MacGuigan appointed the following seven people to form the Special Committee on Pornography and Prostitution: Paul Fraser (chair), Susan Clark, Mary Eberts, Jean-Paul Gilbert, John McLaren, Andrée Ruffo and Joan Wallace. Paul Fraser, a civil and criminal litigation lawyer, was a member of the Vancouver law firm of Fraser and Gifford. He was a past president of the Canadian Bar Association and a former part-time member of the Law Reform Commission of British Columbia. Susan Clark, a sociologist, was the dean of human and professional development and director of the Institute for the Study of Women at Mount St Vincent University in Halifax. Mary Eberts, a civil litigation lawyer, worked for the Toronto law firm of Tory, Tory, DesLauriers and Binnington. She co-edited *Equality Rights Under the Charter of Rights and Freedoms*, and was a member of the Canadian Civil Liberties Association. She later joined the Metro Toronto Action Committee on Public Violence Against Women and Children. Jean-Paul Gilbert was a senior board member (Quebec region) of the National Parole Board; director of the Montreal Police Department from 1964 to 1969; and president of the Quebec Society of Criminology. John McLaren was a professor of law at the University of Calgary. He was previously the dean of law at the University of Windsor and had done research on the control of vice and accident compensation. Andrée Ruffo, a judge, was a barrister and solicitor in private practice in Montreal, working mainly in family law. Joan Wallace, a writer and consultant, was the founding president of the Vancouver Status of Women. She was a member of the Canadian Advisory Council on the Status of Women between 1973 and 1977, and was a former director of the Canadian Research Institute for the Advancement of Women.

The government provided no justification for this selection. From the organizational affiliation provided in the report, however, we can see the significance of the following criteria for the government: (1) geographical representation, because input was required from across Canada; (2) legal and academic representation, because the committee's mandate involved a program of 'socio-legal research'; (3) female representation, because pornography and prostitution were considered women's issues; (4) feminist representation, because of the strength of the feminist discontent with the present state of the Criminal Code provisions relating to pornography and prostitution; (5) social-scientific representation, because the question of the impact of pornography on behaviour and attitudes was a major issue; (6) experience on other commissions of inquiry; (7) and representation from law enforcement agencies, because of their daily experience with the regulation of pornography and prostitution.

Clark explains how the members' background shaped the report:

We took a more theoretical approach to the issues, and a more academic approach, in the sense that we were not prepared to go for just some politically expedient quick fix. So I think that we really did debate the issues and tried to develop an approach towards pornography and prostitution, but particularly pornography, that was defensible in an intellectual sense, it was not just reacting to the fact that people were complaining all the time. We were trying to work out a defensible, principled approach to it. I don't think that we would have gotten that if we did not have those people on the committee, in approaching the law that way.[18]

Both McLaren (1986) and Eberts confirm the determination of committee members to produce a more academic, theoretically informed document rather than a piece of advocacy. Such an approach requires consensus, which at times was difficult to obtain. According to Eberts, the tension between civil libertarian and feminist orientations within the committee accounts largely for the incongruities in the report:

> There are different points of view; the liberal approach to porn is different from the feminist approach. There were people who were more interested in the liberal approach. There was a small critical mass of people who were attracted to the feminist approach. And there were people with their own particular interest, like Andrée Ruffo, motivated by her great concern with children and the advocacy of certain measures with respect to them. To the extent that there are inconsistencies in the report it is because the report is made up by a group of people who had different points of view. You see, we strove to get consensus – that is another factor, [and] it was very important. When you strive to get consensus you get a mix sometimes. It is less coherent than one point of view.[19]

The strain within the committee certainly had an impact on the report; but this can be overstated, so that one reaches an instrumentalist view of the report. In fact, the specific tensions that Eberts revealed constitute a microcosm of the conflicts that typify the wider societal debate on pornography. In other words, the tensions between the feminist anti-pornography position and the civil libertarian approach to pornography which characterize the societal debate were also incorporated in the committee. But since the committee's task was to arrive at a rational consensus, to transform the conflicting viewpoints into 'some kind of coherent whole,'[20] the committee had also to resolve its own antinomies.

The mediation of these tensions was directly contingent upon the committee's legal mandate and policy orientation. As this analysis unfolds, the determining impact of committee members on the report will be seen in a different light, one less instrumental than the one suggested by Eberts.

Criminal Law and the Protection of Fundamental Values

At the outset of its report, the Fraser Committee explicitly reveals the liberal democratic policy orientation that informs its approach.

It affirms that certain values have influenced its thinking on pornography and prostitution, its interpretation and synthesis of the public's views, and the formulation of its recommendations, namely, equality, responsibility, individual liberty, human dignity, and the appreciation of sexuality (Canada, 1985: 23–6). Such values must found public policy and inform any legislation on pornography and prostitution because they are a fundamental part of the fabric of Canadian society: 'These values address the fundamental nature of human beings and the sort of society we consider generations of Canadians have been striving to achieve: sometimes successfully and sometimes not. Our social, economic and legal programs are not only supported but actually reflected in the lives our citizens are able to lead' (Canada, 1985: 102).

The committee subsequently affirms the role of criminal law in protecting and bolstering values essential to Canadians. Drawing on reports from the Law Reform Commission of Canada[21] and the Department of Justice,[22] it claims that criminal law not only must protect citizens from conduct causing serious harm, but, most important, must protect societal values: 'Criminal law has something to say about both the values of society and the need to protect them by a system of proscriptions and punishments' (Canada, 1985: 23).

The committee's policy orientation, however, represents a departure from the traditional distinction in criminal law between the safeguarding of individual liberties and the protection of society, a protection understood in terms of the preservation of moral standards shared by the community of individuals. Drawing on the Canadian Charter of Rights and Freedoms, particularly as it relates to minority groups, the Fraser Committee understands the limitations of individual liberties in terms of legally promoting and protecting the rights of groups, however different from the majority, to be treated as equal citizens. Thus, rather than limiting individual liberty for the protection of the moral fibre of society as a whole, a concept at odds with the variety of lifestyles that characterizes Canadian society, the committee's approach to policy making strikes a balance between the protection of individual and group rights (McLaren, 1986: 46–8).

The committee considers this novel rationale for exercising the criminal law a compromise between the two extreme positions found in the pornography debate: the conservative claim that the portrayal of sex is immoral and that the law must regulate morality, and the liberal claim that any portrayal of sex is fine as long as it does not cause physical harm, at which point the law should intervene. To the committee, the feminist argument that pornography infringes on women's right to equality and must be prohibited in a society committed to equality, appears, in the light of the newly enshrined Charter of Rights and Freedoms, a more reasonable position. In fact, the committee contends that

> there are magazines, films and videos solely for the purpose of entertainment whose depiction of women ... demeans them, perpetuates lies about aspects of their humanity and denies the validity of their aspirations to be treated as full and equal citizens within the community ... Because of the seriousness of the impacts of this sort of pornography on the fundamental values of Canadians, we are prepared to recommend that the Criminal Code has an important role to play in defining what material may be available within our society. (Canada, 1985: 103)

In other words, the committee unambiguously points to sexism as the problem with pornography, and to criminal law as the means to eradicate pornography to sustain and promote women's right to equality.

The committee finds its approach to criminalizing pornography 'rational, realistic and fair' not only because it strikes a compromise between the three main positions on pornography, but also because it is not based on the repression of sexuality. The committee thought it crucial to distinguish its approach to the criminalization of pornography from the conservative outcry to ban every representation of sex, because the committee's approach, like the conservatives', was founded on the preservation of fundamental values. Clark explains this as follows:

> I think one of the reasons we tried to develop the rationale about women and promoting their right to protection was to make a distinction between the fundamentalist Christians, who were the clearest group against pornography and sex. We were trying to support the women's groups; and also because we were very uneasy with the fundamentalist groups, we did not want to bring in a report that banned all sex, except sex between married couples, or whatever they wanted us to do. So we were looking for a rational argument ... that would allow us to differentiate between those two. And [our argument] is in some ways a conservative argument, because it is based on the belief in certain values. Fundamentalists were pushing for traditional family values if

you like, [whereas] we and I think some of the feminist groups were arguing that one of the fundamental values is women's equality, and women's right to a safe society.[23]

To demonstrate that its feminist rationale for criminalizing pornography was not based on the repression of sexuality, the committee acknowledges that all Canadians enjoy and benefit from their need for sexual expression, and that such an 'appreciation of sexuality' is a fundamental value that must inform policy making in Canada (Canada, 1985: 26).

While my analysis confirms public support for the 'appreciation of sexuality,' it shows that people do not share the same appreciation for the public display of sexual representations. The disagreements among and between feminists, civil libertarians, and conservatives presented in this study indicate the lack of consensus on what constitutes acceptable sexual representations. The committee avoids discussing this complex issue by claiming that feminist and conservative organizations favouring the control of pornography – those more troubled by the public depiction of sexual representations – support the production of erotica. As shown in previous chapters, conservative organizations oppose any public display of sexually explicit representations on scientific grounds. Moreover, the feminist position on pornography and acceptable sexual representation is not uniform; some feminists find certain sexual images unacceptable when judged by a feminist ethic, while others defend those same images by pointing to the safe pleasure they provide. Thus, by assuming a consensus on Canadians' 'appreciation of sexuality,' the report glosses over one of the most controversial questions in the pornography debate: what constitutes an acceptable representation of sex?

In sum, in its strategy of negotiating a compromise between the various interests involved in the pornography debate, the report draws on the Charter of Rights and Freedoms to argue that criminal law ought to play a role in promoting and protecting the rights of groups that historically have not been treated equally. Then, recognizing the strength of the feminist position in the balance of social forces in the pornography debate, the report adopts its construction of pornography as a harm to women's right to equality as the most reasonable position in the pornography debate. To make sure that its recommendation to criminalize pornography is not grounded in the repression of sexuality, the report then declares the existence of a consensus among Canadians concerning their 'appreciation of sexuality.' Such a declaration glosses over major differences and incompatibilities among and between the three main positions on pornography; more important, it sidesteps the most contested issue within the pornography debate: the representation of sex. In fact, the notion of 'appreciation of sexuality' tells us nothing about *how* to regulate pornography, for it says nothing about the ways in which sexuality can or cannot be represented.

Ambiguous Logic: A Feminist Rationale Combined with Conventional Ideas about Criminalization

We have seen that the report of the Fraser committee links pornography to sexism and justifies the criminalization of pornography by claiming the need to promote and protect the fundamental value of equality (Canada, 1985: 103). However, when the report becomes specific about the nature of pornography and outlines what is to be prohibited, it finds criminal law 'neither an appropriate nor a practicable means' to counteract the pervasive problem of sexism (Canada, 1985: 264). Then, in a manner directly undermining its initial argument about the role of criminal law in upholding equality rights, the report contends that criminal law should be exercised to prohibit 'any material which is so extreme or harmful in its depictions that it is qualitatively different from the general content [of most pornography] and for that reason deserves to be treated differently' (Canada, 1985: 264).

Thus the committee develops a three-tier definition of pornography and recommends the prohibition of the following material: (1) sexually explicit material produced in such a way that physical harm was caused to any participant (tier 1); (2) material involving the participation of children in sexual conduct (also tier 1); and (3) violent and degrading sexually explicit material (tier 2). (The third tier, 'lawful pornography,' consists of sexually explicit material that does not fall within the two previous tiers; such material would be acceptable on the whole, with criminal sanctions pending improper display and access.)

In the committee's three-tier system, the main characteristic, or the 'general content,' of pornography is sexual explicitness, whereas according to its feminist rationale it was sexism. In the three-tier system, the degree of violence combined with sexual explicitness is what should trigger the criminal law; in the committee's feminist rationale it was the encroachment of women's right to equality. In other words, the recommendation to criminalize pornography is inconsistent with the feminist rationale: the committee reasons that, because of its sexist rather than sexual content, *all* pornography harms women, but it recommends that to ensure women greater equality we should censor *only* the representations combining sex and violence. This recommendation does not logically follow from the explanation given. Furthermore, it does not follow either from the empirical evidence on the content of pornography or from the scientific evidence on the link between pornography and harm provided by the committee itself.

The committee argues for the need to eradicate only the most extreme form of sexually explicit material, despite its contention that 'such depictions appear ... to be in a minority' (Canada, 1985: 95). In fact, the research undertaken for the committee on the content and availability of pornography in Canada does not support the argument that pornography is becoming increasingly extreme in its depiction of violence or sexual abuse:

The research which has been conducted on magazines and videos does not confirm the overwhelmingly awful picture presented by some groups and individuals in their briefs to the Committee ... The view that large amounts of violent pornography or child pornography are being consumed is not substantiated by the research ... [and] the idea that a great deal of the pornography has taken on the worst possible characteristics of the genre is unconfirmed at this time. (Canada, 1985: 93)

Rather than depicting violence or the sexual abuse of children, the bulk of the available pornography in Canada is mainly concerned about the 'basic mechanics' of heterosexual sex:

While both types of videos [adult and triple x] do contain scenes of sexual aggression, *violence and domination are not predominant themes*. Rather, mechanical sexual relations, i.e. an absence of affection, love or passion and a concentration on the pure mechanics of sex between two adults of the opposite sex were by far the most common portrayals. None of the films involved children. (Canada, 1985: 95; emphasis added)

If most available pornography is mainly concerned with fucking, and if the research on pornography and harm to society or individuals 'is so inadequate and chaotic that no consistent body of information has been established' (Canada, 1985: 99), then how can a law prohibiting the few materials in which domination and violence are predominant themes ensure greater equality for women?

I pointed out to Mary Eberts the ambiguous logic of adopting a feminist rationale based on the harm that *any* pornography causes to women's right to equality while maintaining that only *extreme* sexually explicit forms are harmful enough to be proscribed. I suggested that this logic undermines the committee's findings on the scarcity of such material in Canada. She addressed this matter at length:

Well, I guess you have uncovered one of the areas where we were fitting together the different viewpoints of people on the committee. There are two different philosophies on how to control pornography. One says you control it because it is an affront to women's equality and if you follow that line it does not have to be the ultimate in violence in order to be an affront to women's equality and so you control it, you criminalize it if it reaches a certain threshold. The overlay on that is the traditional way of thinking in criminal law that you have to have a fairly high threshold of antisocial conduct before you can criminalize, because the criminal law is the last resort. What is happening in the theory of pornography, in particular, is that you have those who advocate greater control of pornography in the interest of the constitutional value of women's equality. They are saying that the threshold to criminalize pornography should be lower than it traditionally has been. *But part of the Report is coming from the traditional law perspective. It concerns itself with how violent it is, how violent it needs to be. Whereas violence has always been the signal that has made the criminal law respond before*, the new way of looking at it is from the point of view of a clash of values: how much does it have to impinge upon this value [equality] before it is criminalized ... The inconsistencies you see in this report are a reflection of a much broader debate in the law and around the law about what will trigger the criminal law. The infringement of what will trigger the criminal law, and how great an infringement will that have to be, because we never before had constitutional values to put up against the value of liberty. It has only been since 1982 or 1985, if you look at the equality value, that we have had something as strong as our interest in liberty, to throw into the discussion about when to criminalize.[24]

This extract clearly indicates how the legal approach and the liberal democratic orientation circumscribed both the thinking of committee members and their recommendations. In fact, both the legal approach and the liberal democratic policy orientation of committee members framed the report; they provided the lens through which to see pornography as a social problem that the law could eradicate.

The ambiguous logic of establishing a feminist rationale to criminalize pornography based on the harm that any pornography inflicts on women's right to equality, while maintaining the idea that only extreme sexually explicit materials warrant proscription, represents an instance of an interpretive conflict over the meaning of the law. By adopting the feminist argument against pornography, the committee drew on the law to challenge the hegemony of liberty over equality. In prioritizing the value of equality, the committee suggested that criminal law is an instrument of change. However, the committee faced a long tradition of legal practices shaped by a more conventional liberal approach to criminal law. Thus it held to the established notion of a high threshold of harm, implying that criminal law, in this context, is an instrument of punishment as a measure of last resort.

The Marginalization of Alternative Discourses

A significant constraining effect of the legalistic and liberal democratic format used by the committee to construct the issue of pornography was the subsequent marginalization of the viewpoint of feminists against censorship. This format could not accommodate the feminist critique of the idea that legal solutions to pornography would ensure greater equality for women; it could not make sense of a viewpoint that claimed to be anti-pornography *and* demanded more freedom of expression to combat pornography. Consequently, the committee classified the feminist anti-censorship strategies either as Marxist, equating them with the destruction of capitalism and of the values and structures that make that economic system possible (Canada, 1985: 19), or as civil libertarian, equating them with a rejection of any governmental control (Canada, 1985: 76–83). The result of such classifications is obvious. Associated with a philosophical tradition that rejects the foundational principles of Canadian society, the feminist anti-censorship viewpoint on sexism is delegitimized as too radical; associated with the civil libertarian position, the feminist anti-censorship critique – which sees censorship as a discriminatory practice against sexual minorities' attempt to express differences – is delegitimized as quietist. By stripping the feminist anti-censorship position of its analysis of sexism and censorship, the committee lost a potentially powerful critique of both the anti-pornography feminist and the civil libertarian positions.

Clark's explanation for classifying the viewpoint of feminists against censorship as civil libertarian implicitly illustrates the rigidity of the committee's legalistic orientation. While recognizing that they constructed pornography as a woman's issue, the committee, as Clark illustrates, did not see feminists against censorship as truly feminist: 'It is not that they did not recognize the problem [for women] posed by pornography, they just did not agree with the solutions.'[25]

Feminists who opposed censorship were dismissed because 'when you really pushed them, no control is what they wanted.'[26] While agreeing that the report's references to the position of feminists against censorship are inadequate and restricted, Eberts acknowledges the primacy of legal solutions for the committee:

The problem is that if you follow the position of feminists against censorship the result is no regulation. And there was rightly or wrongly a value judg- ment on the part of the group [the committee], in coming to its consensus, that there was more harm to be had in the untrammelled circulation of all pornography than there was in the kinds of restrictions we tried to develop. At the time we tried to make, as I mentioned, a balance of criminal law regime for better or worse.[27]

As we saw earlier, the balance the committee opted for meant a position located midway between the extremes of total control and no control. A feminist position for criminalizing pornography was the best middle ground. Alternative critiques remained confined to the margins of the feminist and artistic community – at least for a time.

The Reliance on Institutional Expertise and Practices

Another factor that structured the committee's recommendations to criminalize pornography was its reliance on the knowledge of certain agents whose expertise came from being in regular contact with pornography (Canada, 1985: 11). After conducting extensive public hearings with people across the country, 'the next phase of our [the committee's] work involved superimposing on the views that we had received from the public, those of the administrators, bureaucrats, researchers and others involved day-to-day with the effects and regulation of pornography and prostitution' (Canada, 1985: 11). When questioned on the methodology of 'superimposition' of the experts' point of view onto that of the public's, both Eberts and Clark denied it was the way the committee operated:

I [Eberts] do not remember thinking about it as being a superimposition. Here is my thinking on it. A valuable part of the commission is to solicit the views of the public. They have very good insight on the ways they think about the issue and the way other people think about the issue. These are the people who have paid attention to the issue and who have it at heart. They are interested in the topic. They will take you in depth in the area by letting you know about their experience, they will help you identify the problems by talking about their experience. But if you reflect only on what you hear there, inevitably you will reflect conflict. There is always conflict in what people tell you at the hearings. Our program ultimately was a blend. We had the public hearings. The Ministry of Justice did an opinion survey of the general population. We also talked to experts, and some of them came to the hearings. We also did a great literature search, so we were right up to date on the issue. We had our own discussions, and we tried not so much to superimpose the views of experts onto everything else but to get a sounding or sampling of different sectors and try to put them in some kind of coherent whole.[28]

In other words, the committee consulted with the agencies that regulate pornography, because those agencies' daily contact with the problems posed by pornography provided them with a certain expertise not shared by those in the public, who were too emotional about the issue. This strategy seems rational, but is it? It is almost like trying to find out what it feels like to ride on a roller-coaster by asking the people who run it rather than the people who ride it.

While the committee relied on the expertise of the regulators, it barely acknowledged the experience of those who were regulated – for example, those who had willingly chosen to work in the sex trade, or those who often had their work censored, particularly feminist, gay, and lesbian artists.[29] Instead, the committee relied on the expertise of people legalistically, scientifically, or professionally trained to deal with the 'problems' of pornography.

The committee's particular reliance on the institutional practices of government administrators, bureaucrats, and law enforcement agencies resulted in a comprehension of pornography as a 'social problem' that more law, more technology of control, and more financial and human resources could, if not eradicate, at least keep in order. Thus a large number of the report's recommendations strengthened government and law enforcement agencies' power (recommendations 17–31).[30] Moreover, reliance on those institutionally and professionally trained to solve the 'problems' of pornography to learn about pornography is ironic: it legitimizes as rational knowledge only that produced by those whose business it is to construct phenomena as social problems (Stehr, 1992; Abbott, 1988; Smith, 1987, 1990; Gusfield, 1989).

The committee's nearly exclusive reliance on institutional knowledge succeeded also in silencing information about how such agencies functioned. Feminists against censorship documented and challenged in court the heterosexism of institutional practices, but their critique was ignored. In addition the many legal challenges against provincial censor boards and Canada Customs were overlooked. However, one recommendation shows the impact of the successful feminist challenge of the Ontario Censor Board: in recommendation 6, the committee argues for the regulation of lawful pornography – sexually explicit material not characterized by violence or degradation – in each province by a system of classification; the standards of acceptability would vary in different regions of Canada. The rationale of provincial variation is undermined, however, by the recommendation of a national standard. Arguing that Canada Customs should not 'defer to the opinions of local boards' but should concentrate on 'developing its own talents in [determining obscenity]' (Canada, 1985: 331), the committee also recommends that Customs add illegal pornography as defined in the report (recommendation 7, 18, 22) to its list of materials prohibited in Canada. However, the committee does not question the existing list and the broad definition of obscenity Customs uses to prohibit entry of material into Canada – a definition that, on the basis of the numerous constitutional challenges it led to, is not compatible with the report's definition of legal pornography (Lacombe, 1988: 85–98; Kinsman, 1985: 96).[31]

The reliance on institutional practices and expertise to evaluate pornography resulted in exclusionary strategies. The viewpoints and experiences of 'knowers' without institutional affiliations, located at the edge of the pornography debate – sex trade workers, alternative artists, and porn consumers – were marginalized. Mediated by institutional practices more than by the practices and consciousness of the people living the reality (a reality always contested, as we have seen in the previous chapters), knowledge appears hierarchically constructed and organized so that the credibility, experience, and practices of those about whom knowledge is produced are marginalized. Thus many potentially valuable viewpoints, viewpoints capable of altering or at least qualifying the common understanding of pornography, were lost. Adding to the anger of the marginalized groups was the fact that the report made no practical suggestions about how to deal with the oppressive aspects of the institutions that were supposed to regulate pornography.

Conclusion

This analysis of the recommendations of the Fraser Committee report suggests the possibility of institutional determinism and instrumentalism, for arguing that law reform was shaped by the committee's membership, its legal and liberal democratic policy orientation, and its consultative procedures. That the report was constrained by these elements does not necessarily mean that it was determined by them. Nor was it necessarily doomed to reproduce the same social order just because it was inscribed in a language favouring law reform.

I have tried to rid my analysis of determinism by conceiving the report in a way that accounts for both agency and structure. I have paid attention to the mutually constitutive or generative nature of agency and structure (Bourdieu and Wacquant, 1992). In that context, the Fraser Committee report cannot be understood without reference to the larger political struggles that gave rise to it, and to our society's particular tradition of addressing social problems. Thus the report appears as an institutional or organizational practice,[32] a negotiation highlighting the strength of the feminist anti-pornography position in society, but in a way that was shaped by the presence of past negotiations and a tradition in which law is central.

The framing of the report in terms of law reform is not an instance of the reproduction of a social order characterized by control (Ericson, 1985, 1987) or of the expansionary logic of social control (Cohen, 1985). While the legal discourse constrained the report's approach (some recommendations were certainly inscribed in a logic of social control), it also enabled the report. The legal discourse was the main instrument used by feminists to criticize the conventionally legalistic liberal approach to criminal law, an approach that traditionally has favoured the constitutional value of liberty over equality.

The struggles over the interpretation of the antagonism between liberty and equality did reproduce the hegemony of the law as the lens through which one should approach the issue of pornography, but by privileging equality these struggles contested the law's preferred focal point. The analogy of the law to a lens emphasizes the constraining and enabling quality of both instruments. A lens is a glass device that either concentrates or disperses light-rays; thus, depending on the image one chooses to produce, the lens allows for a variety of foci. In this sense, the power struggles to define pornography as a harm to women's right to equality, both within the Fraser Committee and the wider society, represent the emerging strength of a new focal point: a feminist interpretation of the law.

Far from being a homogeneous structure determining in a unidimensional way what it comes into contact with, the law is better seen as a powerful convention, an authoritative practice – but one that is never fixed. As demonstrated in this chapter, the development of a feminist rationale to criminalize pornography on the basis that all pornography harms women, while maintaining the idea that only extreme representations of sex ought to be banned, represents an instance of an interpretive conflict over the meaning of the law. The law appears as a contested terrain.

5

Bill C-114:
The First Attempt at
Pornography Law Reform

The anti-pornography bill, Bill C-114, was tabled in June 1986 by the Progressive Conservative government, which had been elected during the Fraser Committee's hearings in the summer of 1984. The government's anti-pornography bill was a more draconian approach to the regulation of sexually explicit material than the approach suggested in the Fraser report (Canada, 1985). Under Bill C-114, sexually explicit material that is neither violent nor degrading (third-tier material considered lawful in the structure of the Fraser report) became unlawful. What people found most disconcerting, though, was Bill C-114's sweeping definition of prohibited pornography: ' "Pornography" means any visual matter showing vaginal, anal or oral intercourse, ejaculation, sexually violent behaviour, bestiality, incest, necrophilia, masturbation or *other sexual activity*' (Bill C-114: 2; emphasis added).

In this chapter I will explore the process leading to this bill. More particularly, I want to address the mechanisms that allowed the Conservative government to avoid consideration of women's concerns. The question will be posed: In the light of the strength of the feminist anti-pornography movement in framing pornography as an issue of violence and harm to women's right to equality and safety, and in the light of that movement's numerous efforts to work with the government at reforming obscenity legislation, how could the government fail to act pragmatically and address women's concerns in its anti-pornography bill?

The Impact of a Change in Government

The first set of factors accounting for the conservative nature of the anti-pornography bill has to do with the change in government in the summer of 1984, the time when the Fraser Committee was holding public hearings. The committee, which was commissioned by the Liberal government and had to report to the minister of justice, produced a report reflecting the policy-making influence of the governing party's liberal, and particularly its liberal feminist, electoral constituency. As was mentioned in chapter 4, the committee couched the entire debate on pornography in legal terms by relating the control of pornography to the defence of liberal democratic principles such as individual liberty, equality, responsibility, and human dignity, which were said to constitute fundamental Canadian values. The Conservative government did not use these terms to frame the pornography issue. In fact, most Tory members of Parliament found the liberal feminist approach of the Fraser report 'totally unacceptable.'[1] The Tories were not interested in discussions about possible encroachments on constitutional rights or about protecting the artistic merit of sexually explicit material. The statement of John Reimer (MP, Kitchener) epitomizes the attitude many Conservative members of Parliament felt for liberal principles in the context of pornography: 'Why is it, then, that we bend over backwards to legitimize pornography on such spurious grounds as artistic merit and individual freedom of choice? Let's stop kidding ourselves. Any depiction of any person as a mere object of sexual self-gratification constitutes a perversion of human sexuality' (Hansard, 3 June 1986: 13910). The Tories wanted true conservative legislation.

Before proposing its anti-pornography bill, the government made explicit, in the November 1984 Speech from the Throne, that it classified pornography as a social welfare issue rather than a legal issue. This meant that any legislative initiatives to control pornography and bring more equality to women had to be related to the support and strengthening of the family. The October 1986 Speech from the Throne reiterated the social policy implications of the family. Commenting on the meaning of the speech, Barbara McDougall, then the minister of state (privatization) and minister of the status of women, establishes clearly the link between the control of pornography and the protection of the family:

As the Speech from the Throne stated, we are dedicated to the pursuit of one goal, that of a modern, tolerant and caring nation in which its citizens are secure and prosperous. To this end we intend to bring before the House some important legislative initiatives to support and strengthen the institution of the Canadian family, among them the introduction of measures to end violent and degrading forms of pornography involving women and men, legislation to take effective action against child prostitution and initiatives against the traffic in illicit drugs, which will help to improve the quality of life for Canadian families, for Canadian parents and, in particular, for Canadian young people. (*Hansard*, 7 October 1986: 166)

Thus the Tories' traditional orientation resulted in the constitution of pornography as a threat to family values rather than to the liberal democratic principles upheld in the Fraser report.

The Tories' position on pornography is simple: by celebrating sex – in particular, violent, abusive, and perverse sex – pornography undermines the values and traditions the family teaches, and consequently leads to an erosion of the quality of life.[2] Defined as a 'dreadful type of cancer,' pornography was often compared to drugs in its addictive and destructive effect on 'the morals and dignity of this country' (Bill Attewell, MP, Don Valley East, *Hansard*, 28 January 1986: 10243). Jim Jepson (MP, London East) expressed the alarm of many Conservatives:

It is quite clear that [pornography] draws people into a vortex of dependency and addiction leading to increasingly more difficult tastes to satisfy and to a host of related personal problems. More importantly, the person who buys pornography contributes to the health of a vast and growing industry. The industry does not exist without supporting a great many undesirable industries, including drugs, crime, and the exploitation of women and children ... The political and social traditions of our country have overwhelmingly supported our community's proper role in defending itself from the creeping social disintegration that is, in a continuous cycle, both a result and a cause of pornography, and a direct attack on the family unit which I believe is the foundation stone of our country. (*Hansard*, 1 October 1985: 7237–8)

By associating pornography with other 'dangerous' problems, such as child abuse, violence against women, and drug addiction, the Conservatives made it a social condition that required immediate reform (Gusfield, 1989).

In sum, when the Conservatives came to power in 1984, they were broadly (but by no means, as we shall see later, unanimously) committed to some sort of moral clean-up of the country, and pornography was part of the filth that had to go.

Pressure from Pro-censorship Forces

The second set of factors accounting for the conservative nature of Bill C-114 has to do with the growing influence of anti-pornography, pro-censorship forces in society during the period between the publication of the Fraser report (February 1985) and the drafting of the bill (June 1986).

The National Action Committee on the Status of Women (NAC), the umbrella group for feminist organizations of varying political orientations, and the Canadian Advisory Council on the Status of Women (CACSW) supported the general intent and direction of the Fraser Committee's recommendations. The CACSW, for example, found that 'the general tenor of the Report and many of the recommendations are excellent, though important modifications could be made to improve them' (1986a: 2).

An examination of the modifications suggested by feminist organizations, however, shows their ultimate dissatisfaction with the report. They criticized the definition of prohibited pornography for being too narrow, the definition of legal pornography for being too enabling, and the punishment for the makers, producers, and sellers of unlawful pornography, especially child pornography, for being too lenient.[3] In sum, feminist organizations criticized the Fraser Committee's recommendations for being too permissive, and asked for an expansion of the scope of the law on pornography rather than a circumscription of it.[4]

Religious and family-oriented forces were also active in their quest for the total restriction of sexually explicit material. They accused the Fraser Committee of being too permissive in allowing the depiction of sexually explicit material. The Interchurch Committee on Pornography urged the government to amend the Criminal Code to prohibit depictions of the following sexual acts – a list that would be later reflected in the definition of pornography of Bill C-114: 'anal or vaginal penetration, masturbation, ejaculation, oral sex and sexual use of other bodily functions such as urination, defecation and vomiting, and portrayal of pregnancy, lactation or menstruation as objects of ridicule or of necrophilia and incest' (Canada, 1986a: 7).

R.E.A.L. Women of Canada approved the report for justifying the exercise of criminal law to protect fundamental values. It accused the Fraser Committee, however, of favouring the feminist viewpoint by considering the value of equality as the only one fundamental enough to require protection by the criminal law. R.E.A.L. Women contended that the values of marriage and family life were equally fundamental to the well-being of Canadians, and that, consequently, sexually explicit material ought to be proscribed (R.E.A.L. Women of Canada, 1985b: 4).

Finally, the United Church of Canada criticized the three-tier definition of pornography for implying that some violent material is less harmful than others (1986: 3). It also declared the Fraser Committee's definition of lawful pornography too permissive in failing to prohibit material that clearly degraded women, such as *Playboy* and *Penthouse* (1986: 3).

The networking that took place between church organizations, Conservative members of Parliament, and senior government officials was crucial in augmenting pro-censorship pressure. The churches organized an intense letter-writing campaign to voice their dissatisfaction with the actual obscenity legislation, the permissive approach proposed by the Fraser Committee report, and their desire for a more restrictive approach to the regulation of sexually explicit material. For example, three months before the tabling of Bill C-114, a priest of the Roman Catholic church informed the Canadian bishops of the possibility of attaining a truly conservative law on pornography if they united their efforts:

In my recent visits to Ottawa, senior government officials have made it clear that if we hope to influence this legislation we must act now. They have also indicated that to be most effective we should join with other churches in a broadly based effort embracing all of Canada. To limit our efforts to one section of the country or a particular denomination would have much less impact. Let me emphasize that many experts feel this may well be the last real opportunity we have to deal with this enormous threat to the moral values of our Canadian society.[5]

Church organizations responded quickly and effectively to the strategy, and so did other groups. Fourteen petitions pressing for more stringent measures to deal with pornography were tabled in the House of Commons during the interim period between the publication of the Fraser Committee report and the drafting of Bill C-114.

These petitions always included numerous signatures from church and other organizations (*Hansard*, 30 April 1986: 12792). According to John Crosbie, then The minister of justice, during the drafting of the bill the Department of Justice was inundated with letters asking for tighter control than was recommended in the Fraser Committee report. An examination of the Commons debate after the publication of the report shows the growing influence of anti-pornography and pro-censorship forces on their members of Parliament. Mounting pressure for a more restrictive approach was translated into repeated calls from both the opposition parties and the Conservative party for strong anti-pornography legislation. For example, Svend Robinson (MP Burnaby), the New Democratic justice critic, asked the minister of justice whether he would 'bring forward quick legislation in order not to block the import of explicit erotica ... but of child pornography and violent pornography?' (*Hansard*, 18 March 1985: 3110). John Nunziata (York South Weston), the Liberal justice critic, also declared his party's support for strict legislation to counter the problem of pornography: 'We in the Liberal Party will support any legislation whatsoever which will deal with this very serious problem of all this smut coming into the country, finding its way into grocery and variety stores, and being available for children and others to see. I can assure the Government on behalf of my Party that we will support legislation which will serve to stop the importation of such material' (*Hansard*, 2 April 1985: 3609).

Support for tightening the law appeared unanimous. The anti-pornography, pro-censorship forces had done their work.

The Policy-Making Process in the Department of Justice

The third set of factors responsible for the conservative nature of the anti-pornography bill involves the consultative process between the minister of justice, John Crosbie, and senior civil servants at the Department of Justice.

Crosbie's appointment as minister of justice came as a surprise to him: his background was in economic issues, and he had served as the party's energy critic. Pornography was never an issue that Crosbie had at heart. An occasional reader of *Penthouse*, Crosbie defines himself in liberal terms: 'I am not a prude myself, I think I am just as interested in sex and erotica as most people out there.'[6] While he did not have a well-defined agenda on the subject, he had several pressing reasons for addressing pornography. First, the Conservative party's promise to act on the issue was part of its campaign platform. Second, the Department of Justice was expected to respond to both the Badgley report (Canada, 1984) on child sexual abuse and the Fraser report (Canada, 1985) on pornography and prostitution, both of which were commissioned by the previous Liberal government. Third, the government, which had inherited a large debt from the Liberals' encouraged policy-making in the field of justice because legal solutions were perceived as the cheapest strategies for a government that needed to show commitment to 'doing something': 'One of the reasons for ... giving Justice issues a major push was the fact that the government did not have much money. The government did not feel it could introduce big spending programs, it had to try to get the deficit under control. Changing the law on pornography, street soliciting, etc., none of this cost the government very much money.' Fourth, 'the boys at Justice,' that is, senior civil servants, made the issue a high priority.[7] Thus, despite himself, Crosbie had to confront the issue of pornography.

A process of consultation ensued between Crosbie, civil servants, and policy and research advisers at the Department of Justice to delineate the ground work for policy-making. The first step that led to the drafting of Bill C-114 involved the outlining of policy options. In this initial phase of policy-making, policy advisers inform the minister about the 'environment' in which the issue under investigation is located. In the case of pornography, the environment consisted of information about the state of the law, the publics involved in the debate, the state of scientific evidence on the effect of pornography on behaviour, and the opinion of experts concerning the regulation of pornography.

Let us examine this environment in more detail. According to one senior policy advisor at Justice, obscenity legislation was characterized in the early 1980s by an increasing process of liberalization. In *R. v. Doug Rankine Co.*, Judge Borins, by affirming that contemporary standards tolerated sexually explicit material that was not degrading, dehumanizing, or violent – a decision clearly inspired by feminist thinking on pornography – suggested the possibility of an appropriate context for displaying sex.[8] Subsequent cases followed this more or less liberal decision. Not every judge, however, shared Judge Borins's tolerant attitude. The Manitoba Court of Appeal, in *R. v. Video World*,[9] argued against the liberal line of authority, stating that the latter did not represent the country as a whole. Consequently, the court declared obscene material that showed simulated vaginal, anal, and oral intercourse, as well as masturbation. This decision was immediately appealed.[10] While Crosbie should have been informed of the controversial and conflictual nature of judicial decisions on obscenity, civil servants depicted the law as becoming increasingly restrictive:

The government in post-1985 was confronted with these conflicting lines of authority. The one which was quite liberal [following the decision of Judge Borins] and the other which represented a more traditional restrictive approach [the decision of the Manitoba Court of Appeal in the *Video World* case]. But the latter had the greater weight of authority behind it; it was an appellate decision as opposed to a decision of an individual trial level judge. It is a very difficult position to be in, in terms of trying to ascertain what is the current state of the law. *And for the Tory government the current state of the law was extremely important.* If you can understand that whatever was done with pornography it would have been very difficult for any government of whatever political stripe to have retreated from the status quo. Given the concerns about pornography, whether one accepted the evidence or not, the pressure was to toughen the law ... As a result, I do not think that there would have been any room for any government to have stepped back and said, we like this more liberal approach and we are going to legislate that, to codify that.[11]

This statement is of importance in understanding the influence of civil servants on the conservatism of Bill C-114. While it is an accepted practice in law to favour appellate decisions because they have greater authority than those of lower courts, civil servants could have been more judicious in relying on the decision of the Manitoba Court of Appeal in *Video World*, because it was itself under appeal. In 1985, when the government thought it essential to ascertain the state of the law, judicial decisions on obscenity not only were controversial, but were influenced to a large extent by feminist thinking on pornography and harm to women.[12] The fact that civil servants presented obscenity legislation as being quite severe, yet in need of reform to tighten it even more, shows how dedicated some of them were to developing a restrictive anti-pornography proposal.

Civil servants also informed Crosbie of the existence of two different communities involved in the campaign to reform the law: feminists and religious and family-oriented groups. While policy advisers understood the feminist position as an attack on the representation of 'power imbalance' rather than of sex, they felt that feminists ultimately favoured tougher controls on the representation of sex than the current obscenity legislation or the Fraser report offered.[13] Thus policy advisers informed Crosbie of the existence of a very strong and well organized public requesting a tightening of the law.

Civil servants paid little attention to the position of feminists against censorship, despite their protests against the criminalization of pornography, the court cases they launched against censorship, and their critique of the Fraser report for ignoring their viewpoint on pornography (Diamond, 1985). This institutional deafness seems to have been partly caused by the lack of mail from feminists against censorship. In fact, civil servants and the minister of justice paid great attention to the large correspondence they received, a correspondence that was mostly in favour of law reform. A policy adviser explains:

The [anti-pornography] community was very, very vocal, and usually by way of writing campaign letters to ministers and local members. And throughout the history of the subsequent bill the mail to the minister of justice was running overwhelmingly in support of the legislative efforts of the government. And it was not unusual to have the entire membership of a particular church writing to the minister of justice thousands of letters. It was the subject of correspondence for a number of years. Certainly up until the abortion decision in the Morgentaler case, it outstripped everything else.[14]

Because pro-censorship forces requested a tightening of the law on the basis of scientific evidence that pornography causes harm, it was imperative for the Department of Justice to evaluate the state of science. 'Research specialists' at the Department of Justice informed policy advisers that the scientific evidence of the impact of pornography on behaviour was inconclusive, and that one could not find scientific support for the feminist proposition that pornography harms women. A senior policy adviser commented that law reform 'cannot be based, or cannot be justified on a scientific analysis of the evidence. That is what our research specialists told us and that is certainly the basis on which we proceeded. If there is a reason for legislating against pornography it is not to be found in scientific evidence.'[15] Consequently, Crosbie was advised that a decision to criminalize pornography could not be based on scientific grounds.

Finally, the findings of both the Badgley report (Canada, 1984) on child sexual abuse and the Fraser report (Canada, 1985) on pornography and prostitution were presented to the minister of justice. It is noteworthy that provincial attorneys general did not support the Fraser Committee's recommendations, which 'would have been too liberal and would have opened up the door to the sale of material [already] banned or made the subject of prosecution.'[16] The opinion of the attorneys general counted a great deal for the Department of Justice because of their expertise in the regulation of the problems posed by pornography. It was clear to civil servants that to get their approval the anti-pornography law had to be more proscriptive than was recommended in the Fraser report.

Thus it is clear that in the event of law reform Crosbie could not rely on the approach recommended by the Fraser Committee – it was too permissive on all counts. The public that favoured law reform and the experts that regulated obscenity legislation rejected it. Ultimately, the most important challenge confronting the government was the possibility of striking a compromise between the demands of a group traditionally opposed to the Conservative party, but popular none the less and willing to work with the government – the coalition of feminist organizations – and the Conservatives' electoral constituency, particularly religious and family-oriented groups. Crosbie describes the dilemma he faced:

They [feminist organizations] hate Conservatives, they hate the Tory government. It is political. We arouse all of their most combative instincts. They are usually allied with the NDP in any event. They are completely ideological; frankly, it is hard to put up with them ... You can live without them, but you certainly can't live with them ... As a politician, I have to do it, but thank God we gave up going to the meetings of NAC. They are insulting; we would ask them a question and they would answer 'booh.' They are a bunch of ignoramuses ... But while they are against violence against women, they are also a very sophisticated group. So they don't want anybody's freedom being cut down. These are inconsistent positions.[17]

Despite Crosbie's difficulties with organized feminist groups, they were a powerful lobby and he had to address their concerns. Karen

Mosher, then Crosbie's legislative assistant, acknowledges her department's desire to reconcile the tension between the two forces; but she also recognizes that the effort failed and that in the end the proposed legislation promoted the interests of religious and family oriented organizations only:

The anti-pornography bill tried to do too much, it tried to cover too many of those interests, and tried to reconcile things which at bottom may not be reconcilable ... I think it started off being primarily a response to women's groups who saw the proliferation of increasingly violent material as a threat to full emancipation, full equality. I think that through the process of debate through caucus it got much more of a family orientation, much more of a protecting people from themselves kind of orientation.[18]

Why did the government not favour a more pragmatic approach, one that would have ensured it the support of women's groups? The answer lies in Mosher's hint that something happened in 'the process of debate through caucus.'

The Consultative Process in the Tory Caucus

The fourth set of factors responsible for making the anti-pornography bill more restrictive than suggested in the Fraser report has to do with the way the federal government embodied the balance of social forces within the pornography debate in its own caucus.

The drafting of any legislation is always done pursuant to a memorandum to Cabinet, approved by Cabinet. After consulting with policy advisers to establish what policy options are available to them, Cabinet members usually decide the particular direction of the legislation they want to put forward. Cabinet subsequently grants the Department of Justice the authority to draft the legislation. This authority, called a record of decision, outlines in detail what the amendments, sections, and subsections of the legislation should look like. In the case at hand, Cabinet decided to consult closely with members of the Conservative caucus before granting Justice the authority to draft the anti-pornography legislation. Why was the caucus so actively involved in the policy-making process?

According to Crosbie, the caucus was divided between the 'liberal sophisticates' like himself, who have few worries about pornography, and the 'fundamentalists' like Jake Epp, who are 'moral-majority-type' people, committed to the eradication of all 'evils.' This division within the party corresponds to a rural–urban split, with a higher concentration of 'fundamentalists' in the rural areas and the Western provinces. It also corresponds to a cultural split: the fifty-two members from Quebec, referred to as the 'Quebec caucus,' were not interested in tightening the law on pornography. In addition to the regional and cultural splits, every member of Cabinet, except for Epp, was a 'liberal sophisticate' on the issue of pornography. Horrified by the permissive attitude of Cabinet and the Quebec MPs, the 'fundamentalists' increased their activism in favour of tightening the law when the government announced its intention to reform obscenity legislation.

Also of significance in explaining the strong reaction of the 'fundamentalists' to the issue of pornography is their disappointment with some 'liberal' initiatives implemented by the Department of Justice.[19] The reform of the Divorce Act, which eliminated default as a ground for divorce and allowed divorce after one year of separation, and the federal response to the report of the Parliamentary Committee on Equality Rights, which potentially banned discrimination on the basis of sexual orientation, seemed to indicate a moral laxity on the part of the government. According to Crosbie, 'the fundamentalists were all full of piss and vinegar' about those reforms. Consequently, when it came time to address the issue of pornography, the 'fundamentalists' were not willing to accept a compromise. They demanded a truly conservative pornography law.

Faced with the dissatisfaction of many backbenchers over Crosbie's liberal reforms and the general lack of consensus within the party as to the best way of dealing with pornography, Cabinet feared the reactions of the most conservative members of its caucus. In Crosbie's view, had the government not involved the 'fundamentalists' in the drafting of the bill and presented them with a law, a free vote might have been necessary, with potentially embarrassing consequences. Crosbie explains that the fundamentalists 'might have voted against the government ... This is an issue where they considered their conscience might overrule supporting the party ... So we had to work hard to make sure that there was a majority within the caucus.'[20]

Knowing that the caucus was divided over social issues and wanting to avert political embarrassment, Cabinet decided to involve the caucus in the policy-making process. Thus the anti-pornography bill ended as a compromise between the 'fundamentalists' and the 'liberal sophisticates' within the Tory caucus.[21]

Crosbie agrees with Mosher's opinion that somewhere in the 'process of debate through caucus' the bill's drafters lost sight of the interests of women's groups, and instead came to represent solely the interests of religious, pro-family groups. He states that in the end the bill 'was not an attempt to pander to women's issues; that was only incidental.'[22] It was instead an effort to overcome the division on social issues within the caucus. Explaining why his party could not adopt the Fraser Committee's approach (Canada, 1985), Crosbie claims that it was 'too liberal with a small "l" for the crew that I had to deal with in the caucus. So it had to be something that would satisfy the moralists and the sophisticates in our caucus, which the Fraser report would not do. So it had to be a compromise somewhere in between those two views.'[23]

Thus the feminist rationale that would have criminalized pornography to promote and protect women's right to equality vanished through the involvement of the Tory caucus in the policy-making process. Caucus members, in consultation with policy advisers at the Department of Justice, devised a rationale whereby the purpose of the criminal law was the protection of people and values and the proscription of inappropriate behaviour. The main question facing the caucus was

whether or not there were something to be gained from the use of the criminal law. And many [caucus members] agreed that yes, it has an educational purpose or role to play, and there was a substantial proportion of the public that was offended by the display and access of pornography. [There was] the issue of convenience stores and what to do with people confronting pornography when they go in to buy their jug of milk. Does the criminal law have a role to play in protecting those people? And the government said yes, it did.[24]

In sum, to criminalize pornography, the caucus opted for a rationale based on the relationship between law, morality, and the protection of society. In this context, the criminal law is not simply an instrument of last resort for the protection of the individual from injury: it must also protect and promote the common political and moral ideas and institutions without which people cannot live together (Devlin, 1959: 23). Pornography thus appeared to the Conservatives as a vice that the law could eradicate through its capacity to educate and intimidate.

The Centrality of Child Sexual Abuse

This analysis of the consultative process within the caucus helps explain the conservative nature of Bill C-114. It has shown how, in the compromise between the 'fundamentalists' and the 'liberal sophisticates' within the Conservative caucus, the drafters of the anti-pornography bill lost track of feminists' concerns about the harm pornography causes to women's right to equality. Instead of addressing women's issues, caucus members were preoccupied with the development of a strategy that ensured the protection of family values – the main issue for the 'fundamentalists' – but also respected people's freedoms – the main issue for the 'liberal sophisticates.' Such a strategy was difficult to arrive at, because many caucus members were committed to the total eradication of sexually explicit material. The end product of this strategy, Bill C-114, disregarded liberty rights by prohibiting the depiction of sex. How could this have happened? How could the civil libertarian elements of the Conservative party have been so minimized? An examination of the way in which the Tories subordinated the issue of pornography to the issue of child sexual abuse is telling.

A corollary of the extensive meetings between Cabinet and caucus members was the subsequent framing of the discussion of pornography and prostitution by the larger phenomenon of child sexual abuse. Both the Badgley report on child sexual abuse (Canada, 1984) and the Fraser report on pornography and prostitution (Canada, 1985) found evidence of extensive child abuse in Canada and pointed to a consensus in society on the need for dealing immediately with the issue. In a document analysing the reports, the government links pornography and prostitution to the more urgent and distressing issue of child sexual abuse:

Pornographic depictions were not infrequently shown to children by abusers to reduce the child's inhibitions and to school the child in the acts to be performed. *The linkage is clear.* Again, it has been found that many juvenile prostitutes have run away from home following incidents of sexual abuse; such may well be the prior history of many adult prostitutes. Finally, completing the vicious circle, the empirical studies show that those who abuse children sexually were very frequently themselves the victims of just such abuse. (Canada, Department of Justice, 1985: 4; emphasis added)

Mobilizing the idea of a 'vicious circle' of pornography, prostitution, and child sexual abuse, the government decided to make child sexual abuse the most crucial issue of its administration.[25] As part of a strategy aimed at demonstrating its deep commitment to eradicating the 'social dimension of the problem,' the government created an interdepartmental committee headed by the minister of health and welfare to 'coordinate *all activities* of the federal government that deal with problems of child sexual abuse.'[26] This interdepartmental committee, then, was responsible for dealing with the problem of pornography.

The hierarchy of the committee had a significant impact on the conservative nature of the anti-pornography bill and its disregard for liberty rights. By giving Health and Welfare the lead in the coordination of activities dealing with pornography, the government strengthened the policy-making influence of the ministry that most directly incorporated family and religious interests. It will be remembered that at the time, Jake Epp, the minister of health and welfare, was the only 'fundamentalist' in Cabinet. By creating an interdepartmental committee headed by the most influential of the fundamentalists, the government secured the support of the most conservative caucus members for its anti-pornography bill. Moreover, once it associated pornography with a problem of such significance as child sexual abuse, the government could not seriously defend pornography on liberal grounds; its immediate eradication became necessary.

To sum up, the making of the anti-pornography bill was not straightforward: it involved a process of consultation, negotiation, and compromise between different agents. None the less, a conservative policy prevailed. Four factors have been identified as directly affecting policy-making. First, with the change from a Liberal to a Conservative government, pornography became constituted as a threat to the family rather than to liberal democratic principles. Second, anti-pornography, pro-censorship forces, dissatisfied with the obscenity provisions of the existing Criminal Code and with the leniency of the Fraser report, engaged in a relentless letter-writing campaign, a campaign so effective that it even led the two opposition parties to clamour for a tougher law. Third, the consultative process with civil servants at the Department of Justice had a significant impact on the conservative nature of Bill C-114. Whereas the state of obscenity litigation in 1985 was conflicting and influenced by feminist thinking to a large extent,[27] civil servants presented judicial decisions on obscenity as becoming increasingly restrictive, yet, according to the public, in need of being tightened even more. This strategy of effacing judicial controversy reveals the zealous attitude of some civil servants in the elaboration of conservative legislation on pornography. Finally, the involvement of the caucus in the policy-making phase minimized the influence of the civil libertarian element within the Conservative party. So powerful was the 'fundamentalist' element in the caucus that it was able to redefine pornography as integrally linked to the most inflammatory of public issues – the sexual abuse of children, a violence which no Canadian could tolerate.

Public Reaction and the Death of Bill C-114

Strong criticism awaited the anti-pornography bill. The arts community, civil libertarians, feminists against censorship, some women's groups, and the media attacked the bill for its concern with sex rather than violence – in other words, for not diverging from the traditional approach to obscenity. Many accused the government of being undemocratic for imposing 'Victorian' morals and values and failing to accept the sexual variety of contemporary society. They argued also that the government capitalized on the horror most Canadians feel about child sexual abuse to launch an open-ended attack on all sexually explicit material. What concerned them most was the all-encompassing provision that defined as pornography depictions of 'other sexual activity.' Alan Borovoy, general counsel for the Canadian Civil Liberties Association, explains the fear many felt about the authoritarianism inherent in Bill C-114:

While the existing law suffered from vagueness, this bill achieved absurdity ... And what are we to make of the concluding words '... or other sexual activity'? I used to think of myself as worldly but, for the life of me, I have been unable to figure out what sexual activity these words include that does not appear in the rather detailed list that precedes them. A number of commentators have conjectured that, if enacted, the bill could prohibit the showing of hugging, kissing, or perhaps even holding hands. Was there ever a more magnificent example of the power-hoarding fallacy? (1988: 60)

The implications of Bill C-114 for censorship of artistic and mainstream films depicting sex between consenting adults were obvious and intolerable. Civil libertarians, artists, and the media demanded that Bill C-114 be abolished.

Women's groups and feminist organizations, however, did not react so unanimously. The National Action Committee on the Status of Women rejected Bill C-114 in its entirety, refusing even to suggest ways to rewrite it. NAC claimed that the bill did not address the power imbalance inherent in pornography and thus could not differentiate between pornography and erotica. Louise Dulude, then the president of NAC, was unequivocal: Bill C-114 'is extremely puritan and totally unacceptable' (*Toronto Star*, 11 June 1986). Not all feminists involved in the anti-pornography movement agreed with NAC's stance. While many felt that 'some very essential parts of [the feminist] speech have not been heard by the government,'[28] they were not willing to lose the chance to legislate on pornography. The Canadian Coalition against Media Pornography (CCAMP) stated: 'If we can come up with some good suggestions as to improve how this definition can be re-written, or parts of it subsumed under the other definitions of pornography, we feel confident that we will be listened to and that amendments will be made' (CCAMP Newsletter, 12 June 1986). Most feminist organizations involved in the anti-pornography movement, in fact, were interested in modifying the bill so that dominance and power imbalance, rather than sexual explicitness, would be at the heart of the legislation.

For example, the Canadian Advisory Council on the Status of Women (CACSW), the Committee against Pornography (CAP), the Canadian Coalition against Media Pornography (CCAMP), and Canadians Concerned about Violent Entertainment (CCAVE), all agreed that Bill C-114 did not go far enough in circumscribing material that is harmful and degrading. They even criticized the bill as being too enabling because it allowed judicial interpretation: 'The present drafting does not go far enough in its application. In its limitation to visual depictions, to "permanent or extended impairment" and its lack of clarity, many foreseeable portrayals of physical harm and violence toward women may be interpreted as being legal under the present draft' (CACSW, 1986b: 5). They argued that Bill C-114 should be modified to prevent the judicial interpretation of the meaning of 'harmful or violent material,' and should be enlarged to encompass written material. They even urged that no defences based on the artistic, educational, or scientific merit of the material should be allowed, because as it was the defences permitted by Bill C-114 could be used to exonerate material truly pornographic – that is, material that denied women full access to legal, social, and economic equality (CACSW, 1986b: 9). In sum, the feminist community was strongly divided in its attitude towards the bill; in fact, CACSW's attitude was at the opposite extreme from NAC's.

Needless to say, most religious and family-oriented organizations were unanimous in their approval of the proposed legislation. The police were also pleased by it. Speaking as the president of the Canadian Association of Police Chiefs, Police Chief Greg Cohoon of Moncton said that the bill's clarity was an improvement over the vagueness of the previous obscenity legislation (*Globe and Mail*, 12 June 1986).

Meanwhile, a ministerial shuffle sent John Crosbie to the Department of Transport and Ramon Hnatyshyn to the Department of Justice. According to a civil servant at the Department of Justice, Hnatyshyn took the public discontent over Bill C-114 seriously and wanted the bill rewritten. Consequently, Bill C-114 was never debated in the House. It died on the order paper on 28 August 1986 with the end of the parliamentary session.[29]

6

Bill C-54:
The Impossible Compromise

Minister of Justice Ramon Hnatyshyn wanted the anti-pornography bill rewritten to please both feminist and religious and family organizations. According to a senior general counsel of the Department of Justice who advised Hnatyshyn, 'The effort, then, was to rewrite [the bill] to try to capture that elusive middle ground, to get enough support so that it would retain the support from those back benchers who reflected the family religious perspective, and so it would be more palatable to the feminist community.'[1] This compromise was difficult because conservative groups rejected sexually explicit material on the grounds that science had proved its danger. A policy adviser to the minister of justice explains the dilemma Hnatyshyn faced:

[Feminists] were prepared to accept anything very explicit so long as it showed the participant on an equal plane. It was not the explicitness that they wanted banned, it was the dominance and violence and the abuse: sexism. However, the family and religiously oriented community did not care about any of that, it was all trash for them, and no matter how nicely portrayed and equally balanced the participants would be, it would still be unacceptable. There were quite a few government back benchers who represented that point of view.[2]

The compromise was finally achieved by including in Bill C-54, the anti-pornography bill, a provision allowing for the display of and access to 'erotica.' Bill C-54 defined erotica as 'any visual matter a dominant characteristic of which is the depiction, in a sexual context or for the purpose of the sexual stimulation of the viewer, of a human sexual organ, a female breast or the human anal region.' Access to erotica of any one under eighteen years of age was prohibited. The display of erotica to anyone was subject to the following regulation: 'Every person who displays any erotica in a way that is visible to a member of the public in a public place, unless the public must, in order to see the erotica, pass a prominent warning notice advising of the nature of the display therein or unless the erotica is hidden by a barrier or is covered by an opaque wrapper, is guilty of an offence punishable on summary conviction.' While pornography was defined along the lines recommended in the Fraser report, Bill C-54 was prohibitive: it forbade the depiction of acts such as vaginal, anal, and oral intercourse, lactation, menstruation, and ejaculation.

After tabling Bill C-54 in May 1987, Hnatyshyn held a press conference in which he praised the anti-pornography proposal, describing it as the result of intense consultations with various groups and individuals committed to the abolition of sexual violence and degradation. He argued that Bill C-54 represented a 'broad consensus in the Canadian public that there is no place for portrayals of child pornography, sexual violence and degradation in a sexual context' (Toronto Star, 23 May 1987). Hnatyshyn praised Bill C-54 as an improvement over the current obscenity legislation, which lacked clarity and precision.

Despite his efforts to strike a compromise between feminist and conservative forces, Hnatyshyn and his government scrapped Bill C-54 in the fall of 1988. What happened? How can one explain this failure in law reform, a failure that took place when all conditions were ripe for a change? In this chapter I will attempt to answer these questions by examining the public reaction to Bill C-54.

Dissenting Reactions from Artists, Civil Libertarians, and the Media

Civil liberties organizations, the arts community, feminists against censorship, gay and lesbian organizations, and the media attacked Bill C-54, which they perceived as anti-sex and anti-democracy. Speaking for the Book and Periodical Development Council, Pierre Berton claimed that if Bill C-54 were enacted it would make Canadian writers the 'laughing stock of the Western World' (Toronto Star, 16 September 1987). The bill not only opposed intellectual freedom, but also seemed to deny sexuality itself. According to the Canadian Rights and Liberties Federation, the bill represented 'an overly-broad assault upon our principles of free speech. If interpreted strictly, it could make it almost impossible even to discuss these topics in any meaningful fashion; discussion of certain elements of sexuality could be reduced to debate without passion, analysis without commitment' (1987: 3).

While all these organizations opposed the exploitation of children in pornography, they criticized the government for implying that by attacking 'kiddie porn' it would solve the problems of sexual abuse (see Canadian Rights and Liberties Federation, 1987). Some argued that 'kiddie porn' had been used by the state as a means to crack down on sexually explicit material. Berton attacked the bill's faulty logic:

I can watch Rambo killing a million 'gooks.' I can, on Elwy [Yost's] TV show, watch Gary Cooper being tortured with burning bamboo splints under his fingernails. I can turn on the television news and see dead bodies strewn all over Nicaragua. I can see films, photographs and TV crime shows in which men and women shoot each other alive – as long as they don't do it in a sexual context. But I am forbidden by a new law to watch a man and a woman lying in each other's arms making passionate and explicit love. (*Toronto Star*, 16 May 1987)

The opponents of Bill C-54 cited the absurdity of proscribing the depiction of explicit sexuality to prevent acts of sexual abuse when representations of violence were so widely available.

In the fall of 1987 many artists protested against Bill C-54 by censoring works that they claimed would be targeted for prosecution if the bill was approved. Nudes by Matisse, Rodin, and Horatio Torres, among others, were covered in brown paper. At the Art Gallery of Ontario, gallery officials posted notices next to thirty-eight artworks that they felt would be affected by the legislation. The Day of Resistance Coalition Against Bill C-54 organized a nationwide protest. People gathered in community centres and art galleries to watch, hear, and discuss sex-related films, videos, and books that were open to prohibition under Bill C-54. The purpose of these events was to dramatize the importance of sex-related material, especially in the era of AIDS, and to show how Bill C-54 would 'curtail our ability to explore and discuss sexual issues' (Day of Resistance Against Bill C-54, 1987).

In sum, those opposed to Bill C-54 reacted strongly to what they perceived as an attempt to instil a puritan, anti-sex mentality at a time when open discussions of sex were central to the development of safe sex practices, the expression of sexual identities marginalized by traditional standards, and the right to free expression.

Mixed Reactions from Feminists

The feminist reaction to the anti-pornography bill was not uniform. While initially it looked as if NAC supported the intent of the bill, some important changes took place within the organization; those changes eventually led to NAC's rejection of the bill on the grounds that it was a superficial, ineffective, and inappropriate means to deal with pornography. Before the bill was tabled, NAC's membership was relatively united on the need to criminalize pornography. However, in its brief to the House of Commons Justice Committee on Bill C-54 (1988), NAC indicated that some fundamental changes had occurred in the organization's attitude towards pornography. In the following section, I will digress briefly to focus on the transformations that took place within NAC, because they point to a shift in the balance of social forces on pornography within the organized feminist movement, a shift that influenced other important players in the fight against Bill C-54.

In its brief NAC proposed four criteria as minimal requirements for any legislative response to pornography:

1. That any legislation focus on violence rather than sex acts;

2. That legislation not affect the distribution of sex education materials to people under 18;

3. That legislation not reinforce heterosexism and thereby discrimination against lesbians and gays and;

4. That any legislation put the onus on the Crown to prove that material charged does not have educational or artistic merit rather than placing the onus on the artist or educator to prove that it does. (NAC, 1988: 4)

These criteria, endorsed at NAC's 1987 annual general meeting, show the influence of feminists against censorship in changing NAC's initial position on pornography. The first criterion indicates that NAC dropped its initial focus on sex *and* violence to focus on violence alone. A focus on violence, however, does not easily translate into a legal scheme for criminalization, since violence is a central theme in most cultural representations. One can imagine the depletion of most libraries and museums in the event of a law banning the representation of violence. Nevertheless, NAC's decision to focus on violence is not simplistic; it suggests that the organization had become less interested in quick fixes, such as criminalizing pornography, and more interested in condemning a ubiquitous aspect of our society. For to address critically the problem of violence, we need the freedom to discuss, express, and represent violence. The second criterion demonstrates a new interest in the production of sexually explicit material, especially that directed at young people, who, according to the socialist feminists on NAC, were more than ever in need of sex information in the age of AIDS.[3] The third criterion acknowledges the dangers to sexual minorities in criminalizing pornography: 'Experience has shown us that sweeping definitions, such as that proposed in Bill C-54, will consistently be used in their broadest possible interpretation to limit and censor materials perceived of as "sensitive" or "abnormal." Lesbian and gay material will clearly suffer under the current proposal and this is not acceptable to NAC member groups' (NAC, 1988: 6). In other words, NAC learned to recognize the implications of criminalizing pornography for the makers and consumers of material that challenged or departed from heterosexual representations of sexuality. The fourth criterion suggests a greater degree of empathy for feminist artists: NAC argues that there is no reason to depart from criminal law in placing the onus of proof.

The strength of feminists against censorship had another important impact on NAC's attempt to comprehend the relationship between pornography and harm to women's right to equality. NAC's critique of Bill C-54 shows an effort to conceptualize women's oppression as 'context-dependent' – that is, as part of the economic, social, cultural, legal, and political inequalities women face daily:

In order to properly address pornography's harm it is essential that greater resources be focused on the full range of services and programs necessary to improve the status of Canadian women. Better funding for a wide range of services for incest survivors, battered women and rape victims, more attention for media literacy education to respond to the problems of sex role stereotyping in the media, greater job training and re-training programs for women and the establishment of effective affirmative action programs – all these are examples of services and programs which must be an essential part of any government response aimed at controlling pornography. (1988: 8)

In this context, pornography becomes part of the totality of social relations that must be addressed if women's inferior status is to change.

While NAC argued that women would benefit more from changing social relations than eradicating pornography, it recognized that some of its member groups supported the control of pornography through the implementation of civil remedies or through human rights legislation and the creation of a statutory right of action grounded in the notion of equality rights. Despite these differences, NAC reported a consensus among its member groups on the inadequacy of Bill C-54 (1988: 4).

Not all feminist organizations agreed with these new developments within NAC. The Committee against Pornography (CAP) opposed NAC's decision to reject Bill C-54. It denigrated NAC's attempts to fight for the right to abortion and equal pay when women's 'right to exist is being challenged' by pornography.[4] CAP withdrew its membership from NAC.

Other feminist anti-pornography organizations, such as the Canadian Advisory Council on the Status of Women (CACSW), the Canadian Coalition against Media Pornography (CCAMP), Resources against Pornography (RAP), the Metro (Toronto) Action Committee on Violence against Women and Children (METRAC), and the Canadian Committee against Violent Entertainment (CCAVE), defended the general aims of Bill C-54, insisting that opposition to the bill showed that there had been a 'lot of misunderstanding' about it (Globe and Mail, 14 August 1987). They studied the bill and made recommendations to the government to improve it (see CACSW, 1988; CCAMP Newsletter, June 1987 to October 1988; RAP, n.d.). To show their support they organized a letter-writing campaign, urging Hnatyshyn to push the bill through second reading.

The mixed reactions of feminist organizations were represented at the federal level by the positions of the New Democratic party and the Liberal party. In their critique of Bill C-54 the two opposition parties generally claimed that women's organizations had condemned the bill and that the government should rewrite it. To the assertion that Bill C-54 was not popular among women's groups, Hnatyshyn replied, 'I should like to point out ... that women's groups are not opposed to the Bill itself, they are against certain definitions. They want explanations and more information, but they are not directly against the Bill' (*Hansard*: 30 November 1987: 11295). Indeed, Hnaty-shyn was right. Women's organizations supplied him with numerous suggestions to improve his bill. The main opposition to Bill C-54 came from elsewhere.

The Revolt of the Librarians

When asked why the government chose to let its anti-pornography bill die, civil servants at the Department of Justice point to the emergence of a new player in the pornography debate: librarians. A policy adviser describes how the Department of Justice was startled by the librarians' outcry: 'And for the first time ever, the librarians of Canada rose up in anger. I had never seen anything like that; they are among the most conservative people collectively and individually. They were greatly offended that the government would do anything that might tell them how to control their collection.'[5]

In the fall of 1987 library boards across Canada voiced their anger at Bill C-54, which they perceived as a threat to cultural freedom and librarians' lawful responsibility. Among the most outspoken of the library boards was the Toronto Public Library Board, which announced its decision to close twenty-eight of thirty-two public libraries in Toronto on 10 December 1987.[6] The chair of the board, Sheryl Taylor-Munro, explained the rationale for this action: 'The bill is a clear threat to a first-class library system ... The Government is saying we are no different than child pornographers. This bill goes against everything like open access to information and freedom of speech' (*Globe and Mail*, 21 November 1987). What led such a normally tranquil group to espouse such an extreme strategy? In the following section I will examine the process whereby librarians came to adamantly oppose Bill C-54.

The activities of the Toronto board were supported by librarians, the artistic community, and civil liberties organizations across Canada. Alan Borovoy, general counsel for the Canadian Civil Liberties Association (CCLA), praised the librarians' protest: 'Librarians don't generally fit the perception of social activists ... When they get as concerned as this, it has got to go a long way to raising the consciousness of the people. It's going to make the people in this com-

munity sit up and take notice' (*Toronto Star*, 26 November 1987).
Borovoy had reason to celebrate the revolt of the librarians. An
excerpt from the CCLA's newsletter reveals that civil libertarians
were more than just approving onlookers:

CCLA members will be happy to know that the idea for this novel tactic came
from us. At the October 28, 1987 meeting of the Toronto Library Board, Alan
Borovoy, CCLA General Counsel, and David Schneiderman, Field Representa-
tive, called upon the Board to adopt a resolution which included '... the
closing of libraries during normal open hours to dramatize the issue ...' CCLA
went on to play a pivotal role in the organization of the protest. *Our representatives planned, badgered, and cajoled to drum up support.* We addressed
conferences, debated on the media, and prepared background material. (Canadian Civil Liberties Association, 1988: 1; emphasis in original)

Borovoy and his organization had, in fact, largely orchestrated the
uprising.

One of the CCLA's strategies was to request the legal opinion of
Edward L. Greenspan, a prominent criminal lawyer, concerning the
potential vulnerability of library personnel to Bill C-54. Greenspan's
detailed opinion (1987), in the form of a letter to the CCLA, is worth
examining because it subsequently formed the basis of the librarians'
official position on the bill.

Greenspan's carefully worded text refers to books that were available in most libraries. Drawing on reports made for his firm about the
content of those books, Greenspan asks whether the members or staff
of Canadian library boards could face criminal prosecution in the
event that Bill C-54, in its present form, became law. The answer is
yes.

He asserts that in law there is a presumption against construing the
words of a statute to attribute redundancy to any of them (1987: 1).
This means that the words 'incites, promotes, encourages, or advocates' (any conduct defined as pornographic under Bill C-54, such
as bestiality and incest) should each be defined uniquely. Greenspan
argues that 'encourages' could mean 'legitimates' or 'presents as
acceptable.' Consequently, it is possible that a book such as Ayn
Rand's *The Fountainhead* could be defined as encouraging sexually
violent behaviour, because the novel's hero sexually abuses the
woman who then becomes his lover, and this aggression is presented
as a component of his individuality (1987: 2). Marian Engel's *Bear*,

Greenspan argues, could be defined as pornography because it either 'incites' or 'promotes' or 'encourages' or 'advocates' bestiality – an act whose representation was prohibited by the bill. (The book contains scenes of sexual contact between a woman and a bear [1987: 2]). Because it depicts a romance between two siblings, Michel Tremblay's play *Bonjour la, Bonjour* could be defined as pornographic for 'inciting, promoting, encouraging, or advocating' incest (1987: 2).

One of the 'degrading acts in a sexual context' Bill C-54 deems pornographic is that in which a person 'penetrates with an object the vagina' of another. This provision could render William Faulkner's *Sanctuary* pornographic; in that novel an impotent man forcibly inserts a corncob into the vagina of a young woman. Moreover, the woman is portrayed as enjoying the man and their sexual encounter (Greenspan, 1987: 2). Another 'degrading act,' according to Bill C-54, occurs when a person 'ejaculates onto another person.' The instructional book *Safe Sex in the Age of AIDS* produced by the Institute for the Advanced Study of Human Sexuality, recommends such a practice: listed among safe sex practices is the act of ejaculating on a partner's back or breasts because it involves no exchange of bodily fluids and thus no danger of infection. It is not farfetched to say, Greenspan argues, that such material 'encourages' some of its readers to ejaculate on each other (1987: 2).

Greenspan is sceptical of Hnatyshyn's claim that library books would be protected by the defences of artistic, educational, scientific, or medical merit. Judgments about the merit of a text are highly subjective, and according to Greenspan neither the minister of justice nor anyone else could provide the library board or its staff with adequate assurance that the defences could be successfully applied in the cases of the material mentioned above. Greenspan also contends that in the past such defences have not prevented prosecutions. He cites the film *Last Tango in Paris* and the book *Show Me*, both of which were alleged to be obscene despite the fact that the former was considered artistic and the latter educational (Greenspan, 1987: 3). While those cases resulted in acquittals, reputable witnesses were involved on both sides. The defences of artistic, scientific, or educational merit and recourse to experts to assess such merit do not necessarily ensure protection from prosecution.

Greenspan notes another potential problems for librarians in Bill C-54: that fear of criminal charges might make the police the paramount judges of what is acceptable. Because criminal prosecution is costly and upsetting, a library board and its staff might follow the directives of the police rather than face a trial (Greenspan, 1987: 3). In other words, the fear of being charged might impel librarians to simply comply with police instructions to remove books. Hence, the police rather than the courts would decide what was pornographic.

Certain sections in the bill described material for which there would be no defence available – in other words, material that 'incites, promotes, encourages, or advocates' sexual conduct involving persons under 18 years of age. The implication of these sections is that many important artistic and educational works could be censored. Petronius's *Satyricon*, Boccaccio's *Decameron*, Nabokov's *Lolita*, and Plato's *Symposium* all contain passages that may 'encourage' sexual intercourse between children or between a child and an adult. Despite the artistic reputation these books have acquired, no defence would be available to the board's members or employees in the event of a criminal prosecution.

Another section of the bill prohibited books that 'incite, promote, encourage, or advocate' masturbation by persons under 18. Planned Parenthood's *How to Talk to Your Child About Sexuality*, Howard R. and Martha Lewis's *Sex Education Begins at Home*, John V. Flowers, Jennifer Horsman and Bernard Schwartz's *Raising Your Child to Be a Sexually Healthy Adult*, and Dr Benjamin Spock's *Baby and Child Care* contain passages 'encouraging' parents to teach or to let their children masturbate because it is considered a healthy practice. Greenspan warns librarians that

there are strong grounds to believe that this type of material would be caught by the Bill. All of these books appear to advocate, promote or encourage masturbation among children. In some of the above instances, parents are even told, in explicit terms, to *encourage* their children to masturbate. Please remember that the defence of educational purpose would not apply in these circumstances. And anyone found distributing such material would be liable to 10 years in jail. (Greenspan, 1987: 4; emphasis in original)

Greenspan acknowledges Hnatyshyn's media announcements stating that the authorities would not be likely to launch a prosecution against the libraries. While acknowledging that this might be true, Greenspan cautions librarians about running such a risk. He contends that unless the minister of justice amends the Bill, the Minister cannot immunize anyone, including library personnel. Whatever law is enacted is likely to be enforced by the Provincial Ministry of the Attorney General and the local police. Even if there were a disposition to trust the good judgment of the existing incumbents in these positions, there would be no way of knowing how their successors might behave. What we do know is that much of the material in the current possession of libraries falls within the wording of the Bill. (Greenspan, 1987: 5)

Propelled by this forceful analysis of the inimical impact of Bill C-54 on library collections and personnel, librarians launched a vehement attack on the proposed anti-pornography legislation. In addition to drawing upon Greenspan's detailed analysis, librarians addressed the feminist concerns about pornography. Mobilizing the expertise of science, they suggested that scientific evidence is inconclusive on the causal relationship between pornography and violence against women. They used the work of researchers referred to by the anti-pornography movement to undermine the claim that legislation prohibiting pornography would improve women's unequal status. Indeed, the recourse to law reform, they argued, was not recommended by those scientists (Donnerstein, Linz and Penrod) from whom the anti-pornography movement had taken its evidence. The librarians quoted these scientists: 'We believe it is premature to advocate either more zealous enforcement of existing obscenity laws or the creation of new laws to curb the distribution of pornography because existing research leaves too many questions unanswered' (quoted in Toronto Public Library Board, 1988: 15).

The librarians were careful to say that their critique of law reform was not based simply on the civil libertarian's argument that unless direct harm is proved, nothing should interfere with one's freedom.[7] Rather, their position on freedom of expression was combined with a profound concern for the women and children who were victims of violence. Drawing on NAC's critique of Bill C-54, which was strongly influenced by feminists against censorship, they supported NAC's recommendations for 'alternative methods of dealing with the serious problem of violence' (Toronto Public Library Board, 1988: 14).[8]

The librarians' challenge was met with 'comforting' statements from the minister of justice. Trying to appease these unlikely radicals, Hnatyshyn asserted that their fears were unwarranted; the proposed legislation was aimed at 'hard-core pornography' rather than at material in libraries. Librarians could not trust him completely, however, in view of the way in which other Conservative members of Parliament had already defended the bill. For example, MP Richard Grisé, parliamentary secretary to the deputy prime minister and president of the Privy Council, had responded to the concerns of librarians in the following fashion:

Librarian groups, for instance, object to this Bill because they will have to reorganize certain documents, books and publications in certain areas of their library. What should be most important in our society today? Not to change anything, or to impose certain standards and restrictions to our library, and we know that an increasing number of young people go to the libraries, which is certainly a good thing! Is it not normal to want to keep such material away from our young people and require that there be a special section in libraries for erotica which will not be accessible to young Canadians? I believe that this is much more important. (*Hansard*, 30 November 1987: 11294)

Such statements energized the librarians' revolt, which grew in scope until a large number of organizations were calling for an end to Bill C-54.

Many within the Department of Justice feel that it was the revolt of the librarians that singlehandedly killed the legislation. An examination of the Commons debates does not indicate that the librarians were perceived as a significant threat. In fact, the opposition parties refused to move the bill to second reading, and they voiced a critique that combined the positions of the librarians, the artistic community, and feminist organizations. Opposition members pointed to the enabling nature of Bill C-54 and its disrespect for Canadians' freedoms and rights. They also attacked the bill as a strategy intended to suppress sexuality, and one that would give wide powers to law enforcement agencies. Indeed, the speeches in the House often celebrated former Prime Minister Pierre Trudeau's comment that the state has no business in the bedrooms of Canadians. The Fraser Committee's report appeared suddenly to be a plausible approach to the regulation of sexually explicit material. Various members of Parliament reprimanded the government for not having taken the committee's report seriously (*Hansard*, 2 December 1987: 11428).

But it was not only the opposition members' critique that made Bill C-54 die on the order paper when Parliament dissolved for the election in the fall of 1988. Holding a majority in the House, the government could have pushed the bill through if it had wanted to. According to a Conservative member of Parliament, the government needed more time and debate: 'We are determined to move ahead with this Bill, but we also are determined to make sure that proper debate is held and that Members do not feel pushed with [an] unreasonable time frame in this regard' (*Hansard*, 28 June 1988: 16846). This comment is interesting when contrasted with the government's original argument that swift action was needed to combat an urgent problem, action which if delayed would mean more violence and harm to women and children. Why was more time and debate needed? Why had the government's laxity not triggered upheaval among the Conservative caucus, or precipitated pandemonium among conservative organizations so committed to law reform on pornography?

The Retreat of the Conservatives

At first, conservative organizations responded favourably to Bill C-54. Lynn Scime, the president of R.E.A.L. Women of Canada, praised the government for finally doing something truly conservative (*Toronto Star*, 24 January 1988). R.E.A.L. Women urged the government not to give in to the objections of the artistic community, civil libertarians, and some feminist organizations concerning the regulation of erotica, because those groups ignored scientific evidence that clearly demonstrated the harm caused by sexually explicit material. R.E.A.L. Women identified some loopholes that could liberalize the bill, and recommended ways of strengthening it (R.E.A.L. Women, n.d.a). None the less, they liked the bill as a whole.

The Coalition for Family Values, like other religious and family-oriented groups, wanted the elimination of the section concerning 'erotica,' because that was simply another term for soft-core pornography. The coalition argued, for example, that depictions of anal sex, which were classified as erotica, were as despicable as depictions of bestiality, necrophilia, and incest, and should therefore be classified as pornography. This feeling was shared by the Reverend Hudson T. Hilsden, chair of the InterChurch Committee on Pornography and the Pentecostal Assemblies of Canada, who declared that 'anal intercourse should be moved into a separate category and artistic merit defences should not apply for the depiction of this conduct. There is no place in Canadian society for conduct that clearly degrades and dehumanizes people' (Hilsden, n.d.).

Conservative organizations also addressed the protection of sexually explicit art, an issue which they thought was at the heart of the objections raised by artists and librarians. For example, the Coalition for Family Values urged the government to draft its legislation in such a way that only material intended for sexual stimulation would be deemed pornographic. The recommendations of the conservative groups did not mean they rejected the bill; on the contrary, they found it acceptable – at least at first.

By March 1988, however, the support for the proposed anti-pornography legislation had faded almost completely. According to Neville Avison, a senior policy adviser at the Department of Justice who was involved in the drafting of Bill C-54, 'suddenly, C-54 started to look like a monstrous liberalization' (quoted in the *Toronto Star*, 11 May 1989). The InterChurch Committee on Pornography (ICCP), which had hired a lawyer to scrutinize Bill C-54, discovered that the bill contained numerous loopholes that could drastically liberalize an apparently conservative law. It would even liberalize the current obscenity provisions, as interpreted in *Video World* by the Manitoba Court of Appeal and upheld by the Supreme Court of Canada.[9] (It will be recalled that the Manitoba Court of Appeal found obscene certain material containing simulation of vaginal, anal, and oral intercourse, as well as masturbation.) The ICCP feared what it saw as the regressive aspects of the bill: 'We are deeply disturbed, however, that the bill as written would actually remove protections which now exist under the obscenity provisions of the Criminal Code ... *Many degrading and abusive images, of which we can give you graphic examples if you wish, would become legal as now they are not* ... Concerns we have voiced about the Bill from the outset have been dealt with, in effect, by the Court, *but the passage of C-54 as written would undo that very good effect.*'[10]

The ICCP and other religious organizations were gravely disappointed by the part of the bill that was supposed to impose controls on the display of and access to adult magazines. The ICCP wanted the minister of justice to 'deal with the images in the magazines and films. *Bill C-54, as written fails to do this adequately.*'[11] In other words, the group wanted not just to restrict the display of adult magazines but to ban them outright. The ICCP also feared that some sections of Bill C-54 would remove the possibility of censoring texts, a power that was available under the existing obscenity provisions. Finally, the ICCP felt that Bill C-54 would not help to control child pornography because it did not prohibit simulated sexual activity with children or the depiction of children as sexual objects. The ICCP, like other conservative groups, threatened to stop supporting – and even to denounce publicly – the government's efforts unless changes were made to the bill.

According to Neville Avison, the churches 'backed off quite rapidly' when they realized that the current obscenity legislation could be used to prohibit the undue exploitation of sex (*Toronto Star*, 11 May 1989). In fact, the realization of the potential efficacy of the existing obscenity provisions led to a new understanding of politics and power for conservative organizations. Dr Suzanne Scorsone explains the change in attitude:

What changed the whole scene was the decision of the Manitoba Court of Appeal [in *Video World*] to enforce the existing obscenity provisions of the Criminal Code. That [case] was appealed to the Supreme Court of Canada, and the Supreme Court of Canada upheld it, saying that the law was clear. And it is here that the churches and the feminists and everybody else comes in, saying we want something done. It was clear that the community at large did not want to tolerate this kind of material. Which means that all of our yelling and screaming and rational arguments and our reasoned presentations had actually been heard by somebody. Maybe Parliament couldn't deal with it, *but in the post-Charter world the centre of power had in fact slid down the Hill into the Supreme Court, from the House to the Supreme Court.* That is what has happened ... It became the case that Bill C-54 would have been retrogressive from our perspective. It would have made things even more open. So we did a one hundred and eighty degree about face and withdrew our support for the bill and I think many feminists did as well, and so the bill crashed ... You see, we were thinking in terms of the old Canada. Canada used to be ruled by Parliament. *It was this particular case [pornography] that opened my eyes certainly to the fact that Parliament no longer rules: the Supreme Court does.* The balance of power, as I said, had slid down the Hill to the Supreme Court ... Parliament can talk, talk, talk, but the judiciary comes along and 'bang': it is gone in five minutes. And we are by no means the only people who have perceived that. Now any time there is a big issue that comes up, people start lobbying the Supreme Court, like they do in the U.S.[12]

The campaign to proscribe pornography came to an end for religious and family-oriented organizations with the recognition that the present obscenity legislation could still be used to ban sexually explicit material. Suddenly, the alleged subjectivity, vagueness, inadequacy, and unenforceability of obscenity legislation, which created the necessity to reform the law in the first place, vanished. It is as if a conservative judicial interpretation suddenly gave obscenity provisions their objectivity.

The Death of Bill C-54: Mixed Results

Faced with such diverse opposition to Bill C-54, the government found it impossible to strike a compromise. The right and the left both opposed the bill, but for very different reasons. A senior policy adviser at Justice explains the government's predicament: 'That is another one of the greatest ironies of the whole process [of drafting the bill]. On one end, hearing from religious and family-oriented groups that the bill was too liberal. And from the other end, that it would be cataclysmic!'[13] In the end, the government ended up opting for a solution that was agreeable to both sides: it scrapped the bill.

The death of Bill C-54 cannot be explained as a victory of the anti-censorship forces, for the bill became less and less popular among its most outspoken supporters, religious and family-oriented organizations. However, the bill's death does attest to the increasing strength of the feminist anti-censorship position in the pornography debate. For instance, the revolt of the librarians, though it drew largely on civil libertarian discourse, might not have been so effective had librarians not articulated a feminist position on pornography. Hnatyshyn's objective was to strike a compromise between feminist and conservative organizations. By articulating the dangers of censorship to freedom of expression *and* women's status, the librarians struck a chord at the Ministry of Justice and in the House of Commons. The government could not dismiss their revolt by equating it with the conventional civil libertarian's opposition to censorship. That the librarians' position on pornography, censorship, and women's status was directly influenced by the activities of civil libertarians attests once again to the strength of the feminist anti-censorship position in the debate on pornography. In fact, the work of feminists against censorship in the pornography debate has had a huge impact on both civil liberties and feminist anti-pornography organizations: civil liberties organizations began to address women's concerns in their critique of censorship, and NAC modified its unequivocal equation of pornography with women's oppression.

While the opposition of the librarians was forceful and well-orchestrated, it would be wrong to believe that it was solely responsible for the failure of law reform. Conservative organizations' support of strong anti-pornography legislation diminished after the bill began to appear to them as a 'monstrous liberalization,' and the bill's most vociferous supporters were thus eliminated. Once these organizations saw that the existing obscenity provisions, which they had originally condemned as vague and impossible to enforce, could actually be used to eradicate sexually explicit material, their desire for law reform waned. In fact, using a strategy of intimidation, they drew on the obscenity provisions to fight for decency at the local level.[14]

Meanwhile, the lack of public support – especially from a large section of the Conservative party's constituency – combined with pending elections and other important issues, such as the Supreme Court's decision in *R. v. Morgentaler*[15] to strike down the abortion provisions of the Canadian Criminal Code and the free trade agreement with the United States, diminished the Tory caucus's interest in pornography.[16]

Five Years Later: The *Butler* Decision

Four years after the failure of his own proposal for law reform, John Crosbie had no regrets: 'This is four years later and there has been no epidemic, right? Canada is just as well off without [a law against pornography]. I am just giving you my opinion. I don't think that we really need legislation.'[17] In 1992, five years after the second effort to reform obscenity legislation with Bill C-54, the Supreme Court of Canada, affirming the constitutionality of the obscenity provisions of the Criminal Code, condemned further legislative attempts to criminalize pornography: 'The attempt to provide exhaustive instances of obscenity has been shown to fail (Bill C-54, 2nd Sess., 33rd Parl.) ... The intractable nature of the problem and the impossibility of precisely defining a notion which is inherently elusive makes the possibility of a more explicit provision remote. In this light, it is appropriate to question whether, and at what cost, greater legislative precision can be demanded.'[18]

There is no more need to reform the law; pornography is under control. How has this happened? Is the situation after the failure of law reform the same as it was before? Are we just witnessing another recurrence of the 'order of things,' or has something changed? If so, what? To begin answering these questions, we need to explore how, despite its failure, the politics of pornography law reform has transformed institutionalized practices.

Although the government failed to reform the law on obscenity, the public campaign to criminalize pornography succeeded. In February 1992 the Supreme Court of Canada unanimously declared in the *Butler* case that while the obscenity provisions of the Criminal Code violated the Canadian Charter of Rights and Freedoms, they were a reasonable and justified limit prescribed by law. The most significant aspect of this ruling is the new test the Supreme court elaborated to determine obscenity – a test that by incorporating the feminist position that pornography harms women brought the feminist campaign to proscribe pornography to an end.

Section 163(8) of the Criminal Code states that 'any publication a dominant characteristic of which is the undue exploitation of sex, or of sex and any one or more of the following subjects, namely, crime, horror, cruelty and violence,' is obscene. Over the years, the courts have attempted gradually to devise a series of 'objective' tests to identify when the exploitation of sex was 'undue.' The most important of theses tests is that of 'community standards of tolerance.' Essentially, judges have tried to evaluate what offends the community's morality on the basis of what they felt Canadians would not tolerate other Canadians' being exposed to. Over time, the courts have developed a second test: they held that the community would not tolerate material that treats sex in a 'degrading or dehumanizing' manner. This test, however, is based on the idea that pornography harms women rather than on the idea that it corrupts morals. The courts have also developed the 'internal necessity' test, or the 'artistic' test. In essence, that test holds that the exploitation of sex will not be considered 'undue' if it is required for the 'serious treatment' of the theme under consideration.

According to the Supreme Court, the problem with those tests is that they are not consistent with each other: what is obscene under one test may not be under another. Moreover, a failure to specify the connection between the tests, particularly between the first two, Justice Sopinka argued in *Butler*, makes it impossible to know on what basis obscenity is determined: 'With both these tests being applied to the same material and apparently independently, we do not know whether the community found the material to be intolerable because it was degrading or dehumanizing, because it offended against morals or on some other basis.'[19] Justice Sopinka states that in the light of the Charter of Rights and Freedoms it would be inimical to our individual freedoms to impose a standard of public or sexual morality. To resolve the inconsistency, he establishes as the prevailing objective of obscenity legislation the avoidance of harm to society: 'The courts must determine as best they can what the community would tolerate others being exposed to on the basis of the degree of harm that may flow from such exposure. Harm in this context means that it predisposes persons to act in an anti-social manner.'[20] Justice Sopinka gives his general definition of harm, however, a specifically feminist content: 'The objective [of obscenity legislation] is the avoidance of harm caused by the degradation which many women feel as 'victims' of the message of obscenity, and of the negative impact exposure to such material has on perceptions and attitudes towards women.'[21]

Then, after stating the impossibility of scientifically establishing a clear link between obscenity and harm to women, Justice Sopinka insists on the reasonableness of assuming that exposure to images is related to changes in attitudes and beliefs. This assumption is grounded in the feminist argument about the indirect and social harms pornography causes women, namely, objectification, degradation and dehumanization. Justice Sopinka prioritizes absolutely the value of equality as the guiding principle to determine 'harm to society,' thereby upholding the rationale feminists developed to criminalize pornography: 'If true equality between male and female persons is to be achieved, we cannot ignore the threat to equality resulting from exposure to audiences of certain types of violent and degrading material. Materials portraying women as a class as objects for sexual exploitation and abuse have a negative impact on "the individual's sense of self-worth and acceptance." '[22] Justice Sopinka's interpretation of obscenity legislation and the test he develops to determine the 'obscene,' then, clearly show the success of feminists in replacing the law's traditional 'moral' understanding of harm to society with a conception of harm based on the promotion and protection of the right to equality.

After stating the objective and rationale of obscenity legislation in feminist terms, the court affirms that there is no need for further attempts at law reform to address the problems posed by pornography: 'The attempt to provide exhaustive instances of obscenity has been shown to be destined to fail (Bill C-54, 2nd Sess., 33rd Parl.). It seems that the only practicable alternative is to strive towards a more abstract definition of obscenity which is contextually sensitive and responsive to progress in the knowledge and understanding of the phenomenon to which the legislation is directed.'[23]

Thus the Supreme Court addresses the current feminist concern over pornography specifically in terms of obscenity. Drawing on the feminist definition of pornography expounded in the Fraser report, the court affirms that (1) the portrayal of explicit sex with violence will nearly always be obscene; (2) the portrayal of explicit non-violent sex that is degrading or dehumanizing is obscene if the risk of harm is substantial; and (3) the portrayal of explicit non-violent sex that is neither degrading nor dehumanizing will not be obscene unless it uses children in its production.[24]

The judgment in *Butler* was an unambiguous victory for anti-pornography feminists; following its announcement, they celebrated. Catharine MacKinnon, who helped prepare the Women's Legal Education and Action Fund brief for the *Butler* case, was euphoric: 'This is a stunning legal victory for women, this is of world historic importance' (*Globe and Mail*, 29 February 1992). The feminist attempt to reform the law by constructing pornography as a problem couched in terms of an infringement on women's right to equality succeeded in transforming the law; time will tell whether the law can succeed in transforming the quality of women's lives.

7

The Enabling Quality
of Law Reform

My examination of the politics of pornography law reform was intended in part as a critique of the essentialism and determinism of most law reform studies. It attempted to integrate law reform into a conception of the social world that assumed the mutually constitutive nature of social structure and agency, but did not reduce this relationship to a unified, homogeneous, or totalizing process. To perform such an integration, it was imperative not to theorize power as global and systematic, as something that operated simply through rationalization and mystification. Instead, drawing on contemporary social research, particularly that of Foucault and Bourdieu, I focused on the contingent, the local, and the conflictual; I focused on the contradictions and inconsistencies within the social world and tried to understand how these were organized in a more or less coherent manner. Drawing on Foucault's relational and productive notion of 'power-knowledge' and his concomitant 'genealogical' approach, I conceived the politics of pornography law reform in terms of a strategy of power, a strategy of force among social agents that produced knowledges about pornography and self, knowledges that both constrained and enabled action. My examination of the politics of pornography law reform concentrated on the truth claims made about pornography by various organizations; it recognized those claims as part of relations of power, that is, relations embedded in historically specific beliefs and values that were themselves precarious for being hegemonically organized. By recognizing the relationship between knowledge and power, then, I was able to generate various observations on the reform process that challenged the conventional wisdom on law reform.

The attempt to criminalize pornography in the 1980s did not result in the reproduction of a unified and controlling social order, but reinaugurated pornography as a contested political terrain. This terrain, still involving issues of censorship, freedom of expression, and harm to society, seemed traditional; it was novel, however, because the knowledges, strategies, and political identities it produced were different from those produced by previous pornography debates.

In the recent attempt to criminalize pornography, feminists were powerful enough to shift the focus of the pornography debate from the immorality and indecency of sexually explicit representations to the sexism and violence of sexual representations of women. This change involved mobilizing scientific and legal discourse. Feminists exposed the sexism of the scientific knowledge that linked pornography to sexual liberation and argued that pornography creates anti-female attitudes that put women at risk, a fact science itself was soon corroborating. Feminists also exposed the sexism of the liberal claim to liberty by arguing that men's right to freedom is premised on the subordination of women. They then argued that pornography must be eradicated to ensure women true equality. Their position on pornography as a threat to women's right to equality provoked a multiplicity of reactions. While more conventional positions reappeared, such as those of conservatives and civil libertarians, new ones also surfaced, such as those of feminists against censorship, sex radicals, and sex workers. In different ways, these positions resisted the feminist knowledge of pornography, sexuality, women, and law.

In sum, by focusing on the truth claims social actors made about pornography and the self, and in understanding how such claims were involved in relations of power, my analysis pointed to the *enabling* quality of the law reform process. As social agents struggled to challenge meanings they experienced as limiting or as not corresponding to their reality, they formed new collective identities, often in conflict with one another, and produced a multiplicity of knowledges with different groundings in both science and the law.

My argument about the enabling nature of law reform is confirmed by an analysis of the institutional responses to the pornography controversy. The failure of the Fraser Committee report to inform policy making on pornography, the failure of the conservative government's attempts to criminalize pornography (Bill C-114 and C-54), and the success of the Supreme Court in integrating the feminist definition of harm in obscenity provisions cannot be analysed in terms of a state logic that assumes the inevitable reproduction of a controlling and constraining social order. The processes of consultation, negotiation, compromise, and mediation involved in these institutional responses should warn us against reifying the 'state,' against depicting it as a unified entity above social relations that represses or monopolizes social agents. Instead, as this study suggests, the state and its apparatuses are better conceived as institutional sites of collective political conflicts, conflicts that are not independent of the social struggles that gave rise to them. The state, in other words, is an institutional complex that conditions and is conditioned by the balance of social forces in society. Any distinction between institutional power and the power of social agents must be rejected (Foucault, 1980b; Jessop, 1982: 220–8). Instead, we must pay attention to the process by which social struggles constitute, protect, defy, and transform institutional practices.

My argument that law reform should be conceived as a mechanism that generates and enables practices does not negate the assertion that law reform is constraining. As the genealogy of changing attitudes towards pornography suggests, the languages of science and law played a crucial role in constituting pornography as an object of knowledge and a target of institutional practices. While these discourses are the structures that have constrained social agents in their attempt to do something about pornography, they have not determined their actions in a unitary way. In the following section I want to illustrate how we can conceive the constraining aspect of these dominant discourses in a way that is neither static nor homogenized – in a way, in other words, that points to the mutually constitutive nature of structure and agency.

Law Reform and Science

All actors involved in the pornography debate mobilized the scientific discourse to justify their respective positions on the criminalization of pornography. As we have seen, there was no consensus on what constitutes pornography or its effects on society; however, there was a sense among most players in the pornography debate that it was just a matter of time before science would reveal the 'truth' about pornography. The hegemonic appeal of science seems to be founded in our modern 'common sense' belief that science, because of its 'objective' nature and methodology, is beyond time and space, and therefore constructs a world of factuality, authenticity, and order (Gusfield, 1981a; 1989; Latour and Woolgar, 1979; Latour, 1988; Clarke and Gerson, 1990). My analysis of the politics of pornography law reform problematizes this appeal to science as the best way to get at the truth of pornography by demonstrating that scientific research on the effects of pornography is profoundly embedded in historically contingent social relations.

For example, during the pornography debate of the 1960s, civil liberties organizations challenged the conservative orthodoxy on the immorality of sex by appealing to the right of each individual to achieve greater sexual freedom. In a context characterized by a strong public desire for sexual freedom, a definite relationship emerged between the scientific approach to produce knowledge about pornography and the particular expectations of a more or less liberal audience. Indeed, the scientific community of the time studied pornography mostly for its sexually liberating effects on society. Scientists designed their research primarily to test whether exposure to pornography would benefit people's sexual lives. They told the Commission on Obscenity and Pornography (United States, 1970) that pornography's main effects were sexual arousal and masturbation. More specifically, scientists alleged that exposure to pornography led to sexually beneficial conduct: it ameliorated couples' sex lives by increasing their sexual activities; it helped couples and individuals to overcome sexual difficulties by increasing their ability to talk about sex and their sexual needs; and it helped couples overcome sexual monotony by offering them a panoply of sexual techniques to enhance their pleasure. Early scientific studies also tried to find out whether pornography had an impact on attitudes. The scientific approach to test for such an impact was conceptualized again in terms of the sexually liberating potential of pornography: science found that exposure to pornography produced tolerance towards pornography's legalization and tolerance towards sex – homosexual, premarital, and non-procreative sex (United States, 1970; Donnerstein et al., 1987). In other words, pornography tended to liberalize attitudes towards sex. Thus scientists concluded that, far from being harmful to society, pornography was an element in the general shift from a conventional to a more open morality. Finally, a few scientific experiments attempted to study whether there was a link between pornography and antisocial behaviour. They sought to relate the incidence of pornography to sex crimes and delinquency; no causal connections were found. It was argued that pornography, by serving as a substitute for a sexual partner, could possibly diminish the incidence of sexual assault.

The scientific consensus on the sexually liberating and beneficial aspects of pornography started to crumble in the late 1970s, when the pornography debate became increasingly characterized in the public culture by the powerful feminist critique of knowledge, sexuality, and the oppression of women in society. It was only in this context that the scientific community became interested in the possible links between pornography and women's oppression. Whereas in the early 1970s scientific studies had started to focus on the impact of non-violent material on same-sex aggression (Zillman, 1971), in the late 1970s they focused primarily on the link between violent material and violence against women (Donnerstein et al., 1987). Scientists designed their experiments primarily to discover whether pornography, in both its violent and non-violent forms, caused violence to women, and whether it changed attitudes towards women to such a point that it could be detrimental to women's efforts to be treated as equal citizens. They attempted to determine whether exposure to pornography caused anti-female attitudes, leniency towards rapists, sexist opinions, aggressive conduct towards women, and desensitization or inability to empathize with female victims of rape. It is obvious that we are now far from the scientific model of the late 1960s. This change in scientific design posed problems for anyone interested in evaluating people's use of pornography. For example, the U.S. Department of Justice reported in 1986 that pornography was used mostly as a masturbatory aid; recent scientific experiments, however, do not even offer masturbation as a possible choice in their design. Most experiments today are concerned with the link between pornography and sexism, not with the link between pornography and sexual arousal. It is clear, therefore, that since the late 1970s there has existed a strong relationship between the scientific approach to obtain knowledge about pornography and the particular expectations of a feminist audience.

I do not want to suggest that the recent scientific findings about pornography and sexism are more biased than those that appeared in 1970. Nor do I agree with Hawkins and Zimring (1988) who suggested, in their study of the politics of pornography commissions and policy recommendations, *Pornography in a Free Society* (1988), that the differing conclusions concerning pornography's effects were a function of the political orientation of the commissions, not of the nature of the evidence. Instead, I see in those contradictory scientific results a change of scientific format that indicates the embeddedness of scientific endeavour in historically contingent power relations. In other words, the new 'facts' about pornography are not simply the products of 'objective' science (Childress, 1991), but are the result of a wider societal shift in attitudes towards pornography.

Science, a hegemonic process of organizing the world in a logical and coherent way, certainly constrained the way in which social agents organized their positions on pornography. However, as a series of operations and devices necessarily embedded in historically specific cultural, social, and political practices, science was itself shaped by the power relations characterizing the pornography debate. The changing relations between culture and scientific endeavour demonstrate how the constraining aspect of a powerful discourse is also capable of generating practices. Science was actively mobilized; it was acted upon to produce different knowledges about pornography; it was shaped by power relations and the knowledges produced by those relations; and it was resisted.

The most surprising resistance to science in the pornography debate originated within the scientific community itself. Donnerstein, Linz, and Penrod, the scientists to whom the anti-pornography movement most frequently referred, mobilized their own knowledge to produce in *The Question of Pornography* (1987) a trenchant critique of the scientific rationale for criminalizing pornography. Their latest experiments, which compare pornography with slasher films, prime-time TV, and R-rated Hollywood movies, point to the danger of ignoring the impact of non-sexually explicit cultural representations on attitudes. These experiments were clearly influenced by the position of feminists against censorship; violence, for the scientists, was now the main element that triggered anti-female attitudes. In an interview conducted by Donald Alexander Downs (1989), Edward Donnerstein emphasizes the ubiquity of violent messages in our culture: 'We say that certain messages have negative attitudinal effects. The problem is that these messages are all over the place, not just in pornography. For example, a recent *Time* magazine advertisement for an ABC show about a woman who fell in love with the man who raped her and killed her husband. What we're trying to say is that violent forms of pornography have that message, but, unfortunately, so does all the media' (in Downs, 1989: 189–90). Donnerstein and other scientists cautioned the anti-pornography movement and policy makers against focusing primarily on sexually explicit material (pornography) to search for the causes of the increase in sexual violence: in their view we should be concerned with what is on the shelves of video stores rather than with what is beneath the stores' counters (Donnerstein et al., 1987: 91, 173–4; Childress, 1991: 194).

Thus, while the politics of pornography law reform legitimized and reproduced science as an authoritative discourse, the lack of consensus within the scientific community led to a decrease in the usually powerful hold of science on law reform. The failure of science's authority can best be seen in institutional practices. The Fraser Committee report, the two anti-pornography bills (Bill C-114, Bill C-54), and the decision in R. v. Butler all were admissions that the rationale for prohibiting pornography cannot be founded on science, because science is thoroughly inconclusive on the link between pornography and harm to society. Consequently, institutions concurred that a moral rationale for criminalizing pornography – such as one based on notions of equality and human dignity – should replace a scientific rationale.

Law Reform and the Politics of Rights

Scholars of the new social movements of advanced capitalist societies agree that liberalism (in particular, the legal recourse to rights) provides those movements with the political language to struggle against subordination and make demands on the state to eradicate inequality. While some analysts see in the liberal democratic tradition a radical potential for a truly plural and transformative politics, others see in it a discourse essentially supporting the status quo.[1] The politics of pornography law reform, and in particular the ability of the feminist movement to institutionalize its definition of pornography in the obscenity provisions of the Criminal Code, provide the ground for a critique of the position negating the transformative potential of the politics of rights. In the following section I want to demonstrate how, in the light of the feminist victory, critics of the politics of rights must re-evaluate their position on law and power.

Critics of the politics of rights condemn the growing tendency of victims of discrimination to resort to law and to couch their demands in the language of rights, because this strategy essentially reproduces the hegemony of law, which in turn ensures the perpetuation of a social order characterized by inequality. Carol Smart, in *Feminism and the Power of Law* (1989), cautions feminists against the recourse to law because 'the extension of rights has ... been linked to the growth of the technology of the disciplinary society. More rights come at the cost of the potential for greater surveillance and greater conformity and the claim for new rights brings about the possibility of new forms of regulation' (1989: 162). In other words, Smart, drawing on Foucault's notion of discipline as a technology of power in modern society, conceives the politics of rights as a technology of the power of law. Conceptualized as intrinsic to disciplinary and patriarchal society, rights discourse can only lead to the production and extension of patriarchal control in the whole of the social body: the recourse to law cannot be transformative.

In the light of this widening of the net of patriarchal control, Smart argues that the language of rights, as a strategic component in political struggles, has become an 'exhausted' rhetoric – one that 'may even be detrimental' to women (1989: 139). Providing numerous examples that support her thesis about 'the failure of feminism to affect law and the failure of law to transform the quality of women's lives' (1989: 5), Smart asserts that the 'rights discourse has become more of a weapon against women than in favour of feminism' (1989: 3). In fact, legalized politics 'empowers law' in ways that are far from transformative: it deradicalizes women's demands, disqualifies women's experiences, and reasserts the law's traditional control over women by allowing men counter-rights. Consequently, Smart contends that to counteract the repressive patriarchal power of law, feminists must develop an alternative discourse – one that is external to law. It seems as if only outside the law will feminists succeed in transforming the quality of women's lives.

Judy Fudge and Harry Glasbeek, in 'The Politics of Rights: A Politics with Little Class' (1992), make a similar argument, but from a Marxist point of view. They criticize the use of liberal legal discourse as a means of effecting radical change, because this discourse does not redress social and economic inequalities; on the contrary, 'the entrenchment of civil, political and human rights in constitutional documents and the enactment of wide-ranging human rights legislation is compatible with the perpetuation, and even the furthering, of a great deal of social and economic inequality' (1992: 51). Their evaluation of Canadian constitutional rights litigation is bleak: 'As a transformative instrument [the Charter] has been a disappointment'

(1992: 52). Most Canadians have no more rights than they did before the Charter. When rights guaranteed in the Charter have been promoted, the results have been gloomy: Nazis claimed the right to speak; commercial speech became as worthy of protection as political speech; rape shield laws, aimed at protecting victims of sexual attacks from being cross-examined on their past sexual experience, were removed to assure the accused a fair trial; and capitalist corporations became legal subjects with a right to privacy (1992: 52–6). While Fudge and Glasbeek acknowledge positive outcomes, the outcomes' signification for the politics of rights is automatically devalued for not being radical enough; the changes have not pre-empted 'the ability of the state to use legal coercive powers' (1992: 54). They conclude their evaluation of the Charter on a fatalistic note:

In Canada, the Charter has not had anything like the impact those who favour constitutional rights litigation would have desired. The argument here is not that there are never any welcome results ... Rather, the point is that the outcomes of Charter litigations cannot be characterized as being transformative in nature. On the contrary. Precisely because the entrenched rights are abstract and universal and only bind the state, they tend to reinforce those aspects of the Canadian polity which need to be challenged: libertarian individualism and their commodification of everything ... Under documents like the Canadian Charter, legal political rights claims can be used to further commodification and consumerism, exactly those characteristics of a post-fordist society which fuel differences and inequalities. (1992: 55)

Their argument is problematic because, on the·one hand, it reduces the expression of human diversity and the creation of all relations of subordination to the class division of capitalist societies, and, on the other, it supposes that the discourse of rights, because of its universal ideal of liberty and equality, simply mystifies that class division and ultimately serves the reproduction of capitalism. This kind of thinking flies in the face of recent critiques of essentialism, reductionism, and positivism. The argument is also problematic because of the authors' implicit association between the liberal democratic principles – liberty and equality for all – and capitalism. While it is difficult not to think of liberalism in terms of the defence of private property and the capitalist economy, this association is not a necessary one. As shown by a variety of political theorists, even some liberals, the association was born out of historically specific political struggles. Consequently, it is possible to disentangle political liberalism from economic liberalism (Macpherson, 1962, 1977; Mouffe, 1992; Rawls, 1972; Golding, 1992). Sue Golding, in *Gramsci's Democratic Theory: A Contribution to Post-Liberal Democracy*, succinctly argues the case for the political potential of rights: 'It would seem reasonable, in other words, given the historic specificity of liberal democracy, to acknowledge the best parts of that tradition, particularly around civil rights and the notion of self-development – around, that is to say, the diversity of humankind – without having to accept the market assumptions that seemed inherent in this notion of modernity' (1992: 8).

Critics of the politics of rights are pessimistic about the transformative potential of the recourse to law because, despite disclaimers about the unity and coherence of the social body,[2] they still hold on to a notion of the social world that is static and rigid. In fact, to conceive the politics of rights as the concealment of capitalist relations, as Marxists do, or of (patriarchal) social control, as some Foucauldians do,[3] is to reduce social practices to a unitary logic, one that works to reproduce a unified social body. Law and knowledge, then, appear as the passive supports of a structure that is independent of the activities of social agents (Bourdieu and Wacquant, 1992).

The political theorist Claude Lefort's impressive analysis of the democratic revolution in *The Political Forms of Modern Society* (1986) and *Democracy and Political Theory* (1988) can help us criticize the view of modernity as leading to a unified social body. He argues that traditional societies were organized around a 'theologico-political experience' (1988: 213) from which the king derived his sovereign justice and reason. Society, or the kingdom, was conceived like a body, the 'king's body'; society's unity – that is, the hierarchy of its members and the knowledge of one's place in relation to the other – resided in an unconditional order (Lefort, 1988: 17). With the advent of democracy, the unity of the social body became indeterminate; with the death of the king, power became an 'empty space':

Once power ceases to manifest the principle which generates and organizes a social body, once it ceases to condense within it virtues deriving from transcendent reason and justice, law and knowledge assert themselves as separate from and irreducible to power. And just as the figure of power in its materiality and its substantiality disappears, just as the exercise of power proves to be bound up with the temporality of its reproduction and to be subordinated to the conflict of collective wills, so the autonomy of law is bound up with the impossibility of establishing its essence. (Lefort, 1988: 17–18)

The democratic revolution, with its disembodiment of power from the king and the subsequent lack of unity between power, law, and knowledge, thus inaugurates a new type of society: a society without a body or an organic identity, a society without clearly defined boundaries (Lefort, 1988: 18; Mouffe, 1988b: 33). This lack of unity of the democratic social body implies the radical transformative potential of law, because law becomes deprived of its foundations; in fact, by virtue of the declaration of natural rights, 'rights' become fixed to a new point, 'man,' whose nature is paradoxically uncircumscribable:

The rights of man are declared, and they are declared as rights that belong to man; but, at the same time, man appears through his representatives as the being whose essence it is to declare his rights. It is impossible to detach the statement from the utterance as soon as nobody is able to occupy the place, at a distance from all others, from which he would have authority to grant or ratify rights. Thus rights are not simply the object of a declaration, it is their essence to be declared. (Lefort, 1986: 257)

An important consequence of the indeterminacy of 'man,' as well as the separation of power, knowledge, and law in democratic society, is the impossibility of determining the content of rights. Democratic rights are open to countless possibilities:

The rights of man reduce right to a basis which, despite its name, is *without shape*, is given as interior to itself and, for this reason, eludes all power which would claim to take hold of it – whether religious or mythical, monarchical or popular. Consequently, these rights go beyond any particular formulation which has been given of them; and this means that their formulation contains the demand for their reformulation, or that acquired rights are not necessarily called upon to support new rights ... From the moment when the rights of man are posited as the ultimate reference, established right is open to question. (Lefort, 1986: 258; emphasis added)

By inaugurating a society in which power, law, and knowledge have lost their foundations, the democratic revolution shattered the principle of unity of the social body. Democracy became, according to Lefort, the 'theatre of an uncontrollable adventure' (1986: 305) and an unprecedented 'voyage of self discovery' (1988: 21).

It is by using Lefort's analysis of democratic rights that we can best understand the transformative potential of politics. The centrality of rights claims in the pornography debate cannot be overstated. In the name of their right to equality, liberty, dignity, freedom, and justice, social actors produced diverse and contradictory knowledges concerning pornography and the self. For example, anti-pornography feminists sought to criminalize pornography to eradicate a fundamental obstacle to women's right to full equality. Conservatives supported law reform to entrench a traditional social order, an order in which the right of women to be equal and free could not be easily maintained. Civil libertarians fought against the criminalization of pornography in an effort to preserve the right to free speech. Feminists against censorship, sex radicals, and sex workers fought against criminalization to protect and even expand the right of minorities to express their differences. Thus social actors mobilized principles partly embodied in law to amend existing legal arrangements that restricted their identity. Ultimately, rather than being a mechanism of repression, reappropriation, or recuperation, the liberal legal discourse was, for them, a highly effective body of resources.

The success of feminists in institutionalizing their definition of pornography will probably not radically change the quality of women's lives, nor will it eradicate economic inequalities; but it certainly testifies to the existence of new collective identities and needs and to 'a new sensitivity to these needs' (Lefort, 1986: 261). Moreover, despite their failure to change the law, the truth claims of all other social actors in the pornography debate, and the demands they made on the state, testify to the rise of competing political identities and needs. It can be argued that the symbolic dimension of liberal democratic rights, far from masking a fundamental oppression, is actually constitutive of politics and identities.

In his work on the nature of the individual's relation to the political order, Foucault (1986; 1988; 1991) maintains that liberalism, as an 'art of government,' is a rationality that has given us the forms of existence through which political action – that is resistance – is made possible. Foucault is unambiguous about the potentiality of resistance inherent in liberalism: 'Liberalism is not a dream which clashes with reality and fails to insert itself there. It constitutes – and this is the reason both for its polymorphous character and for its recurrences – an instrument for the criticism of reality' (quoted in Gordon, 1991: 31). While Foucault conceives liberalism as a form of governmental rationality designed to limit established power, initially the power of the sovereign, he argues that liberalism is not limited to the practice of opposition or negation. Liberalism is equally a practice of the elaboration of mechanisms of 'biopower': techniques to maximize life by providing security, assurances, and predictability. Thus liberalism is a rationality that seeks to render us governable by interpellating us as members of a nation, a state, or a population;[4] but because it is an instrument with which to criticize state reason, liberalism also provides us with the seed for a counter-power or counter-politics. It gives us a rationality to make demands on, or against, the state in order to maximize our life (Burchell, Gordon, and Miller, 1991).

Lefort's claim that democratic rights are constitutive of politics and the 'nature of man' and Foucault's claim that liberalism is a political rationality for the critique of state reason to maximize life both emphasize how political action is born out of the existing arrangements, or forms of existence, that have sought to render us governable. Struggles for equality and liberty in every aspect of social life, expressed as they are through the discourse of rights, must be seen therefore as explorations and pursuits of what is intimated in the liberal democratic tradition (Mouffe, 1988b: 39). The liberal democratic tradition thus provides the symbolic resources to struggle against all forms of subordination; it offers a discourse that enables the production of new social and political subjectivities and new ways of governing.

Critics of the politics of rights are certainly correct to caution us about the ubiquity of liberal legal discourse in everyday practices and the accompanying implications for social control; but they are incorrect to see the increased penetration of law in every realm of social life in terms of the reproduction of a repressive social order. The law is certainly a dominant discourse, as this analysis of the pornography debate has shown. It constrains the way social agents produce knowledges about pornography and make demands on the state; but the law does not determine these agents' activities, nor does it determine the results of those activities. While it is true that by mobilizing the law to eradicate pornography, the feminist movement accepted 'the significance of law in regulating the social order' (Smart, 1989: 161), it also contested the manner in which law has traditionally regulated obscenity and the portrayal of women, and thus challenged the power conferred on law. In other words, the institutionalization of the feminist position on pornography by the Supreme Court in the *Butler* decision must be seen in the light of the law's transformative potential, rather than as another instance in the reproduction of the social order. Feminists themselves mobilized the law; the law did not deradicalize their demands. In fact, feminists actively sought to contest, undermine, and modify the conventional legal wisdom on obscenity. They challenged the hegemony of the law by re-evaluating legal values and norms, by offering different interpretations of the law, its purpose, and their relationship to it, and by making their position appealing to the public. Thus feminists not only reproduced the law as an authoritative discourse, but also gave it a different mandate.

Law therefore must be understood as a hegemonic *process*: it is produced not given. It is only through political struggles over meanings that it exists. To hold on to the notion of it as a system of domination is to ignore the dynamic process by which the law becomes dominant in the first place and to fail to see how the law, as an institutional practice, includes certain meanings and excludes others. As a contested terrain for the negotiation of social struggles, the law does not provide equal access and opportunities to all social agents. This is so because the institutional arrangements in place are the partial resolutions of earlier conflicts. The negotiation of new struggles therefore is shaped by the institutional terms that derive from past conflicts. In other words, what law institutes is never fixed but always precarious; the law inevitably contains ambiguities and contradictions and thus offers the possibility of its own radical renewal.

To summarize, I want to reiterate how my analysis of the politics of pornography law reform supports the argument about the pervasiveness of rights discourse in everyday practices but nevertheless points to the inherent lack of fixity of that discourse and to the diverse political strategies it enabled. Given a tradition in which liberal legal discourse is powerful, it is not surprising that social actors framed the pornography debate in terms of law reform. Given that as an authoritative discourse the law has interpellated us as equal members of a nation whose essence is to claim the individual right to self-determination, it is hardly surprising that social agents drew upon this discourse to challenge the practices they perceived as limitations on such a right. By mobilizing the ideals of liberty and equality, social actors asserted a variety of identities and produced a multiplicity of knowledges concerning pornography, sexuality, society, and self. The strategy of appropriating the law necessarily involved the reproduction and legitimation of this discourse as hegemonic, but it also enabled a reconfiguration or a different articulation of its discursive elements. Far from simply reproducing the 'order of things,' the liberal legal discourse enabled a critique of this 'order' and of the forms of existence in which social agents found themselves. My case study suggests that the law is best conceived as an ensemble of symbolic resources that social actors draw upon to claim self-determination and to articulate new identities and knowledges. While the law in some cases may reproduce order, in many others it has the potential to radically destabilize that order.

Conclusion

Rather than resulting in consensus, the attempt to reform obscenity legislation inaugurated a controversial politics involving various actors claiming a plurality of positions, positions with conflicting grounds in science and law. The lack of consensus that characterizes the contemporary politics of pornography is not unique. Donald Alexander Downs, in *The New Politics of Pornography* (1989),[5] argues that in the United States the recent conflictual debate over pornography is part of an ongoing controversy, dating back to the 1970s, over democratic principles, particularly the nature of liberty and freedom. For Downs, conflicts over abortion and sexual orientation demonstrate the lack of societal consensus on the substantive content of civil or individual rights and the lack of state neutrality in promoting these rights (Kellough, 1990; Petchesky, 1984; Weeks, 1977; 1981). The significance of the anti-pornography feminist critique, Downs argues, is the challenge it poses to the foundation of the modern liberal doctrine of free speech. Indeed, by exposing sexism, feminists anti-pornography have confronted the Enlightenment claim that liberal democratic rights are ultimately founded in the universality of 'man.' By deconstructing the claim to universality embedded in such notions as 'individual freedom,' 'equality,' and 'liberty,' feminists have challenged an element of patriarchal society. While Downs supports the challenge feminism creates for liberalism, he rejects feminist anti-pornography politics. He sees in the totalizing approach to women's oppression a real possibility of jeopardizing the quality of both public discourse and democratic debate (1989: xv–xix).

I agree with Downs's critique of the rigidity of the feminist anti-pornography approach. As I have emphasized in this study, it was the awareness of 'right' – the liberal democratic social imaginary – and the experience of discrimination that made possible the feminist practice of struggling for the extension of rights. Although feminists rejected liberalism, out of liberalism's recognition of the universality of individual rights they were able to find the symbolic resources for their own pursuit of equality. While anti-pornography feminists struggled for the expansion of rights, they did so in a way that condemned the liberal claim of 'sameness.' Feminists asserted a special status for women, a specificity that they demanded be recognized. Indeed, they sought to criminalize pornography by invoking gender differences; they claimed that all women are angered by pornography, that all women are victimized by pornography, and that all pornography is bad for women.

The problem with the politics of the feminist anti-pornography movement is that it universalizes gender differences by invoking a feminist common good that itself cannot allow for the plurality of subject positions that women occupy. This common good is exclusionary because it is founded on an *already constituted* gender identity. Gender identity is better conceived as something derived from the historical process, something that is incessantly in formation and always conflictual. The public reaction to the attempt to criminalize pornography involved various collective identities that claimed recognition through the construction of different and divergent realities, truths, and knowledges. The recognition on the one hand of multiple and conflicting realities about self and the social world and on the other of the indeterminacy of power, knowledge, and law (Lefort, 1986, 1988) necessarily problematizes any attempt to ground politics in a 'substantive common good' (Mouffe, 1988b; 1992). What is needed to evaluate politics, it seems to me, is a political common good that is capable of addressing the common desire for recognition – the right to full equality – in a way that allows for differences and diversity – the right to self-development, to liberty. Weeks expresses a similar view when he claims that 'to be able to deal with the world as it is, and to change it, we need a language of politics that is able to speak to differences and uncertainties within a framework of common principles' (1991: 194). This suggests a political common good that does not assume already constituted identities. Such a common good would attend to the fluidity of political identities, and their continual development, in a way that is truly democratic and plural (Laclau and Mouffe, 1985; Mouffe, 1992; Golding, 1992). This political common good cannot be legitimized in some absolute or spontaneous desire or in abstract principles, because, as we have seen, it comes out of the forms of existence in which we find ourselves (Foucault, 1991). Struggles for equality and liberty are the product of an 'art of government,' a tradition of behaviour and a form of existence that puts these values at the heart of social life. These values, then, are the historically contingent grounds on which any contemporary struggle can be evaluated (Foucault, 1991; Lefort, 1986; 1988; Mouffe, 1988b).

From this perspective we can evaluate the various and conflicting truth claims about pornography and self that were deployed during the debate over the criminalization of pornography. Both the feminist and conservative attack on pornography criticized the liberal conception of the individual as a bearer of rights who exists independently from his insertion in a community. Feminists and conservative organizations demonstrated how this legalistic and atomized conception of the individual pays attention neither to the ways those rights are exercised nor to the content of those rights. Their critique of liberalism revived communitarian notions of civic duties and virtues. Their attempt to go beyond liberal individualism to questions of justice, equality, and the community is certainly a necessary step in the development of a radical plural democracy. The problem, as we have seen, is that both the feminist and the conservative common good is conceived as existing prior to, and independent of, individual freedoms, desires, and interests. Consequently, neither common good allows for diversity.

The struggles of sex radicals over sexuality, sexual representations, and freedom of expression are more in line with a view of politics that assumes a community of equals who share liberty rights and social responsibilities because of their common place in an 'art of government' founded on freedom and equality for all. Sex radicals' resistance to the positions of both the anti-pornography movement and civil libertarian organizations did not result in a totalization of women's experience of pornography, women's identity, and the pornographic genre itself. In other words, sex radicals' idea of the common good did not imply the acceptance of a single substantive principle of the 'good life.' Instead, they paid attention to the particular and the heterogeneous to construct a position that would assure individuals who were excluded by the concept of 'man' the means to pursue liberty and equality.

Epilogue

Postmodern Art in the Age of Obscenity

In 1962, at the finale of a widely publicized trial, Mr Justice Judson of the Supreme Court of Canada summarized his reasons for declaring D.H. Lawrence's *Lady Chatterley's Lover* not obscene:

The use of the word 'undue' recognizes that some exploitation of the theme is of common occurrence. What I think is aimed at is excessive emphasis on the theme for a *base purpose*. But I do not think that there is undue exploitation if there is no more emphasis on the theme than is required in the *serious treatment of the theme of a novel with honesty and uprightness*. That the work under attack is a serious work of fiction is to me beyond question. It has none of the characteristics that are often described in judgments dealing with obscenity – *dirt for dirt's sake, the leer of the sensualist, depravity in the mind of an author with an obsession for dirt, pornography, an appeal to a prurient interest,* etc. The section recognizes that the *serious-minded author* must have freedom in the production of a *work of genuine artistic and literary merit* and the quality of the work, as the witnesses point out and common sense indicates, must have real relevance in determining not only a dominant characteristic but also whether there is undue exploitation.[1]

The *Lady Chatterley's Lover* decision was an epochal event in Canada, as it was in England. It signified the arrival of a sexually enlightened society, a society in which works of art dealing with mature themes could be freely consumed and openly discussed. After the trial, Canada witnessed 'the opening of the floodgates': long-suppressed classics and newer works of erotica, including *My Secret Life* (1988), John Cleland's *Fanny Hill* (1966), Pauline Réage's *The Story of O* (1972), and Henry Miller's *Tropic of Cancer* (1961), were quickly published and widely distributed (Williams, 1989: 88–91; Kendrick, 1987: 202–4). It was society's reverence for art that made this glasnost of the erotic possible.

Indeed, throughout the vagaries of the obscenity and pornography debates traced in this book, the artistic defence has remained relatively stable. For example, in 1992 the Supreme Court of Canada set out to redefine obscenity in terms of harm to women, rather than in terms of traditional standard of propriety; but it still made room for the artistic defence: 'Materials which have scientific, artistic or literary merit are not captured by the provision ... Materials such as photographs, prints, books and films which may undoubtedly be produced with some motive for economic profit, may nonetheless claim the protection of the Charter in so far as their *defining characteristic is that of aesthetic expression, and [they] thus represent the artist's attempt at individual fulfilment.*'[2] Thirty years after the *Lady Chatterley's Lover* case, the Supreme Court of Canada has defended potentially suspect works by, once again, pointing to their 'artistic' or 'literary' merit – that is, by differentiating them from the purely 'obscene.'

In the 1980s and 1990s, however, with the arrival of postmodernism, many have begun to question the binary logic of obscenity legislation. They ask: Can we really distinguish between art and obscenity? If so, how? Who, for example, should be entitled to make such a distinction? What is at stake in this distinction? Whose interests does such a distinction serve? How those questions were arrived at and what they imply needs to be explored in more detail.

Some recent sociological and literary theory has explored the formation of cultural hierarchies, seeking to discover how certain works are deemed 'great' and certain cultural attitudes revered as 'sophisticated' while other works are labelled 'rubbish' and other attitudes scorned as 'vulgar.' Particularly interesting in this regard is Barbara Herrnstein Smith's *Contingencies of Values: Alternative Perspectives for Critical Theory* (1988). Drawing on Pierre Bourdieu's seminal work, *Distinction: A Social Critique of the Judgement of Taste* (1979), Herrnstein Smith shows how our valorization of art and the refined, discerning, and disinterested sensibility able to appreciate it have been contingent upon the marginalization of 'mere' entertainment and the unthinking hordes who pay for it. Her argument thus acknowledges that aesthetic distinctions are never objective processes of finding the truth of some work, as the courts in obscenity cases would have us believe.[3] Rather, distinctions such as that between art and entertainment and art and obscenity are about power. They are part of the symbolic logic through which class differences are constituted and perpetuated:[4]

The logic is itself based on distinction: 'legitimate' (that is, elite or canonical) culture and the elective tastes of the socially dominant classes define themselves and acquire their distinguishing features in contradistinction to the ('ordinary,' 'vulgar,' 'barbaric') tastes of the socially dominated. In particular, the ascetic ideals of disinterest, disembodiment, purity, and autonomy that are associated with 'the Kantian aesthetic' and exhibited in aristocratic tastes emerge as a symbolic counterpart and active sign of the objective and subjective distance of members of the dominant classes from practical urgency and economic necessity, whereas the inverse – that is, the 'popular aesthetic,' which favours substance over form, quantity over quality, and utility, immediate consumption, and bodily sensation over the 'detached gaze' of aesthetic contemplation – is the symbolic counterpart and objective product of the socioeconomic status, history, and trajectory of members of the dominated classes. (Herrnstein Smith, 1988: 75–6)[5]

While neither Herrnstein Smith nor Bourdieu talks explicitly about pornography, it is not difficult to see how their theories might apply to the politics of obscenity. Consider the cherished distinctions of anti-pornography feminists between pornography and 'erotica,' of anti-censorship feminists between pornography and 'alternative,' 'feminist,' 'sex positive' porn, and of moralists between 'filth' and 'art' – in other words, between 'dirt for dirt's sake' and 'dirt for art's sake' – are they not just other ways of inscribing the art/entertainment dichotomy? Indeed, in obscenity cases, the authors and producers of erotica and its equivalent are depicted as 'serious minds,' whereas the producers and consumers of pornography are painted as 'leering sensualists.' The erotician is detached, the pornographer obsessed. As I stated above, such high/low splits *always* involve power relations. In the case of censorship, that power is quite explicit: the unsuspecting porn reader is always in danger of having her entertainment snatched rudely from her hands.

The institutions that legitimate art and repress the obscene, then, are not so benign as they seem:

The cultural objects and practices favoured by the dominant classes (these include types of clothing, sports activities, food preparation, and so on, as well as music and other artforms) are legitimated as intrinsically superior by the normative institutions controlled by those very classes; at the same time, the tastes of the dominant *for* those objects and practices are interpreted as evidence of their own natural superiority and cultural enlightenment and thus also their right to social and cultural power. (Herrnstein Smith, 1988: 76: emphasis in original)

Indeed, in most obscenity cases, the judiciary and its appointed 'experts' (usually university professors) have paraded the prized concepts of the Kantian aesthetic tradition – seriousness, purposefulness, disinterestedness, formal complexity – to defend or condemn works whose morality or benevolence was in question.

To determine whether *Lady Chatterley's Lover* was obscene, for example, Mr Justice Judson relied heavily on the oral evaluations of three Canadian literary experts (Hugh MacLennan, Morley Callaghan, and Harry T. Moore) and on the written statements from 'outstanding literary critics in the United States':

There is real unanimity in their opinions that the book is a *true* and *sincere* representation of an aspect of life as it appeared to the author ... Lawrence had certain opinions about the organization of modern industrial society and its effects upon the relations between man and woman. He chose to express these opinions in a work of *imagination*, written about an adulterous relationship between the wife of an impotent man of property and that man's servant. Whether his choice of medium was a good choice for the preaching of his ideas and whether the ideas themselves were foolish and wrong-headed are matters upon which there may be a difference of opinion. But a theme of adultery, and what to some readers – and there must be many of these – appears to be a stilted assertion that there exists an important connection between the organization of an industrial society and the sexual relations between man and woman, do not, in themselves, give the book a dominant characteristic condemned by the section of the Code.

This novel is a *complex piece of writing*. It is, in part, but only in part, the story of the development of the relationship between the man and the woman and an outspoken description of their sexual relations.[6]

Several years later another classic was 'set free' for similar reasons. *Fanny Hill*, 'the first masterpiece of English pornography' (Hyde, 1964), was initially found obscene, because it contained 'perversions' – lesbianism, voyeurism, seduction, orgies, oral sex, and flagellation

– whose publicity could be dangerous.[7] The decision was appealed, and the Ontario Court of Appeal found that the book did, after all, have artistic merit. Relying on the experise of Robertson Davies (then the master of Massey College and a professor of English at University College) and Arnold Edinborough (then the editor of *Saturday Night* and formerly a teacher of English at various universities) the court held that the author's 'realistic,' 'sincere,' 'formal,' and 'humorous' representation of 'a seamy side of the life of his time' was, despite its dominant sexual content, a serious and purposeful project.[8] In other words, the court declared *Fanny Hill* a valuable contribution to culture, not a mere frolic in the gutter. More recently, Chief Justice Freedman of the Manitoba Court of Appeal found that the film *Last Tango in Paris* was not obscene because, according to experts, the director had a 'serious' purpose and presented his subject in a 'thoughtful' manner, creating visual effect through 'skilful' camera techniques.[9] However, in cases involving the magazines *Dude* and *Escapade*, and the film *Dracula Sucks*, the courts, with the help of experts, confidently revealed the absence of artistic merit.[10] The court held that 'the photographs' in *Dude* and *Escapade* 'lack the charm, the grace and the poetry that we associate with great works of art. They are executed with technical skills but it would appear that the main purpose is to stress and underline the sex appeal of their subjects, and nothing else.'[11] In the case of *Dracula Sucks*, the trial judge described the film as 'tasteless,' preoccupied with 'unnecessary sex,' and having 'no plot'; in other words, the film possessed 'absolutely no artistic merit whatsoever.'[12]

Thus what appeared the apogee of enlightened tolerance – the *Lady Chatterley's Lover* decision – was actually the entrenchment of a particular modernist aesthetic, an aesthetic that was a perpetuation of, not a departure from, the aesthetic that has been hegemonic in the West since the eighteenth century.[13] Amy M. Adler, in 'Post-Modern Art and the Death of Obscenity Law,' argues that the *Miller* test, the American counterpart to our Canadian obscenity test, 'etched in stone a theory of art that was itself a product of only a transitory phase in art history – the period of late Modernism' (1990: 1364). Such an 'etching in stone' has occurred in a number of English speaking countries, including Canada, and the political consequences are readily apparent: all that falls outside the modernist standards of purity, stylistic integrity, and originality is automatically suspect and in danger of suppression. Just ask the fans of *Dracula Sucks*.

Recognizing the hidden politics of the triumph of modernist aesthetic standards, 'postmodern' artists, such as Karen Finley and Annie Sprinkle, have made their works explicit and often shocking challenges to the distinction between art and the obscene.[14] In her performance art, Finley strips off her clothing, smears food over her body, and confesses to violent sex acts with relatives and priests, while raving, screaming, and accusing. Her work has been called 'obscenity in its purest form' (Adler, 1991; Dubin, 1992). Sprinkle, a former porn star, uses her performances to recount her experience of the porn trade; the performances themselves are virtually indistinguishable from 'pornography.' Finley's and Sprinkle's works quite deliberately transgress the dichotomies of acceptable and unacceptable, of high and low, of art and obscenity – dichotomies that as Bourdieu (1979) and Herrnstein Smith (1988) have shown, function to exclude, to strengthen the powers that be.[15]

While the artistic defence has been attacked for what it *excludes*, it has also been criticized for what it *includes*. Witness the Conservative member of Parliament Jim Jepson (London East) addressing the House of Commons:

Mr. Speaker, yesterday I read on the front page of *The Ottawa Citizen* that, believe it or not, pornographic videos were being shown under the guise of so-called art at the new National Art Gallery. One video, according to the article, showed a close-up of male genitals and intercourse between males as well as other homosexual acts.

The assistant curator of film and video was quoted as saying that the work being shown is unquestionably art. The curator says they explore the difficult questions of our time: sexual identity and the role of the media in our lives.

With such comments as this, is it any wonder some people in the art community have successfully persuaded the Justice Department officials to deep-seat the Government's pornography Bill, Bill C-54, in spite of overwhelming public support and mail to the Justice Department? *How much garbage such as these videos is society to tolerate in the name of so-called art?*[16]

Similarly, Mr. John Reimer, also a Tory MP (Kitchener), decries the artistic defence, brushing aside the concerns of civil liberties organizations and artists: 'Why is it, then, that we bend over backwards to legitimize pornography on such spurious grounds as artistic merit and individual freedom of choice? Let's stop kidding ourselves. Any depic-

tion of any person as a mere object of sexual self-gratification constitutes a perversion of human sexuality.'[17] Jepson and Reimer attack
the artistic defence as an apology for filth, a hole in the law that
allows dangerous material to flood the country. Puritanical tirades
against the artistic defence are not uncommon, and there are a great
many on the right who would like to see its scope drastically limited.
But conservatives were not alone in their rejection of the artistic
defence. Anti-pornography feminists strongly criticized the Conservative government's attempt to maintain the defence of artistic merit
in Bill C-54. The Canadian Advisory Council on the Status of Women
asked the government to eradicate the artistic defence of Bill C-54
because it could be used to 'exonerate material truly pornographic'
(1986b: 9). As was shown in a previous chapter, the anti-pornography
feminist Susan Cole (1989) had little concern for art and the protection of feminist art from obscenity legislation, because she believed
that pornography was, for women, a matter of 'life and death.' In the
light of this extreme reaction to the artistic defence, it is necessary
to admit that the defence, while based on exclusion, has a strategic
value. Without it artworks such as those of video artists Richard
Fung ('Chinese Character') and Joe Sarahan ('Holly Joe'), condemned
by Jepson as 'garbage,' might be censored. Drawing on notions of
'artistic merit' and 'seriousness,' curator Susan Ditta claimed their
videos were 'definitely' artistic because they explored difficult contemporary problems, those of 'sexual identity and the role of the
media in people's lives.'[18] Even charges of obscenity directed at Karen
Finley were opposed by affirmations of the seriousness of her art: she
is a body artist, critics argued, she uses her body as a canvas, she
inverts order by making the private public, she challenges fundamental boundaries, and she speaks out against violence, sexual abuse, and
racial hatred (Dubin, 1992; Adler, 1991). Similarly, Annie Sprinkle's
performances were described as art: critics argued that her experience
of the porn trade became the text through which she expressed herself (Dubin, 1992). While these cases were not the subject of obscenity prosecution, they are examples of art critics' attempting to save
controversial artworks by reinscribing the modernist distinction
between art and obscenity.

   A powerful instance of the efficacy of the artistic defence occurred
in Toronto in May 1985. Police seized the multimedia installation
'It's a Girl,' by the feminist trio of artists called Woomers, from the
display window of Pages Books and Magazines. Both the owner and

the manager of the bookstore were charged with exhibiting obscene material. The police laid charges, contending that parts of the display – including plaster penises, an infant's mobile made of birth control devices, women's lingerie, and a pile of sanitary napkins splattered with red paint – were obscene. The courts decided on the basis of the artistic defence that the installation had artistic merit and a serious social purpose. While one regrets the actions of the police, one has to admit that in this case the 'artistic defence' was indispensable. Moreover, while one regrets that the display's 'artistic value' had to be established, one acknowledges the efficacy of establishing artistic value *in this context*.

To conclude, I would like to emphasize how, in the light of the postmodern critique of aesthetic value, it has become difficult to legitimate the obscenity provisions of the Criminal Code. Once we realize the embeddedness of art and aesthetic values in their historical, cultural, and political contexts, the attempt to 'objectively' circumscribe the 'obscene' or the 'pornographic' appears doomed to failure. Postmodernism provokes us to reconceive the aesthetic in a way that integrates it into power relations. It incites us to examine aesthetic values as products of struggle, not gradual enlightenment. The politics of modernism and the whole axiological heritage of the West have been exposed as parts of a system of symbolic domination. However, that same heritage still provides tools that can be used strategically to defend this or that controversial work. Indeed, it is all we have, and there are more than a few angry citizens who see society's reverence for art as just liberal feebleness and who would dearly love to see the last of the 'artistic defence.' If they succeed in their campaign, our society will be tragically diminished.

The politics of art versus obscenity promises to be volatile in the years to come. As long as postmodern artists and scholars continue to challenge the distinction between art and obscenity, legal institutions will have a difficult time defining and thus regulating 'harmful' material. However, as long as others cry out about the permissiveness of obscenity legislation and call for censorship, the artistic defence will continue to be mobilized – often by the same people who criticize it. Such is the paradox of contemporary blue politics.

Appendix

List of Sources

The following people were interviewed or consulted:

Bell, Shannon. A self-defined 'pornographic woman,' a video artist, and at the time a PhD candidate in political science at York University.

Brock, Debbie. Member of the International Women's Committee.

Brown, Mary. Chairperson of the Ontario Censor Board (1984).

Clark, Susan. Member of the Special Committee on Pornography and Prostitution (1983–5).

Cockerline, Danny. A sex worker in Toronto.

Cole, Susan. A feminist, writer, and journalist active in the anti-pornography movement.

Crosbie, John. Minister of Justice (1984), Progressive Conservative Party.

Eberts, Mary. Member of the Special Committee on Pornography and Prostitution (1983–5).

Flemming, John. Former Canada Customs officer.

Fournier, Kathryn.   Member of the Pornography Committee, National Action Committee on the Status of Women (1985–7).

Gillis, Margaret.   Manager, Prohibited Importations, Tariff Programs, Customs Programs, Revenue Canada, Customs and Excise.

Kran, Marcia V.J.   Counsel, Criminal Law Policy Section, Department of Justice, Ottawa.

Lambertson, Ross.   President of the Canadian Rights and Liberties Federation, Victoria.

Landolt, Gwen.   Chairperson of R.E.A.L. Women of Canada.

Leaher, Wendy.   Former member of Project P.

Lehman, Ken.   Senior Program Officer, Field Appraisal Section, Entry, Postal and Appraisal Division, Revenue Canada, Customs and Excise.

Mosher, Karen.   Special assistant to the Minister of Justice, John Crosbie. Formerly with the Federal/Provincial Relations Office of the Privy Council Office.

Murphy, Linda K.   Director, Prohibited Importations, Tariff Programs, Customs Programs, Revenue Canada, Customs and Excise.

Nisonen, Elsie.   Executive Assistant, METRAC, Metro (Toronto) Action Committee on Public Violence against Women and Children.

Royalle, Candida.   Former porn star; now the owner of, and producer for, Femme Productions, a production company that makes 'adult or couple erotica with an emphasis on women's sexuality.'

Scorsone, Suzanne.	Head of Family Life, Roman Catholic Archdiocese of Toronto.
Pollock, Nancy.	Head of Canadians for Decency (1984).
Tomczack, Kim.	Chairperson of V-Tape, Toronto, and a video artist.
Yael, b.h.	Video artist, Toronto.
Name withheld.	Senior General Counsel, Department of Justice, Ottawa.
Name withheld.	Member of Project P (1984).
Names withheld.	Sex workers and members of the Canadian Organization for the Rights of Prostitutes.
Names withheld.	Counsellors for the AIDS Committee of Toronto.

Notes

Chapter 1: Introduction

1 Lord Campbell's Publications Act of 1857 (1857, vol. 146, *Hansard's Parliamentary Debates* 3d series, 329)
2 *R. v. Hicklin*, (1868) LR 3 QB 360, at 371. The Hicklin case involved Henry Scott, a devout member of a Protestant group known as the 'Protestant Electoral Union,' whose activities consisted of selling pamphlets that exposed the practices of the Roman Catholic church. Scott purchased pamphlets, which he then sold to disseminate information on what he considered to be depraved practices. He was prosecuted for selling a pamphlet that had been available since 1836 in various editions. The pamphlet, entitled *The Confessional Unmasked: Showing the Depravity of the Romish Priesthood, the Iniquity of the Confessional, and the Questions Put to Females in Confession*, purported to reveal techniques used by priests to extract erotic confessions from their female penitents. Copies of the pamphlet were brought before the judges, one of whom was Hicklin, who found the pamphlet obscene and ordered the destruction of all copies. Scott appealed the judgment. On the basis that Scott had no intention to either sell the material for gain or to prejudice good morals, it was decided that the distribution of the pamphlet was, despite its obscene character, not a misdemeanour. The Queen's Bench reversed this decision, holding that the publisher's innocent motive was irrelevant to a finding of obscenity.

According to Gerber's (1965) examination of *The Confessional Unmasked*, it was the following discussion of fellatio that offended the judges:

But is it always a mortal sin, if the husband introduces his – into the

mouth of his wife? It is denied by Sanchez and others, provided there
be no danger of pollution. But it is more truly affirmed by Spor. de
Matrim, and others, both because in this case, owing to the heat of
the mouth, there is proximate danger of pollution, and because this
appears of itself a new species of luxury, repugnant to nature (called
by some, *Irrumation*), *for as often as another vessel than the natural
vessel ordained for copulation, is sought by the man, it seems a new
species of luxury.* However, Spor. and others make an exception, if
that be done casually; and, in truth, Sanchez seems to be of this
opinion, whilst he excuses that act from mortal sin, should all danger
of pollution cease. Pal., also, makes an exception, 'if the husband
does this to excite himself for natural copulation.' But, from what
has been said before, I think neither ought to be admitted. In the
same manner, Sanchez condemns a man of mortal sin, who, in the
act of copulation, introduces his finger into the hinder vessel of the
wife, because (he says) in this act there is a disposition to sodomy.
But I am of opinion that such effect may be found in the act; but,
speaking of itself, I do not acknowledge this effect natural in the act.
But I say that husbands practising a foul act of this nature, ought
always to be severely rebuked. (quoted in Gerber, 1965: 82–3)

3 *R. v. Butler*, [1992] 1 SCR 452, at 470–1

4 Mr Justice Judson of the Supreme Court of Canada declared that the
novel *Lady Chatterley's Lover* was not obscene because its exploitation
of sex was not 'undue,' and it was not 'dirt for dirt's sake' (*Brodie,
Dansky and Rubin v. R.* (1962), SCR 681).

5 In finding that the obscenity test must be based on 'contemporary' and
'tolerant' community standards, Mr Justice Freedman alludes to the
increased politicization of sex that is taking place in the wider society:
'Community standards must be contemporary. Times change, and ideas
change with them. Compared to the Victorian era this is a liberal age
in which we live. One manifestation of it is the relative freedom with
which the whole question of sex is discussed. In books, magazines,
movies, television, and sometimes even in parlour conversation, various aspects of sex are made the subject of comment, with a candour
that in an earlier day would have been regarded as indecent and intolerable. We cannot and should not ignore these present-day attitudes
when we face the question whether [girlie magazines] are obscene according to our criminal law' (*Dominion News and Gifts (1962) Ltd. v.
R.*, [1963] 3 CCC 103, at 116–17).

6 While the critique of sex radicals initially was directed mainly at the

feminist anti-pornography movement, it also rejected the moralism implicit in the argument espoused by some feminists against censorship that pornography is bad and that all women are – or should be – angered by it. See, in particular, the feminist discussion concerning the correctness of certain sexual practices: Valverde, 1980; Califia, 1981; Orlando, 1983; Wilson, 1983; Rubin, 1984.

7 Cohen, 1979; 1983; 1985; Ericson, 1985; 1987; Ericson and Baranek, 1982; 1985; Chan and Ericson, 1981; Gusfield, 1981a; 1989; Giffen and Lambert, 1988; Hall et al., 1978; Katz, 1968; McBarnett, 1981; Melossi and Pavarini, 1981; Rock, 1986; 1988; Scull, 1979; Small, 1988; Taylor, 1980; Watney, 1987; Ben-Yehuda, 1985; 1986.

8 The notion of hegemony, especially as it relates to cultural processes, has been developed by Antonio Gramsci (1971) and has been elucidated by R. Williams (1977). Williams demonstrates the difference between ideology and hegemony by emphasizing the constitution of cultural hegemony rather than its imposition, as is the case with the notion of a 'dominant ideology.' He says:

'Hegemony' is a concept which at once includes and goes beyond two powerful earlier concepts: that of 'culture' as a 'whole social process,' in which men define and shape their whole lives; and that of 'ideology,' in any of its Marxist senses, in which a system of meanings and values is the expression or projection of a particular class interest.

'Hegemony' goes beyond 'culture' as previously defined, in its insistence on relating the 'whole social process' to specific distributions of power and influence. To say that 'men' define and shape their whole lives is true only in abstraction. In any actual society there are specific inequalities in means and therefore in capacity to realize this process. Gramsci therefore introduced the necessary recognition of domination and subordination in what has still, however, to be recognized as a whole process.

It is in just this recognition of the wholeness of the process that the concept of 'hegemony' goes beyond 'ideology.' What is decisive is not only the conscious system of ideas and beliefs, but the whole lived social process as practically organized by specific and dominant meanings and values ... Hegemony is ... a whole body of practices and expectations, over the whole of living: our senses and assignments of energy, our shaping perceptions of ourselves and our world. It is a lived system of meanings and values – constitutive and constituting – which as they are experienced as practices appear as reciprocally confirming (108–10).

Ernesto Laclau and Chantal Mouffe have concentrated on the question of the organization of the 'whole lived social process' in terms of dominant values and beliefs. They define the process as the materialization of a social articulation among different social relations. They see the articulation as never fixed but always precarious, therefore containing in it the seeds for a radically different articulation. See Laclau and Mouffe, 1985; Mouffe, 1988a.

9 Foucault's latest work, on sexuality (1980a) and governmentality (1986; 1988; 1991), is evidently a significant step in our understanding of the ways discourses to which we are subjected can be drawn upon to forge critiques of the social order – 'the order of things.' There are, of course, a variety of other empirical studies we can draw on to illustrate the mutually constitutive nature of structure and agency. The seminal body of work of the sociologist Pierre Bourdieu, who examined the mechanisms of symbolic domination by which social agents, through their practices, reproduce the existing social order in a variety of fields (education, art, science, religion, and law), is certainly instructive (1977; 1979; 1980; 1987; for an introduction to the work of Bourdieu, see Harker, Mahar, and Wilkes, 1990; Coombe, 1989a). From a Marxist perspective, there is also the excellent work on slavery in the United States by the Marxist historian Eugene D. Genovese. In *Roll Jordan Roll: The World the Slaves Made* (1976), he demonstrates, for example, that while slaves were constrained by a dominant paternalist ideology, they appropriated it and in the process transformed it into a tool for resisting the degradation they experienced under slavery. Similarly, but from a feminist perspective, historians have demonstrated how the constraining and objectifying ideologies of 'true womanhood' and the 'separate sphere' were appropriated by middle-class women for their own ends. In fact, the preoccupation with domestic issues strongly shaped the struggle and demands of the women's movement as it emerged in the second half of the nineteenth century. In both public and domestic spheres, women appropriated their identity as 'maternal' as a way to justify increased power in these spheres (Kealey, 1979; Prentice and Trofimenkoff, 1985). Because of their roles as mothers of the next generation, women fought for the right to gain access to higher education in order to improve their own situation and to be in a better position to socialize their children. While they drew upon evangelical, liberal, and socialist rationales to inspire their reform campaigns, the maternal feminist ideology – that of 'true womanhood,' 'virtuosity,' 'purity,' etc. – was the most effective in confronting men

who had much to lose in both the public and private spheres if women attacked their patriarchal privileges (see 'Education' in Cook and Mitchinson, 1976; Prentice, 1975; for a discussion of the American context see Lesbock, 1984). Nineteenth-century women involved in the social purity movement also drew upon their status as 'virtuous,' but this time to calm men's 'passions' and 'vices.' Instead of challenging the double standard of sexuality which constrained them, these women appropriated it to seek greater control over their bodies. In other words, middle-class women appropriated the claims that constrained, but constructed them to expand the scope of their activities (Jeffreys, 1982; DuBois and Gordon, 1983; see the special issue on 'Politics and Culture in Women's History: A Symposium,' (Spring 1980) 6 *Feminist Studies*; and for a discussion of the appropriation of gender ideology in the contemporary feminist movement see Bland, 1983). These studies illustrate the need to investigate empirically the process by which social agents make their world comprehensible as they produce knowledges of themselves and the world.

10 Foucault's discussion of peripheral sexualities best illustrates the way power through processes of objectification (normalizing techniques) and subjectification (resistance) constructs and organizes identity. He argues that the concern with peripheral sexualities undergoes a major shift in the nineteenth century. For example, the act of sodomy, according to the ancient civil code, was prohibited because it belonged to a category of forbidden acts. The emphasis on wrongdoing was directed at the act rather than the perpetrator, who was nothing more than the one who engaged in a prohibited act. This classical vision and practice was transformed in the nineteenth century with the emergence of a legal subjectivity embodied in 'the criminal.' The perpetrator of the act of sodomy gradually acquired a subjectivity, a case history, a psychology, a morphology, an anatomy, and a curious physiology: he was a homosexual. While he was now at the mercy of the powerful discourses that named his conditions, the homosexual was also in a position to resist them because of his newly acquired identity. According to Foucault, once he acquires his identity, the homosexual can use his special positionality and assert his new identity by showing off, scandalizing, resisting, or passively accepting that he is sick. Therefore, the growth of the perversions, of the unorthodox sexualities, is for Foucault 'the real product of the encroachment of a type of power on bodies and their pleasures' (1980a: 48). It is in that sense, then, that 'power is not an institution, and not a structure' (1980a: 93), but more clearly a relation,

a practice, or a strategy. Although, power does not imply an 'above,' as in a force imposed from above, it does not necessarily negate the existence of a 'below.' This is the case because power, as a relation of forces, implies the immediate effects of inequalities and, most important, resistance: 'Where there is power, there is resistance, and yet, or rather consequently, this resistance is never in a position of exteriority in relation to power ... one is always "inside" power, there is no "escaping" it' (1980a: 95).

Chapter 2: The Emergence of a Feminist Position on Pornography

1 Reformers welcomed the publication of books such as *Pamela* for the eleemosynary and edifying impact they might have on the treatment of wives, daughters, and servants. The plot of this popular novel by Samuel Richardson, the greatest moralist of English fiction in the eighteenth century, involves a young female servant's stoic preservation of her own chastity when she is confronted with the lascivious advances of her aristocratic employer.
2 For example, in 1877 Charles Bradlaugh and Annie Besant were prosecuted for publishing Charles Knowlton's *Fruits of Philosophy*, one of the most widely circulated books on the subject of birth control in the nineteenth century. The prosecution argued that once the fear of pregnancy was removed, promiscuity was bound to follow. According to the solicitor general, if the book were allowed to circulate it would be 'permitted to circulate through *all classes* of society at 6d. a copy' (*The Times*, 19 June 1877, in Thomas, 1969: 4; emphasis added). This rationale, which became embodied in obscenity legislation, was still solidly ingrained in the British *Lady Chatterley's Lover* trial of 1960. While the prosecution lost, it nevertheless asked the jury the notorious question: 'Is it a book that you would even wish your wife or your servants to read?'
3 For a discussion of the Roman Catholic church's position on obscenity, see Chandos, 1962; Kronhausen and Kronhausen, 1964; Gardiner, 1975.
4 The term 'sexual materials' is used in the report to refer 'to the entire range of explicit sexual depictions or descriptions in books, magazines, photographs, films, statuary, and media. It includes the most explicit depictions, or what is often referred to as "hard-core pornography"' (United States, 1970: 72, note 2).
5 For a further discussion of the violence and anti-woman messages of

pornography, see the feminist anti-pornography anthology, *Take Back the Night: Women on Pornography*, edited by Laura Lederer (1980).

6 Dworkin made that statement at the Conference on Media Violence and Pornography held at the Ontario Institute for Studies in Education, on 5 February 1984.

7 The statement consisted of a petition circulated by feminists attending the Conference on Media Violence and Pornography. The petitioners wanted to make sure that the audience understood the indisputable link between pornography and violence against women. Quoted in Lacombe, 1988: 74.

8 See, in particular, (1984) 9 *Status of Women News*, at 20; McDonald, 1983; Cole, 1989; MacKinnon, 1987.

9 See in particular Donnerstein, Linz, and Penrod, 1987; Malamuth and Donnerstein (eds.), 1984; Malamuth and Check, 1981; Malamuth and Donnerstein, 1983; Gray, 1982; Russell, 1980. For a critique of the social learning hypothesis used in the abovementioned texts see McCormack, 1978; 1985; Brannigan and Kapardis, 1986; Segal, 1993.

10 National Action Committee on the Status of Women, 1984: 21; see also the brief prepared for the same committee by the Canadian Advisory Council on the Status of Women (CACSW), 1984; and a summary of the feminist position of pornography in *The Report of the Special Committee on Pornography and Prostitution*, Canada, 1985: 18–22.

11 This list is based on the Minneapolis civil remedy ordinance drafted by Dworkin and MacKinnon, and which was passed by the Minneapolis city council in 1983. The ordinance was subsequently vetoed twice (Downs, 1989). The list includes the following depictions:

a) women are presented dehumanized as sexual objects, things or commodities; or b) women are presented as sexual objects who enjoy humiliation and pain; or c) women are presented as sexual objects who are being raped or sexually assaulted in any other manner, or who experience sexual pleasure in being raped, or sexually assaulted in any other manner; or d) women are presented as sexual objects, tied up, cut up, mutilated or bruised or physically hurt; or e) women are presented in postures or positions of sexual submission, servility or display; or f) women's body parts – including but not limited to vaginas, breasts or buttocks – are exhibited such that women are reduced to these parts; or g) women are presented being penetrated by objects or animals; or h) women are presented in scenarios of degradation, injury, torture, shown as filthy or inferior, bleeding, bruised or hurt in a context that makes these conditions sexual; or i) women are presented in scenarios of lactation, childbirth or pregnancy in a context that makes these into acts that are understood to be sexually gratifying for another adult or k [sic]) women, including women who are or who appear to be under the age of eighteen, are presented in scenarios that are described as or suggestive of incest' (Cole, 1989: 98).

12 For further discussion, see the debate between reader-response literary critics: Iser, 1978; Fish, 1980; 1981; Mailloux, 1982. For a critique and politicization of the concepts of 'interpretive communities' and 'interpretive conventions,' see Ellsworth, 1985.

13 Given that society, for anti-pornography feminists like Cole, is a patriarchy in which only men possess true autonomy, any institution in such a system is the quintessential expression of male interests and values. Consequently, 'consent' in any social practice is 'a liberal fiction': 'The idea of free choice in sexuality is a liberal fiction feminists have to expose and then bury. If the forces of political dominance have been so rigorous and so careful to appropriate every other avenue of expression and social change, why and how can we imagine that they would have left sexuality out?' (1989: 110).

Chapter 3: Compliance with and Resistance to the Feminist Claim of Harm

1 Interview, August 1990

2 Ibid.

3 *Toronto Star*, 4 January 1986

4 This view is most characteristic of the 'institution' of the church and of the more fundamentalist religions (Scorsone, Interview, August 1990; Gwen Landolt, interview, April 1990; Coalition for Family Values; see also Canada, 1985). The United Church of Canada, one of the most progressive churches, has increasingly changed this view of sex with its acceptance of homosexuality and sex outside the confines of marriage.

5 Interview, April 1990

6 While conservative organizations refer in their analysis of pornography to the same scientific studies anti-pornography feminists use, they also often cite the following studies: J.V.P. Check, 'The Effects of Violent and Nonviolent Pornography' (Ottawa: Department of Supply and Services Contract no. 05SV 19200-3-0899, Department of Justice 1985); D. Zillman and J. Bryant, 'Pornography, Sexual Callousness, and the Trivialization of Rape,' (1992) 32 *Journal of Communication*, 10–21;

'Effects of Pornography Consumption on Family Values,' *Journal of Family and Marriage*, forthcoming; 'Pornography's Impact on Sexual Satisfaction,' *Journal of Applied Social Psychology*, forthcoming (I have been unable to locate any of the articles that, according to R.E.A.L. Women of Canada, were forthcoming); T. Minnery, ed., *Pornography: A Human Tragedy* (Wheaton: Tyndale House Publishers 1986); W. Marshall, *Report on the Use of Pornography by Sexual Offenders*, prepared for the Department of Justice (Ottawa 1984); *Attorney-General's Commission on Pornography: Final Report*. United States, 1986.

7 R.E.A.L. Women of Canada, n.d.a: 7; Scorsone, interview, August 1990; Landolt, interview, April 1990; Interchurch Committee on Pornography, 1986a, 1986b)

8 Interview, August 1990 (emphasis added)

9 For my research I examined the following organizations: the Canadian Civil Liberties Association (CCLA), the British Columbia Civil Liberties Association (BCCLA), the Manitoba Association For Rights and Liberties (MARL), the Canadian Rights of Liberties Federation (CRLF), and the Victoria Civil Liberties Association (VCLA).

10 Several other reasons explain why this different approach was adopted. First, the sexual essentialism that dominated the feminist discourse on sexuality and pornography, and that necessarily turned every woman into a sexual victim, denied the sense of agency and pleasure experienced by a growing number of pornography-reading women, especially lesbians. Second, there was a growing dissatisfaction among certain feminists with the essentialism and reductionism of both radical and Marxist feminism and with the inattention to structural impediments to women's equality of liberal feminism. (For an interesting archaeology of 'feminisms' see Jaggar, 1983.) Third, the enactment of the Canadian Charter of Rights and Freedom in 1982 allowed feminist artists as well as gays and lesbians to successfully challenge the power to censor of law enforcement and other agencies, such as Canada Post, Canada Customs, and several provincial film boards. Fourth, feminist gays distanced themselves from the non-feminist civil libertarian position of most upwardly mobile gay professionals (Kinsman, 1987).

It is at the intersection of these different struggles that a socialist feminist position on pornography took form, as a theory and practice for the end of gender, class, and sexual oppression. This theory led to the creation of a feminist anti-censorship position that challenged both the pro-censorship and the civil libertarian forces.

11 For an account of the censorship experience of feminist, gay and les-

bian art in Canada, see King, 1985; Diamond, 1985; Burstyn 1985; and A Space, 1985.

12 For example, she argues that the story of the sexual desires of nuns and ex-nuns has a very different meaning when it is excerpted in a feminist publication rather than in a men's magazine like *Forum*. While the story remains the same, in the context of *Forum* it is read as a form of titillation (Valverde, 1985).

13 For an excellent analysis of the nature and extent of sadomasochistic pornography in the United States, see Williams, 1989.

14 According to *Time* magazine, women in the United States account for approximately '40% of the estimated 100 million rentals of X-rated tapes each year' (30 March 1987: 63). For an analysis of women as pornographers, see Williams's account of Femme Productions, owned by the ex-porn star Candida Royalle (1989).

15 The papers presented at the conference are published in Bell, ed., *Good Girls/Bad Girls: Feminists and Sex Trade Workers Face to Face* (1987).

16 During the pornography debate in the early 1980s, the sex trade organized and formed the Canadian Organization for the Rights of Prostitutes to oppose the enactment of laws to either criminalize or legalize prostitution. Although porn workers and performers joined the organization, prostitution was the main issue in their struggle. Consequently, they did not constitute an organized voice on pornography. See Delacoste and Alexander (1987), and Bell, ed., 1987 for a multifaceted account by sex workers themselves of their experience of the sex industry; see also *Stiletto*, the newsletter of the Canadian Organization for the Rights of Prostitutes.

17 Bernard Arcand (1991) has written a fascinating anthropological account of pornography, relating it to our modernity. However, in his analysis of the contemporary debates on pornography, especially as it involves the feminist position and its mobilization of science, Arcand suggests that history repeats itself. Thus we hear the same arguments linking pornography and violence that we heard twenty or thirty years ago. Arcand argues that the arguments on the effects of pornography follow un mouvement de balancier toujours en réaction avec la mode. Au cours des années 50 et 60, lorsque la censure de toutes représentations de la sexualité demeurait encore très présente, la majorité des commentaires étaient encore convaincus que la pornographie n'entraînait pas les catastrophes psychologiques et sociales qu'une certaine morale conservatrice prédisait mais qu'elle relevait au contraire d'une libéralisation des moeurs aussi attendue que souhaitable ... Dix

ans plus tard, quand la pornographie était devenue omniprésente, on vit apparaître de plus en plus d'études qui entendaient démontrer qu'elle n'était pas si offensive et que sa prolifération soulevait quelques questions sociales importantes et urgentes. Au milieu des années 80, lorsqu'une partie du mouvement féministe et la droite (qui s'exprimait très nettement au sein de la Commission Meese) dénonçaient unanimement la pornographie, on assista à la reprise d'arguments entendus vingt ou trente ans plus tôt. En somme, les discours suivent le cours des fluctuations politiques sans arriver à résoudre la question. (1991: 87)

My analysis demonstrates that the discourses on pornography not only follow political fluctuations, but also transform the nature of the debate on pornography. In that sense, history does not repeat itself; what we witness are different hegemonic articulations linking pornography with different problematizations of the self and sex. In the 1960s, pornography was articulated in the discourse produced by the fight to free oneself from sexual orthodoxy; in the 1980s, it was inscribed in the discourse produced by the fight to free women from subordination. The new scientific 'facts' about pornography emphasize the strength of the change that took place with the construction of pornography as harm to women. I will come back to this point in the conclusion.

Chapter 4: The Special Committee on Pornography and Prostitution

1 Interview, September 1990
2 Interview, August 1990
3 *R. v. Doug Rankine Co.* (1983), 9 CCC (3d) 53 (Ont. Co. Ct.); *R. v. Ramsingh* (1984), 14 CCC (3d) 230 (Man. QB); *R. v. Wagner* (1985), 43 CR (3d) 318 (Alta. QB)
4 *R. v. Doug Rankine Co.* (1983), supra note 3, at 70
5 *R. v. Saint John News Co. Ltd.* (1982), 124 APR 91 (NBQB), at 100
6 *R. v. Sutherland, Amitay and Bowie* (1974), 18 CCC (2d) 117 (Ont. Co. Ct); *R. v. Harris* (1977), 43 APR 104 (NS Co. Ct.)
7 *R. v. Sidey* (1980), 52 CCC (2d) 257 (Ont. CA)
8 *R. v. Szunejko* (1981), 61 CCC (2d) 359 (Ont. Prov. Ct.) and *R. v. Gray* (1982), 65 CCC (2d) 353 (Ont. HC)
9 *R. v. Campbell* (1974), 17 CCC (2d) 180 (Ont. Co. Ct.)
10 *R. v. Kleppe* (1977), 35 CCC (2d) 168 (Ont. Prov. Ct.)
11 NAC correspondence, January 1985; see also MacDowell, 1985: 68.
12 Interview, October 1990

13 Interview with senior counsel, Department of Justice, October 1990; see also Canada, 1985: 131–5.

14 For example, in 1978, Justice Minister Basford proposed a crackdown on pornography by altering the Criminal Code to make the production and distribution of material depicting obscene acts involving children an offence punishable by up to ten years in prison. This change was part of a larger law reform package that addressed a number of issues such as rape, prostitution, parental kidnapping, child abuse, loan sharking, alternative sentencing, and matters dealing with trial procedures. Lost in this melting-pot of pressing issues, pornography was not given serious attention. In 1982 Justice Minister Jean Chrétien proposed legislative changes to prohibit the production and distribution of 'kiddie porn.' At the time, however, Canada's archaic rape law was perceived as a more pressing issue, and the proposed changes to pornography law were withdrawn.

15 While the courts declared the censorship power unconstitutional and the requirement to approve all films and videos for public exhibition invalid, the government of Ontario granted the Ontario Censor Board a 'stay of execution' on the ruling. This meant that the board could continue its operation until the Supreme Court of Canada heard the appeal. The board's legitimacy, however, was in jeopardy. The government of Ontario responded to the charge that the board acted in an arbitrary and unaccountable fashion by introducing amendments to the Ontario Theatres Act. The amendments defined the board's role, duties, and powers in a formal and legal document. Bill C-82 had the appearance of transforming a body increasingly perceived as autocratic and coercive into a body whose practices were subject to the rule of law, and it transformed the board's power to censor into the power to 'remove from the film any portion that' the board did not approve subject to its regulation (Theatres Act, RSO 1980, c. 498, as amended by SO 1984, c. 56). Although the board still has the power to demand cuts, its review power now has the appearance of clarity, precision, objectivity, and accountability. The establishment of regulatory guidelines has given the Ontario Censor Board – interestingly renamed with Bill C-82 'The Ontario Film Review Board' – its constitutional character. After the enactment of Bill C-82, the government of Ontario dropped its appeal of OFAVAS's victory. OFAVAS persisted, and in March 1985 it launched another court challenge against the board for demanding cuts to the public-screening print of Amerika. In its judgment, the Supreme Court of Ontario cleverly avoided deliberating on the constitutionality

of the board's power to demand cuts. Instead, it argued that the board did not use its own regulations and hence had made an error of judgment by not considering the film in its entirety and the film's general character and integrity. (See *Ontario Film and Video Appreciation Society v. Ontario (Film Review Board)* (1986), 57 or (2d) 339 (Div. Ct.); Lacombe, 1988; King, 1985).

16 It should be mentioned that Minister of Justice Mark MacGuigan, who established the Fraser Committee, had a strong personal interest in the control of pornography and other moral issues, which stemmed from his own rather than the Liberal government's initiatives (personal communication with Lorna Marsden, 1991).

17 For example, the committee recommended increases to both the funding and the personnel of law enforcement agencies involved in detecting violent pornography; upgrading of equipment for more efficient detection; the development of mechanisms to ensure better cooperation, communication, and coordination between law enforcement agencies in order to increase their efficiency in spotting a type of material that, according to the Fraser Committee, was practically nonexistent (see recommendations 17-31).

18 Interview, September 1990

19 Interview, July 1990

20 Ibid.

21 'The criminal law serves partly to protect against harm but more importantly to support and bolster social values. Protection against harm it seeks to achieve through deterrence, rehabilitation and – most successfully – prevention. Support of social values it manages through 'morality play' technique – by reassuring, by educating and above all by furnishing a necessary response when values are threatened or infringed. And this on the face of it suggests using criminal law only against conduct causing harm or threatening values': Law Reform Commission of Canada, *Limits of the Criminal Law, Obscenity: A Test Case* (Ottawa 1975).

22 'The purpose of the criminal law is to contribute to the maintenance of a just, peaceful and safe society through the establishment of a system of prohibitions, sanctions and procedures to deal fairly and appropriately with culpable conduct that causes or threatens serious harm to individuals or society': Department of Justice, *Criminal Law in Canadian Society* (Ottawa 1982).

23 Interview, September 1990

24 Interview, July 1990

25 Interview, September 1990
26 Ibid.
27 Interview, July 1990
28 Ibid.
29 It should be noted that the Fraser Committee commissioned research on prostitutes, which involved talking to them. See in particular Lowman, *Vancouver Field Study of Prostitution, Research Notes* (1985). John McLaren, a member of the Fraser Committee, commented on the marginalization of some key 'knowers' in the sex industry:

> Although we did make provision for private sessions, and found them valuable, I think we could have conducted more of them, and actively encouraged individuals or the representatives of groups who would avoid speaking in a public forum to come and share their views with us. The result of the rather perfunctory nature of these encounters was that, as a Committee, we had all too little input from important players in the world of commercialized sex, such as prostitutes and the producers and users of pornography. While this shortcoming was to some extent offset by the research done for us through the Department of Justice, it meant that we lacked that element of personal contact which helps in focusing not only on the problem but also on what motivates people and how they feel about what they are doing. (1986: 43)

Although the voices of the prostitutes were 'academically mediated,' they could not be silenced, since prostitutes were organized and their position already embodied in the position of various feminist organizations fighting against law reform. In the case of pornography, there was no organized movement of porn workers. Committee member Mary Eberts mentioned that few ex-porn models asked for private sessions with the committee. Their experience of the industry, according to Eberts, was clearly that of victimization and brutalization. The experience of artists, as agents 'regulated' by the law on obscenity, was not considered as such, for artists were perceived in the same way as any other members of the general public with a view on the issue.
30 To ensure consistent and efficient detection of pornography, the committee recommended the following: the upgrading of Canada Customs' database; adequate technology to ensure cooperation, communication, and coordination between different sources of information; centralization of data; the creation of a new class of specialists for the determination of prohibited goods; and better funding for Customs (recommendations 17 to 29). It is interesting to note that the Fraser Committee constructed what is essentially a problem of interpretation – determin-

ing whether the material reaching the border is obscene – as a problem
of information resources and professionalism: the better equipped and
professionalized Customs becomes, the more objective and rational its
practices. Technology, it appears, can bring consistency without even
addressing the problem of objectivity!

31 At the height of the pornography debate, in March 1985, the Federal
Court of Appeal struck down Tariff Item 99201-1 of the Customs Tariff
Act prohibiting the importation of 'immoral and indecent' material into
Canada, for being so vague and difficult to apply that it violated the
right to freedom of expression as specified in the Charter of Rights and
Freedoms. As a result, goods confiscated and held by Customs were
automatically released and could freely enter Canada. Confronted by
pressure from a dissatisfied and frightened public and an impatient
House, the Conservative government reinstated the power of Customs
to prevent the entry of obscene material into Canada by making Customs guidelines consistent with the obscenity provisions of the Criminal Code. Despite the establishment of the new 'objective' guidelines,
Customs is not at the end of its troubles: importers are challenging
increasingly the objectivity and constitutionality of Customs
guidelines. For example, in 1986 Customs banned the importation of
The Joy of Gay Sex (1977), although it had been available in Canada for
ten years. In 1987 Customs seized Anne Cameron's Dzelarhons, a
novel based on an Indian legend about a woman who has children with
a bear. The book, which was to be shipped to a gay and lesbian bookstore in Vancouver, was deemed obscene by Customs although it was
available in most Vancouver public libraries. In March 1990 Customs
seized The Young in One Another's Arms, by the lesbian novelist Jane
Rule, although the book had been available in Canada for the past thir-
teen years. In 1991 Customs banned Geoff Main's nonfiction study of
sadomasochism, Urban Aboriginals. Also in 1991 Customs detained
How to Be a Happy Homosexual at the border for one month. In June
1992 Customs intercepted a Canadian manuscript on its way back from
a U.S. literary agent. The RCMP, informed by Customs of the obscene
nature of this unpublished manuscript, went to the author's home in
Alberta to seize the original. Subsequently, the Ministry of the Attorney General found the manuscript, entitled Heroes, Dreams and Incest
to be a legitimate work of fiction that did not violate the Criminal
Code. The author wrote to Customs informing them about the ministry's ruling in the hope of getting his manuscript back, but it was too
late: Customs had already destroyed it. The list goes on.

The majority of the court challenges against Customs involves gay and lesbian bookstores, because one guideline specifically prohibits depictions of anal penetration. The Canadian Coalition Against Canada Customs finds this specific guideline unconstitutional, because it directly discriminates against the sexual practices of a minority group. Moreover, this organization accuses Customs officers of impartiality when it comes to examining shipments heading for gay and lesbian bookstores. As was mentioned above, many books deemed obscene by Customs are available in most Canadian public libraries. Customs officials resolutely deny that their practices are biased against gay and lesbian materials. While statistics are unavailable, Canada Customs asserts that the bulk of the prohibitions, even prohibition of works depicting anal penetration, pertain to heterosexual material (interview with the director and manager of Prohibited Importations Tariff Programs, Canada Customs, September 1990). Customs also argues that its guidelines are applied equally. And, like any law enforcement agents, Customs officers will apply whatever law or guidelines it receives. Thus, as long as depictions of anal penetration are included in their guidelines, gay and lesbian bookstores will experience problems with Customs.

It is fair to say that the decision to include anal penetration in the guidelines has little to do with Customs. The decision is directly linked to the involvement of the Department of Justice in the process of making Customs guidelines consistent with the obscenity provisions of the Criminal Code. We have seen that since the 1960s the jurisprudence on obscenity has become increasingly tolerant towards representations of sex as long as they are not considered 'undue' or, more recently, 'degrading and dehumanizing' by the community (R. v. Doug Rankine Co., R. v. Ramsingh, and R. v. Wagner, supra note 3). Despite this growing recognition of an appropriate context for representing sex, a context determined by a series of tests, the jurisprudence on obscenity was inconsistent and contradictory. The difficulty in determining the obscene resulted in a diversity of judgments which, of course, did not facilitate the task of the Department of Justice in drawing guidelines for Customs. Overall, Justice referred to a variety of judgments, more or less embodying the feminist discourse on the relationship between pornography and harm to women, to establish the bulk of the guidelines. These judgments were far from articulating a position against the explicit representation of sexual activity, the main target being the sexual portrayal of women in positions of subordination, servile submission, or humiliation. On the basis of these judicial decisions, however, Justice could not rationalize prohibiting the depiction of anal sex. Nonetheless, it found a way. To do so, it had to abide by a more conservative judgment. In 1985 the Manitoba Court of Appeal decided that material simulating masturbation or vaginal, anal, or oral intercourse was obscene. By relying on this more restrictive decision, Justice was able to write a ban on depictions of anal sex into Customs guidelines. This strategy of favouring a conservative decision to specifically ban anal sex, despite the chaotic state of the law and the use of more 'liberal' judgements to establish Customs guidelines tolerating heterosexual activities, shows that Justice had serious difficulty with the notion of anal sex per se.

32 I am specifically referring to Bob Jessop's definition of 'the state' as an institutional and organizational site conditioning and conditioned by the balance of social forces in society. See Jessop, 1982 and Hall, 1986; for a discussion of institutional definitions of 'the state,' see Guenther, 1988.

Chapter 5: Bill C-114: The First Attempt at Pornography Law Reform

1 See *Hansard*, October 1985 to June 1986, 7237–9, 12792, 13710, 13910, 14143, 14163.

2 See in particular *Hansard*, November 1984 to August 1986, 7237–8; 7880; 10243; 13710.

3 More specifically, material prohibited under 'pornography causing physical harm' (tier one material) was said to be too narrow in its definition of 'physical harm.' NAC suggested including 'any form of physical injury, as well as pain, *or the threat of physical harm*' (NAC, 1985: 8; emphasis added). It did not matter to NAC and CACSW if the acts depicted were real or simulated, or if there was actual physical pain or harm at the production level. The threat of pain or assault should be in itself sufficient to prohibit the material. Feminist organizations found the list of material defined as 'sexually violent and degrading pornography' – bestiality, incest, and necrophilia – too restrictive. They proposed to enlarge the definition of 'degrading material' by including acts such as defecation, urination, and the treatment of a human being as an animal. They also criticized the definition of child pornography, whereby the depiction of a person under eighteen years of age in sexual conduct was prohibited. They argued that the law should be expanded to proscribe depictions of people who appeared to be under eighteen. Moreover, CACSW did not want the law on pornography to be limited

to sexually explicit visual material; it suggested expanding the reach of the law to written material that was sexist (CACSW, 1986a: 10–12).

4 This view of the feminist organizations' reaction to the Fraser report and their call for more restrictive legislation on pornography were reiterated in the interviews with a senior general counsel, Department of Justice; Mr. John Crosbie, then the minister of justice; and Karen Mosher, a legislative assistant to Crosbie.

5 Archives of the Roman Catholic Archdiocese of Toronto

6 Interview, October 1990

7 Ibid.

8 There was a growing recognition in court cases during the 1980's that material portraying sex in a 'degrading and dehumanizing' fashion exceeded the community standards test. For example, Judge Borins stated:

> Films which consist substantially or partially of scenes which portray violence and cruelty in conjunction with sex, particularly where the performance of indignities degrade and dehumanize the people upon whom they are performed, exceed the level of community tolerance ... [However,] contemporary community standards would tolerate the distribution of films which consist substantially of scenes of people engaged in sexual intercourse ... scenes of group sex, lesbianism, fellatio, cunnilingus and oral sex. (R. v. Doug Rankine Co. (1983), 9 CCC (3d) 53 (Ont. Co. Ct.))

Subsequent decisions held that the element of violence or cruelty was not necessary to render representations of sex 'degrading or dehumanizing'; see R. v. Ramsingh (1984), 14 CCC (3d) 230 (Man. QB) and R. v. Wagner (1985), 43 CR (3d) 318 (Alta. QB)

9 (1985), 36 Man. R. (2d) 68, 22 CCC (3d) 331 (Man. CA)

10 The Supreme Court of Canada upheld the decision of the Manitoba Court of Appeal (R. v. Video World Ltd., [1987] 1 SCR 1255). This decision contributed to the failure of Bill C-54, as will be demonstrated in chapter 6.

11 Interview, civil servant, Department of Justice, September 1990 (emphasis added)

12 See in particular the review of obscenity case law the Supreme Court of Canada provided in R. v. Butler, [1992] 1 SCR 452

13 Interview, September 1990

14 Ibid. It is ironic that so much attention was given to the mail received by the government, because it was civil servants who informed the anti-pornography movement of that strategy (Archives of the Roman Catholic Archdiocese of Toronto).

15 Interview, September 1990

16 Interview, senior general counsel, September 1990

17 Interview, October 1990

18 Interview, September 1990

19 These reforms correspond to Bill C-27, an Act to amend certain Acts in order to ensure compliance with the Canadian Charter of Rights and Freedoms. See Crosbie's speech, *Hansard*, 1985: 3418–23.

20 Interview, October 1990

21 Neither Crosbie nor Mosher denies the possibility that the conservative nature of the anti-pornography bill could have been an attempt to 'appease and please' the fundamentalists (Interview, Crosbie, October 1990). In other words, Bill C-114 constituted an effort to 'balance that fairly progressive agenda [the Divorce Act and human rights legislation] with some piece of legislation which more traditional members might have thought spoke to their interests' (interview, Mosher, September 1990).

22 Interview, October 1990

23 Ibid.

24 Interview, Civil servant, Department of Justice, September 1990

25 Canada, Department of Justice, 1985; Canada, Ministry of Justice and Attorney General of Canada and the Ministry of Supply and Services, 1986a, 1986b.

26 Interview, John Crosbie, October 1990, emphasis added

27 *R. v. Doug Rankine Co.*, *R. v. Ramsingh*, and *R. v. Wagner*, supra note 8, and *R. v. Video World*, supra note 10

28 (1986) 1(8) *Feminist Action* 8

29 When a parliamentary session ends, all pending legislation automatically dies. To be considered again, the proposed legislation has to be reintroduced.

Chapter 6: Bill C-54: The Impossible Compromise

1 Interview, September 1990

2 Interview, September 1990

3 Interview, D. Brock, October 1990

4 Letter from CAP to NAC, 15 December 1987

5 Interview, October 1990

6 Among those actions were '(1) the exhibiting of books that could be banned under the Bill, (2) The distribution of material to book borrowers requesting that they write to the Minister expressing opposition to the Bill, 3) The convening of workshops on the Bill for staff and

public and the closing of libraries during normal open hours to dramatize the issue and to facilitate maximum attendance and pressure, [and]
(4) an attempt to persuade library boards in other jurisdictions and
other community agencies to take comparable action' (Toronto Public
Library Board, 1988).

7 The influence of feminists against censorship on the position of the
libraries is also a reflection of their larger impact on civil liberties
organizations. As noted earlier, CCLA orchestrated the revolt of the
librarians. The CCLA's increased concern for women's issues, especially as they relate to pornography, is shared by most civil liberties organizations in the post-Bill C-54 era. For example, these organizations are
more likely to address freedom of expression in a way that takes into
account women's concerns about pornography. Alternative solutions to
criminalization are explored and speak directly to women's need for
safety, protection, and emancipation. Civil liberties organizations also
referred to the anthology *Women Against Censorship* (1985), edited by
Varda Burstyn, and adopted its solutions to empower women. See Victoria Civil Liberties Association, 1987; Borovoy, 1988; Russell, 1989. In
addition to integrating a feminist critique of censorship in their attack
on the criminalization of pornography, civil liberties organizations,
especially the BCCLA, have increasingly accommodated the concerns
of sexual minorities regarding the homophobic practices of regulatory
and law enforcement agencies.

8 See NAC's recommendations in 'Brief to the House of Commons Justice Committee on Bill C-54,' National Action Committee on the
Status of Women, prepared by Kate Andrew and Debra J. Lewis, February 1988.

9 (1985), 36 Man. R. (2d) 68, 22 CCC (3d) 331 (Man. CA); *R. v. Video
World Ltd.*, [1987] 1 SCR 1255

10 Archives of the Roman Catholic Archdiocese of Toronto, letter from
ICCP to the minister of justice, 15 March 1988 (emphasis in original)

11 Ibid., emphasis in original

12 Interview, August 1990

13 Interview, September 1990

14 Religious and family-oriented organizations have been successful in
removing children's books from the shelves in elementary schools on
the grounds that the books' immoral character could influence the
upbringing of children. For example, an elementary school in Orleans,
Ontario, banned the award-winning Canadian children's novel *Who is
Frances Rain* (1987), by Margaret Buffie, from its library and classes.

The book is about the story of fifteen year-old Lizzie, who comes to terms with her mother's new husband: it was found obscene for using words such as 'hell' and 'bastard.' In Essex County, Ontario, parents are still fighting to get the school board to ban the allegedly obscene novels *The Apprenticeship of Duddy Kravitz* by Mordecai Richler, *Catcher in the Rye* by J.D. Salinger, *A Clockwork Orange* by Anthony Burgess, *One Flew over the Cuckoo's Nest* by Ken Kesey, *Of Mice and Men* by John Steinbeck, and *Deliverance* by James Dickey. *Little Red Riding Hood* has been singled out for encouraging children to drink wine. In March 1990 the Middlesex County Board of Education banned *Giant, or Waiting for the Thursday Boat* by the acclaimed children's writer Robert Munsch: the depiction of God as a young girl was found blasphemous.

15 *R. v. Morgentaler, Smoling and Scott* (1988), 37 CCC (3d) 449 (SCC)
16 Interview, John Crosbie, October 1990; interview, senior policy counsel, Department of Justice, September 1990; see also *Toronto Star*, 14 March 1988.
17 Interview, October 1900
18 *R. v. Butler*, [1992] 1 SCR 452, at 506, per Sopinka J
19 Ibid., at 483
20 Ibid., at 485
21 Ibid., at 507
22 Ibid., at 469–7
23 Ibid., at 506, per Sopinka J
24 Ibid., at 485

Chapter 7: The Enabling Quality of Law Reform

1 For the transformative potential of the liberal democratic tradition, see, among others, Laclau and Mouffe, 1985; Mouffe, 1992; Golding, 1992; Bowles and Gintis, 1986; Hunt, 1990; and Herman, 1993. For a critique of this position, see, among others, Fudge and Glasbeek, 1992; Smart, 1989; and Mandel, 1989)
2 Smart (1989) carefully points to the danger of seeing law as a unified realm above social relations. She even asserts the need to think of law as a terrain of struggle. However, her overemphasis on the constraining power of law gives it the status of an actor, a subject that exercises power to reproduce itself.
3 I am referring specifically to the tradition of social constructionist accounts of law reform, a tradition that uses Foucault's productive

notion of power to develop the thesis that law reform leads to the intensification of social control mechanisms in the whole of the social body (Cohen, 1979, 1983, 1985; Ericson, 1985, 1987; Ericson and Baranek, 1982, 1985; Garland, 1985; Giffen and Lambert, 1988; Ratner, ed., 1987; Smart, 1989; Small, 1988; and Watney, 1987. For a critique of this position see Ignatieff, 1983; Mayer, 1979; Rothman, 1983; and Lacombe, 1993.

4 Initially developed by Louis Althusser in his famous article 'Ideology and Ideological State Apparatuses,' in *Lenin and Philosophy and Other Essays,* translated by Ben Brewster (London: New Left Books, 1971), 'interpellation' refers to the process by which ideology calls or hails the individual as a subject, and thus determines subjectivity. The concept has been correctly criticized for reducing agency to the structure. Nonetheless, I think 'interpellation' is a useful concept, one we might want to keep to emphasize the role of discursive practices in constructing subject position. Foucault's analysis of liberalism demonstrates precisely the power of discourse in shaping our subjectivity, while at the same time allowing us to resist further objectification. For a discussion of the possibility of using the concept of interpellation in a way that accounts for resistance, see Paul Smith, *Discerning the Subject* (Minneapolis: University of Minnesota Press, 1988).

5 This study is, to my knowledge, the only comprehensive attempt at understanding the relationship between the recent politics of pornography and law reform. His main focus is the enactment, in America, of a feminist policy in the form of a civil right – the Minneapolis and Indianapolis ordinances. (This policy is the product of the work of Andrea Dworkin and Catharine MacKinnon, whose feminist views on pornography, sexuality, and women's oppression were presented in chapter 2. The policy in question is identical to the one Susan G. Cole proposed for Canada.) Downs criticizes both the feminist and civil libertarian approaches for being absolutist. However, assuming a view of human nature that is both animalistic and rational, and embracing the scientific evidence linking violent sexually explicit representations of women with social harm, he proposes to retain the actual obscenity legislation, but to expand it to include feminist values in its definition.

Epilogue

1 *Brodie, Dansky, and Rubin v. R.,* [1962] SCR 681, at 704–5; emphasis added

2 *R. v. Butler*, [1992] 1 SCR, at 505 (per Sopinka J.; emphasis added)

3 Mr Justice Judson affirmed the superiority of the new statutory definition of obscenity (1959) over the *Hicklin* test by pointing to the objective nature of its tests: 'I think that the new statutory definition does
give the Court an opportunity to apply tests which have some certainty
of meaning and are capable of objective application and which do not
so much depend as before upon the idiosyncrasies and sensitivities of
the tribunal of fact, whether judge or jury' (*Brodie, Dansky, and Rubin
v. R.*, [1962] SCR 681, at 702).

4 I am using 'class' here in a non-Marxist sense. See Bourdieu, *Distinction: A Social Critique of the Judgement of Taste* (1979).

5 See also Bourdieu, *Distinction*, 41–65.

6 Supra note 1, at 703–4 (emphasis added)

7 *R. v. C. Coles Company Limited* (1964), 42 CR 368 (Ont. Co. Ct.).

8 *R. v. C. Coles Company Limited* (1965), 44 CR 219, at 224.

9 *R. v. Odeon Morton Theatres Ltd.* (1974), 16 CCC (2d) 185, at 194.

10 *R. v. Dominion News & Gifts (1962) Ltd.* [1963] 2 CCC 103; *Towne
Cinema Theatres Ltd. v. The Queen*, [1985] 1 SCR 494

11 [1963] 2 CCC, at 110, per Schults, JA

12 Statement of the Court of Appeal of Alberta in dismissing the appeal,
quoted in *Towne Cinema Theatres Ltd. v. The Queen*, supra note 10,
at 499–500, per Dickson CJ.

13 Modernism is an aesthetic movement that is very much continuous
with the post-Kantian effort to develop the spheres of science, morality,
and art according to their own internal logic. In the Enlightenment
tradition there is an elaboration of the principles of an allegedly universal rationality governing all specific fields of knowledge. Art, or the
aesthetic realm, is conceived as separate from other spheres of life.
Theories of modernist art are founded on the desire to discover the
essence or limit of each art practice (Greenberg, 1961). The art theorist
Brian Wallis argues in *Art After Modernism: Rethinking Representation* (1984) that the modernist goal – the pursuit of purity, the attain-
ment of high quality, achievement, and progress – was to be determined by 'self-criticism, self-definition, and elimination of elements
from other disciplines' (1984: xii). The critic Stephen Connor claims
that a strong tendency of modernism is to posit art works as the product of an autonomous realm, detached from culture, politics, and the
economy – that is, as disengaged from the 'impurities' of the everyday
world. In *Postmodernist Culture: An Introduction to Theories of the
Contemporary*, Connor characterizes modernism as 'the commitment

to produce a work of art that will know no other rules but its own, and will transform the vulgar contingency or worldly relations into purified aesthetic terms' (1989: 108). Modernism attempts to 'purge' art of what it is not – in Connor's words, 'to expel the improper from the domain of art' (1989: 93), or, in Howard Fox's words, to exclude from art 'the prevailing aesthetic, ethical, and moral codes of the larger culture' (1987: 29–30). Implicit in this valorization of purity is the valorization of another cherished ideal: originality. Indeed, in spite of the anti-romantic credos of many modernist artists, the modernist claim that the art work is independent of all references makes it not only a 'pure' sign of nothing but itself, but also a unique product of a great individual mind.

14 Emphasizing the embeddedness of every artwork in its particular social context, postmodern artists refuse to celebrate the cult of the artist standing above and outside the social, cultural, economic, and political realms of life. Instead, they explore the relationship between art and its context. Commenting on the denial of the modernist search for a realm of 'purity,' Fox defines postmodern art as 'neither exclusionary nor reductive but synthetic, freely enlisting the full range of conditions, experiences, and knowledge beyond the object. Far from seeking a single and complete experience, the Post-Modern object strives toward an encyclopedic condition, allowing a myriad of access points, an infinitude of interpretive responses' (1987: 29–30). Connor argues that postmodernism challenges the modernist binary logic whereby art can be purged of its impurities (art being 'pure' and everyday life being 'impure') through a 'deconstructive intensification of that logic ... to the point where the two binary extremes are seen to include and imply each other' (1989: 93). Consequently, the place of art can no longer be conceived as being above the realm of everyday experiences, as it is in the modernist distinction between high and low art – in other words, between art and entertainment. Postmodern art, by embracing artificiality and incorporating a multiplicity of styles and methods such as kitsch, popular entertainment, and mainstream media, mocks the modernist distinction between high and low art (see B. Wallis, 1984).

15 Because works such as those of Finley and Sprinkle are difficult to justify on modernist grounds, these artists have had their funding cut off and live in fear of censorship. The American Congress targeted Sprinkle's and Finley's shows, among many others, when it criticized contemporary art and arts funding (Adler, 1990: 1371; Dubin, 1992). In fact, since the raging controversy over the exhibit of the late Robert

Mapplethorpe's classicized and elegant photographs – which often portray men in homoerotic, and/or sadomasochistic situations – Congress decided in 1989 to eliminate federal funding for any sexually explicit art that fails the Miller 'serious value' test of obscenity. The ultra-conservative Senator Jesse Helms, in a speech to the Congress, displayed some of Mapplethorpe's photography and begged Congress to approve a bill that would crack down on government funding for such art. While Helms's bill was defeated, Congress nevertheless incorporated the Miller artistic value test in the new standard for federal funding. Works, in other words, that fail to fit the modernist description of art will no longer be entitled to federal grants (see Pub. L. No. 101-121, 304, 103 Stat. 741, 741-42 (1989)). In Canada, artists exploring issues of sexuality in particular have experienced dramatic changes in funding and even the cancellation of their exhibitions by gallery owners who feared that charges of obscenity would be laid (Butler and Ellis, 1990).

16 *Hansard*, 12 August 1988, 18259 (emphasis added)
17 Ibid., 3 June 1986, 13910
18 *Globe and Mail*, 12 August 1988

Bibliography

Abbot, A. 1988. *The System of Professions*. Chicago: University of Chicago Press

Abercrombie, Nicholas, Stephen Hill, and Bryan S. Turner. 1980. *The Dominant Ideology Thesis*. London: George Allen and Unwin

Abson, Jill. 1983. 'On Censorship.' *Fuse* (January–February) 255–9

Adler, Amy M. 1990. 'Post-Modern Art and the Death of Obscenity Law.' 99 *Yale Law Journal* 1359–78

Albert, Leo M. 1938. 'Judicial Censorship of Obscene Literature.' 52 *Harvard Law Review* 40–76

Alliance of Canadian Cinema, Television and Radio Artists. 1984. 'ACTRA Policy on Censorship and Pornography'

Anderson, Perry. 1983. *In the Tracks of Historical Materialism*. London: Verso

Arac, Jonathan, ed. 1988. *After Foucault: Humanistic Knowledge, Postmodern Challenges*. New Brunswick: Rutgers University Press

Arcand, Bernard. 1991. *Le Jaguar et le Tamanoir: Vers le degré zéro de la pornographie*. Montreal: Les éditions du Boréal

A Space. 1985. *Issues of Censorship*. Toronto: Our Times Publishing

Association of Library Boards of Ontario. 1987. 'The Library in Criminal Jeopardy: A Critique of Bill C–54.' prepared by Sam Coghlan

Baber, Zaheer. 1991. 'Beyond the Structure/Agency Dualism: An Evaluation of Giddens' Theory of Structuration.' 61(2) *Sociological Inquiry* 219–30

Baert, Renée. 1984. 'Sex Politics and Censorship.' 9(2) *Parallelogramme* 38

Bakhtin, Mikhail. 1981. *The Dialogic Imagination*. C. Emerson and M. Holquist, trans. Austin: University of Texas Press

Barbach, Lonnie. 1984. *Pleasures: Women Write Erotica*. Garden City: Doubleday

Barber, D.F. 1972. *Pornography and Society*. London: Charles Skilton

Bart, Pauline B., and Margaret Jozsa. 1980. 'Dirty Books, Dirty Films, and Dirty Data.' In Laura Lederer, ed., *Take Back the Night: Women on Pornography*. New York: Bantam

Barthes, Roland. 1975. *The Pleasure of the Text*. R. Miller, trans. New York: Hill and Wang

Beauvoir, Simone de. 1972. *Faut-il Brûler Sade?* Paris: Gallimard

Becker, Howard. 1973. *Outsiders*. New York: Free Press

Bell, Laurie, ed., 1987. *Good Girls/Bad Girls: Feminists and Sex Trade Workers Face to Face*. Toronto: Women's Press

– 1986. 'The Sociology of Moral Panics: Towards a New Synthesis,' 24(4) *The Sociological Quarterly* 495–514

Beneviste, Emile. 1971. *Problems in General Linguistics*. M.E. Meek, trans. Coral Gables: University of Miami Press

Benjamin, Jessica. 1983. 'Master and Slave: The Fantasy of Erotic Domination.' In A. Snitow et al., eds., *Powers of Desire: The Politics of Sexuality*. New York: Monthly Review Press

Ben-Yehuda, Nachman. 1985. *Deviance and Moral Boundaries*. Chicago: University of Chicago Press

Bersani, Leo. 1977. 'The Subject of Power,' *Diacritics* (September) 2–21

Bland, Lucy. 1983. 'Purity, Motherhood, Pleasure or Threat? Definitions of Female Sexuality 1900–1970.' In Sue Cartledge and Joanna Ryan, eds., *Sex and Love*. London: Women's Press

Bocock, Robert. 1986. *Hegemony*. London: Tavistock Publications

Borovoy, A. Alan. 1970. 'Law Enforcement Policies in Obscenity Matters.' *The Canadian Civil Liberties Association* 26 November

– 1988. *When Freedoms Collide: The Case for Our Civil Liberties*. Toronto: Lester and Orpen Dennys

Bourdieu, Pierre. 1977. *Outline of a Theory of Practice*. R. Nice, trans. Cambridge: Cambridge University Press

– 1979. *La Distinction: Critique Sociale du Jugement*. Paris: Les Editions de Minuit

– 1980. *Le Sens Pratique*. Paris: Les Editions de Minuit

– *Distinction: A Social Critique of the Judgement of Taste*. Richard Nice, trans. London: Routledge and Kegan Paul

– 1987. *Choses Dites*. Paris: Les Editions de Minuit

Bourdieu, Pierre, and Loïc J.D. Wacquant. 1992. *An Invitation to Reflexive Sociology*. Chicago: University of Chicago Press

Bowles, Samuel, and Herb Gintis. 1986. *Democracy and Capitalism: Property, Community and the Contradictions of Modern Social Thought*. New York: Basic Books

Brannigan, Augustine. 1986. 'Crimes from Comics: Social and Political Determinants of Reform of the Victorian Obscenity Law 1938–1954.' 19 *Australia and New Zealand Journal of Criminology* 23–42

Brannigan, Augustine, and Sheldon Goldenberg. 1986. 'Social Science versus Jurisprudence in *Wagner*: The Study of Pornography, Harm, and the Law of Obscenity in Canada.' 11(4) *Canadian Journal of Sociology* 419–31

Brannigan, Augustine, and Andros Kapardis. 1986. 'The Controversy over Pornography and Sex Crimes: The Criminological Evidence and Beyond.' 19 *Australia and New Zealand Journal of Criminology* 257–84

Bronski, Michael. 1984. *Culture Clash*. Boston: South End Press

Browne, Alister. 1989. 'Response to the Fraser Committee Recommendations on Pornography.' In John Russell, ed., *Liberties*. Vancouver: New Star Books

Brownmiller, Susan. 1975. *Against Our Will*. New York: Simon and Schuster

Burchell, G., C. Gordon, and P. Miller, eds. 1991. *The Foucault Effect: Studies in Governmentality*. Hertfordshire: Harvester Wheatsheaf

Burstyn, Varda. 1982a. 'No to Censorship: A Feminist View.' *Fuse* (May–June) 21

– 1982b. 'Experimental and Radical Films? "Criminal Language" – A Case in Point.' *Fuse* (September) 138–42,

– 1983. 'Art and Censorship.' *Fuse* (September–October) 84–90

– 1984a. 'Censorship Problems and Alternatives.' 9(3) *Parallelogramme* 44–7

– 1984b. 'Anatomy of a Moral Panic.' *Fuse* (August) 30–8

– 1984c. 'The Wrong Sex.' *Canadian Forum* (August–September) 29–35

– 1985. 'Political Precedents and Moral Crusades: Women, Sex and the State.' In V. Burstyn, ed., *Women Against Censorship*. Vancouver: Douglas and McIntyre

Burstyn, Varda, ed. 1985. *Women Against Censorship*. Vancouver: Douglas and McIntyre

Butler, Jack, and Scott Ellis. 1990. ' "Women and Desire" Censored in Manitoba.' *Fuse* (Summer) 14–15

Butler, Judith. 1990. 'The Force of Fantasy: Feminism, Mapplethorpe, and Discursive Excess.' 2 *Differences: A Journal of Feminist Cultural Studies* 105–25

Califia, Pat. 1980. 'Califia: Anti-Anti-Porn.' *Off Our Backs*, (February) 20
– 1981. 'Feminism and Sadomasochism.' 33 (Spring) *Co-Evolution Quarterly*
– 1982. 'Public Sex.' *Advocate*, (30 September)
– 1983a. 'Doing It Together: Gay Men, Lesbians, and Sex.' *Advocate* (7 July)
– 1983b. 'Gender Bending.' *Advocate* (15 September)
Canada. Committee on Sexual Offences against Children and Youths. 1984. *Report*, 2 vols. Robin F. Badgley, chair. Ottawa: Ministry of Supply and Services.
Canada. Department of Justice. 1982. *The Criminal Law in Canadian Society*. Ottawa: Ministry of Supply and Services
– 1983. Special Committee on Pornography and Prostitution. 'Pornography and Prostitution, Issues Paper,' Ottawa: Ministry of Supply and Services
– 1985. 'General Summary of the Discussions during the National Consultation with Non-governmental Organizations on the Recommendations of the Badgley and Fraser Committee.' Prepared by Neville H. Avison. Ottawa: Ministry of Supply and Services
– 1986a. 'Guide to the Federal Government's Response to the Reports on Sexual Abuse of Children, Pornography and Prostitution' (June)
– 1986b. 'Discussion Paper: The Report of the Committee on Sexual Offences against children and Youths and the Report of the Special Committee on Pornography and Prostitution'
Canada. Minister of Justice. 'Statement by the Honourable Mark MacGuigan, Minister of Justice and Attorney General of Canada, on Pornography and Prostitution.' (June)
– 1987. 'Amendments to the Criminal Code Regarding Pornography: Statement by the Honourable Ray Hnatyshyn.' (May)
Canada. Departement of Justice and the Ministry of Supply and Services. 1986. 'Guide to the Federal Government's Response to the Reports on Sexual Abuse of Children, Pornography and Prostitution.' (June)
Canada. Parliament. House of Commons. Standing Committee on Justice and Legal Affairs. 1978. *Report on Pornography*. 30th Parliament, 3d session, no. 18. Ottawa: Queen's Printer
Canada. Parliament. Senate. 1952. *Proceedings and Report of the Special*

Committee on the Sale and Distribution of Salacious and Indecent Literature. Ottawa: Queen's Printer

Canada. Special Committee on Pornography and Prostitution. 1985. *Report,* 2 vols. Paul Fraser, chair. Ottawa: Ministry of Supply and Services

Canadian Advisory Council on the Status of Women. 1983. 'Bibliography on Pornography,' prepared by Jillian Ridington

– 1984. 'On Pornography and Prostitution. Brief Presented to the Special Committee on Pornography and Prostitution,' April

– 1986a. 'A Critique of the Strengths and Weaknesses of the Fraser Report as Draft Legislation,' January

– 1986b. 'A Critique of Bill C–114 as Proposed Legislation on Pornography: Principles and Clause-By-Clause analysis.' Prepared by Joan Bercovitch and Ginette Busque, September

– 1988. 'Pornography: An Analysis of Proposed Legislation (Bill C–54).'

– *Annual Report* (1975–88)

Canadian Artists Representation/Le Front des Artistes Canadiens. 1987. 'A Brief Submitted to the Minister of Justice Regarding the Proposed Bill to Amend the Criminal Code on Pornography'

Canadian Book and Periodical Development Council. n.d. 'Bill C-14 – Key Points of Concern'

Canadian Civil Liberties Association. 1970. 'Law Enforcement Policies in Obscenity Matters.' Submission to the Board of Commissioners of Police Metropolitan Toronto. Prepared by A. Alan Borovoy (November)

– 1984. 'Pornography and the Law.' Submission to the Special Committee on Pornography and Prostitution. Prepared by A. Alan Borovoy and Louise Arbour

– 1987. 'Proposed Resolution for Toronto Public Library Board.' Prepared by A. Alan Borovoy and David Schneiderman, (28 October)

– 1988. *CCLA News Notes* (April–May)

Canadian Coalition Against Media Pornography. 1983. 'Hard Core Pornography, Which Often Emphasizes Violence and Degradation of Women, Has No Place in Canadian Society.' *Newsletter* (December)

– 1984a. 'Position Paper – Federal Initiatives'

– 1984b. *Newsletter* (February)

– 1984c. *Newsletter* (June)

– 1984d. 'Position Paper – Federal Initiatives'

– 1985. 'Highlights of the Report of the Special Committee on Pornography and Prostitution' (May)

– 1986. 'The Proposed Legislation – Bill C–114.' *Newsletter* (June)

– 1988a. 'Bill C–54.' *Newsletter* (February)

– 1988b. 'The Election.' *Newsletter* (October)

Canadian Coalition against Violent Entertainment. 1984. 'A Brief Summary of Recent Research in Aggressive Pornography.' Prepared by David Scott

Canadian Conference of Catholic Bishops. 1983. 'Letter of the Canadian Conference of Catholic Bishops Episcopal Commission for Social Communications to the CRTC.' (January)

– 1984. 'Submission of the Canadian Conference of Catholic Bishops to the Special Committee on Pornography and Prostitution' (March)

– 1986. 'Letter to Fr. Williams F. Ryan, SJ, for the Canadian Conference of Catholic Bishops' (January)

Canadian Rights and Liberties Federation. 1987. 'Brief on Bill C–54, Amendments to the Canadian Criminal Code Respecting Sexual Depictions' (December)

Canadians for Decency. 1984a. *Newsletter* no. 15

– 1984b. *Newsletter* no. 16

– 1984c. *Newsletter* no. 17

Cappon, Daniel. 1984. 'Social Decency.' Pamphlet distributed by Canadians for Decency

Carter, Angela. 1978. *The Sadeian Woman and the Ideology of Pornography*. New York: Pantheon

Chan, J., and R.V. Ericson. 1981. *Decarceration and the Economy of Penal Reform*. Research Monograph no. 14. Toronto: Centre of Criminology, University of Toronto

Chandos, John, ed. 1962. *To Deprave and Corrupt*. London: Souvenir Press

Charles, W.H. 1966. 'Obscene Literature and the Legal Process in Canada.' 44 *The Canadian Bar Review* 243–92

Childress, Steven Alan. 1991. 'Reel "Rape Speech": Violent Pornography and the Politics of Harm.' 25(1) *Law and Society Review* 177–214

Church Gibson, Pamela, and Roma Gibson, eds. 1993. *Dirty Looks: Women, Pornography, Power*. London: British Film Institute Publishing

Clark, Lorenne M.G. 1983. 'Liberalism and Pornography.' In D. Coop and S. Wendell, eds., *Pornography and Censorship*. New York: Prometheus Books

Clark, Lorenne M.G., and D. Lewis. 1977. *Rape: The Price of Coercive Sexuality*. Toronto: Women's Press

Clarke, A.E., and E.M. Gerson. 1990. 'Symbolic Interactionism in Social

Studies of Science.' In H. Becker and M. McCall, eds., *Symbolic Interaction and Cultural Studies*. Chicago: University of Chicago Press

Clifford, James, and George E. Marcus. 1986. *Writing Culture: The Poetics and Politics of Ethnography*. Berkeley: University of California Press

Clor, Harry M. 1969. *Obscenity and Public Morality: Censorship in a Liberal Society*. Chicago: University of Chicago Press

Coalition for Family Values n.d.. 'Brief of the Coalition for Family Values to the Legislative Committee Respecting Bill C–54.' Statement prepared by Robert D. Nadeau

Cohen, Stanley. 1972. *Folk Devils and Moral Panics: The Creation of the Mods and Rockers*. London: MacGibbon and Kee

– 1979. 'The Punitive City: Notes on the Dispersal of Social Control.' 3 *Contemporary Crises* 339–63

– 1983. 'Social-Control Talk: Telling Stories about Correctional Change.' In David Garland and Peter Young, eds., *The Power to Punish: Contemporary Penality and Social Analysis*. London: Heinemann Educational Books; Atlantic Highlands, N.J.: Humanities Press

– 1985. *Visions of Social Control: Crime, Punishment and Classification*. Cambridge: Polity Press

– 1987. 'Taking Decentralization Seriously: Values, Visions and Policies.' In J. Lowman, R.J. Menzies, and T.S. Palys, eds., *Transcarceration: Essays in the Sociology of Social Control*. Aldershot: Gower House

Cohen, Stanley, and Andrew T. Scull. 1983. *Social Control and the State: Historical and Comparative Essays*. Oxford: Martin Robertson

Cole, Susan G. 1989. *Pornography and the Sex Crisis*. Toronto: Amanita Enterprises

Collins, Jim. 1989. *Uncommon Cultures: Popular Culture and Postmodernism*. New York: Routledge, Chapman and Hall

Committee against Pornography. 1986. 'Answers to Common Clichés about Pornography' (September)

Connor, Steven. 1989. *Postmodernist Culture: An Introduction to Theories of the Contemporary*. Oxford: Basil Blackwell

Cook, Ramsay, and Wendy Mitchinson, eds. 1976. *The Proper Sphere: Women's Place in Canadian Society*. Toronto: Women's Press

Coombe, Rosemary J. 1989a. 'Room for Manoeuver: Toward a Theory of Practice in Critical Legal Studies.' 14 *Law and Social Inquiry* 69–121

- 1989b. ' "Same as It Ever Was": Rethinking the Politics of Legal Interpretation.' 34 *McGill Law Journal* 601–52
- 1991. 'Encountering the Postmodern: New Directions in Cultural Anthropology.' 28 *Canadian Review of Sociology and Anthropology* 188–205

Coop, David, and S. Wendell, eds. 1983. *Pornography and Censorship.* New York: Prometheus

Cousins, Mark. 1984. *Michel Foucault.* London: Macmillan

Coward, Rosalind. 1982. 'Sexual Violence and Sexuality.' 11 *Feminist Review* 9–22

- 1985. *Female Desire: Women's Sexuality Today.* London: Paladin Books
- 1987. 'Sexual violence and Sexuality.' In *Sexuality: A Reader.* London: Virago

Culler, Jonathan. 1982. *On Deconstruction: Theory and Criticism after Structuralism.* Ithaca: Cornell University Press

Curtis, Anne M.K. 1979. 'Criminal Law: Obscenity.' 11 *Ottawa Law Review* 501–08

Day, Gary, and Clive Bloom, eds. 1988. *Perspectives on Pornography: Sexuality in Film and Literature.* New York: St Martin's Press

Day of Resistance Against Bill C–54. 1987. 'Statement of the Day of Resistance Against Bill C–54'

Day of Resistance Coalition. n.d.. 'Statement'

Delacoste, Frédérique, and P. Alexandra, eds. 1987. *Sex Work: Writings by Women in the Sex Industry.* San Francisco: Cleis Press

Deleuze, Gilles. 1975. 'Ecrivain non: un nouveau cartographe.' *Critique* 1207–27

Devlin, Sir Patrick. 1959. *The Enforcement of Morals.* Maccabaean Lecture in Jurisprudence. London: Oxford University Press

Diamond, Irene. 1980. 'Pornography and Repression: A Reconsideration of "Who" and "What." ' In Laura Lederer, ed., *Take Back the Night: Women on Pornography.* New York: Bantam

- 1984. 'Pornography and Repression: A Reconsideration.' 5(4) *SIGNS* 686–701

Diamond, Sara. 1984. 'Class and Women's Writing.' *Fuse* (February) 209–12

- 1985. 'Against Censorship.' *Socialist Studies Bulletin* (no. 3) 5–20

Dickie-Clark, H.F. 1984. 'Anthony Giddens's Theory of Structuration.' 8(1–2) *Canadian Journal of Political and Social Theory* 92–110

Dickson, Donald T. 1968. 'Bureaucracy and Morality: An Organizational Perspective on a Moral Crusade.' 16(2) *Social Problems* 143–56;

Dixon, John. 1989a. 'The Bessie Smith Factor.' In John Russell, ed., *Liberties*. Vancouver: New Star Books

– 1989b. 'The Porn Wars.' In John Russell, ed., *Liberties*. Vancouver: New Star Books

Donnerstein, Edward, and Daniel Linz. 1984. 'Sexual Violence in the Media: A Warning.' *Psychology Today* (January)

Donnerstein, Edward, Daniel Linz, and Steven Penrod. 1987. *The Question of Pornography: Research Findings and Policy Implications*. New York: Free Press

Dooley, David. 1982. 'Censorship in a Pluralistic Society.' *Christian Pamphlet* (no. 8)

Downs, Donald Alexander. 1989. *The New Politics of Pornography*. Chicago: University of Chicago Press

Dreyfus, Hubert L., and Paul Rabinow. 1982. *Michel Foucault: Beyond Structuralism and Hermeneutics*. Sussex: Harvester Press

Dubin, Steven C. 1992. *Arresting Images: Impolitic Art and Uncivil Actions*. New York: Routledge

DuBois, Ellen Carol, and Linda Gordon. 1983. 'Seeking Ecstasy on the Battlefield: Danger and Pleasure in Nineteenth-Century Feminist Sexual Thought.' 9(1) *Feminist Studies* 7–25

Dudar, Helen. 1977. 'America Discovers Child Pornography.' *Ms.* (August)

Duggan, Lisa, Nan Hunter, and Carole S. Vance. 1985. 'False Promises: Feminist Antipornography Legislation in the U.S.' In V. Burstyn, ed., *Women Against Censorship*. Vancouver: Douglas and McIntyre

Dworkin, Andrea. 1976. *Woman Hating*. New York: Harper and Row

– 1977. 'Feminists to Focus on Pornography, Violence Major Concern.' *FAAR News*, (July–August)

– 1979. *Pornography: Men Possessing Women*. New York: Perigee Books

– 1980. 'The Prophet of Perversion.' *Mother Jones* (April)

– 1981. 'Pornography's Exquisite Volunteers.' *Ms.* (March)

– 1987. *Intercourse*. New York: Free Press

Eckersley, Robin. 1987. 'Whither the Feminist Campaign? An Evaluation of Feminist Critiques of Pornography,' 15 *International Journal of the Sociology of Law* 149–78

Edmondson, N.H., and J.A. Wright. 1958. 'Canadian Obscenity Law

Archaic Trends.' 16 *University of Toronto Faculty of Law Review*
95–8

Ehrenreich, Barbara, E. Hess, and G. Jacobs. 1986. *Re-Making Love: The
Feminization of Sex*. New York: Anchor Press

Einsiedel, Edna. 1988. 'The British, Canadian, and U.S. Pornography
Commissions and Their Use of Social Science Research.' 38 *Journal of
Communication* 108–21

Ellis, Kate, N.D. Hunter, B. Jaker, B. O'Dair, and A. Tallmer. 1986.
Caught Looking: Feminism, Pornography, and Censorship. Seattle:
Real Comet Press

Ellsworth, Elizabeth. 1985. 'Illicit Pleasures, Feminist Spectators, and
Personal Best.' 8(2) *Wide Angle* 45–55

English, Deirdre, Amber Hollibaugh, and Gayle Rubin. 1982. 'Talking
Sex: A Conversation on Sexuality and Feminism.' 11 *Feminist Review*
40–50

Erasmus, Janet. 1985. 'Pornography: Obscenity Re-examined.' Ottawa:
Law Reform Commission of Canada

Ericson, Richard V. 1985. 'Legal Inequality.' 7 *Research in Law,
Deviance and Social Control* 33–78

– 1987. 'The State and Criminal Justice Reform.' In R.S. Ratner and J.L.
McMullan, eds., *State Control: Criminal Justice Politics in Canada*.
Vancouver: University of British Columbia Press

Ericson, Richard V., and Patricia M. Baranek. 1982. *The Ordering of
Justice: A Study of Accused Persons as Dependants in the Criminal
Process*. Toronto: University of Toronto Press

– 1985. 'Criminal Law Reform and Two Realities of the Criminal Process,' In Anthony N. Doob and Edward L. Greenspan, eds., *Perspectives in Criminal Law*. Toronto: Canada Law Book

Ewald, François. 1975. 'Anatomie et corps politiques.' *Critique*
1228–65

Faust, Beatrice. 1980. *Women, Sex, and Pornography*. London: Melbourne House

Feinberg, Joel. 1973. *Social Philosophy*. Englewood Cliffs, N.J.: Prentice-
Hall

Finn, Geraldine. 1985. 'Patriarchy and Pleasure: The Pornographic Eye/I.'
Canadian Journal of Political and Social Theory 81–95

Fish, Stanley. 1980. *Is There a Text in This Class? The Authority of
Interpretive Communities*. Cambridge: Harvard University Press

– 1981. 'Why No One's Afraid of Wolfgang Iser.' 11 *Diacritics* 2–13

Fisher, William A. 1985. 'Erotica, Pornography and Behavior: A Critical Discussion of Some Scientific and Political Issues.' 19(3) *Sex Education and Information Council of Canada Newsletter*

– 1986. 'The Emperor Has No Clothes: On the Fraser and Badgley Committee's Rejection of Social Science Research on Pornography.' In J. Lowman, M.A. Jackson, T.S. Palys, and S. Gavigan, eds., *Regulating Sex: An Anthology of Commentaries on the Findings and Recommendations of the Badgley and Fraser Reports.* Burnaby: School of Criminology, Simon Fraser University

Foster, Hal, ed. 1983. *The Anti-Aesthetic: Essays on Postmodern Culture.* Port Townsend, Wash.: Bay Press

Foucault, Michel. 1979. *Discipline and Punish.* A.M. Sheridan, trans. Harmondsworth: Penguin

– 1980a. *The History of Sexuality: Vol. 1 – An Introduction.* New York: Vintage Books

– 1980b. *Power/Knowledge: Selected Interviews and Other Writings 1972–1977.* Colin Gordon, ed. New York: Pantheon Books

– 1982. 'The Subject of Power.' In H.L. Dreyfus and P. Rabinow, *Michel Foucault: Beyond Structuralism and Hermeneutics.* Sussex: Harvester Press

– 1984a. 'Nietzsche, Genealogy, History.' In P. Rabinow, ed., *The Foucault Reader.* New York: Pantheon Books

– 1984b. 'What Is an Author?' In P. Rabinow, ed., *The Foucault Reader.* New York: Pantheon Books

– 1986. 'La Gouvernementalité.' 54 *Actes* (Summer) 6–15

– 1988. 'An Aesthetics of Existence.' In *Politics, Philosophy, Culture: Interviews and Other Writings 1977–1984*, Lawrence D. Kritzman, ed. New York: Routledge Chapman and Hall

– 1991. 'Governmentality.' In G. Burtchell, C. Gordon, and P. Miller, eds., *The Foucault Effect: Studies in Governmentality.* Hertfordshire: Harvester Wheatsheaf

Fox, Howard. 1987. 'Avant-Garde in the Eighties.' In Charles Jencks, ed., *The Post-Avant-Garde: Painting in the Eighties.* London: Academy Editions

Fox, Richard G. 1967. *The Concept of Obscenity.* Melbourne: The Law Book Company

– 1972. 'Study Paper on Obscenity.' In *Obscenity.* Ottawa: Law Reform Commission of Canada

Fran, Christie. 1982. 'Not a Love Story Exposed.' Review of *Not a Love Story*, Bonnie Klein, director. *Plexus* (November) 9–18

Friedman, Deb. 1977. 'Pornography: Cause and Effects.' *FAAR News* (July–August) 16–21

Friedman, Lawrence. 1985. *Total Justice*. New York: Russell Sage

Fudge, Judy, and Harry Glasbeek. 1992. 'The Politics of Rights: A Politics with Little Class.' 1(1) *Social and Legal Studies* 45–70

Galliher, John F., and J.R. Cross. 1983. *Morals Legislation without Morality: The Case of Nevada*. New Brunswick: Rutgers University Press

Gardiner, Harold J. 1975. 'Moral Principles: Towards a Definition of the Obscene.' In Ray C. Rist, ed., *The Pornography Controversy*. New Brunswick: Transaction Books

Garland, David. 1985. *Punishment and Welfare: A History of Penal Strategies*. Aldershot: Gower

– 1990. *Punishment and Modern Society: A Study in Social Theory*. Chicago: University of Chicago Press

Geertz, Clifford. 1973. *The Interpretation of Cultures: Selected Essays*. New York: Basic Books

– 1983. *Local Knowledge: Further Essays in Interpretive Anthropology*. New York: Basic Books

– 1988. *Works and Lives: The Anthropologist as Author*. Stanford: Stanford University Press

Genovese, Eugene. 1976. *Roll Jordan Roll: The World the Slaves Made*. New York: Vintage Books

Gerber, Albert B. 1965. *Sex, Pornography, and Justice*. New York: Lyle Stuart

– 1967. *Art and Culture*. New York: Beacon

– 1977. 'Looking for the Avant-Garde.' 52(3) *Arts Magazine* 86–7

– 1980. 'Modern and Post-Modern.' 54(6) *Arts Magazine* 64–6

Giddens, Anthony. 1976. *New Rules of Sociological Method*. New York: Basic Books

– 1979. *Central Problems in Social Theory*. London: Macmillan

– 1981. *A Contemporary Critique of Historical Materialism*. Berkeley: University of California Press

– 1982. *Profiles and Critiques in Social Theory*. Berkeley: University of California Press

– 1984. *The Constitution of Society*. Berkeley: University of California Press

– 1987. 'Structuralism, Post-Structuralism and the Production of Culture.' In A. Giddens and J.H. Turner, eds., *Social Theory Today*. Cambridge: Polity Press

Giffen, James P., and Sylvia Lambert. 1988. 'What Happened on the Way to Law Reform?' in Judith C. Blackwell and Patricia G. Erickson, eds., *Illicit Drugs in Canada: A Risky Business*. Toronto: Nebon

Golding, Sue. 1992. *Gramsci's Democratic Theory: Contributions to a Post-Liberal Democracy*. Toronto: University of Toronto Press

Gordon, Bette. 1984. 'Variety: The Pleasure in Looking.' In C.S. Vance, ed., *Pleasure and Danger: Exploring Female Sexuality*. Boston: Routledge and Kegan Paul

Gordon, Colin, ed. 1980. *Power/Knowledge: Selected Interviews and Other Writings 1972–1977*. New York: Pantheon Books

Gordon, Linda. 1976. *Woman's Body, Woman's Right: A Social History of Birth Control in America*. New York: Grossman

Gramsci, Antonio. 1971. *Selections from the Prison Notebooks*. Quinton Hoare and Geoffrey Nowell Smith, eds. New York: International Publishers

Gray, Susan H. 1982. 'Exposure to Porn and Aggression Toward Women.' 29(4) *Social Problems* 387–98

Greenberg, Clement. 1961. 'Modernist Painting.' *Arts Yearbook* (no. 4) 48–67

Greenspan, Edward L. 1987. Correspondence to the Canadian Civil Liberties Association re the potential vulnerability of library personnel to Bill C–54

Gronau, Anna. 1984. 'Censorship Caught in the Crossfire.' 9(3) *Parallelogramme* 42–44

– 1985. 'Women and Images: Toward a Feminist Analysis of Censorship.' In V. Burstyn, ed., *Women against Censorship*. Vancouver: Douglas and McIntyre

Guenther, Len. 1988. 'Economic Policy Making and State Capacity.' 26 *Studies in Political Economy* 149–72

Gusfield, Joseph. 1968. 'On Legislating Morals: The Symbolic Process of Designating Deviance.' 56(1) *California Law Review* 54–73

– 1981a. *The Culture of Public Problems: Drinking-Driving and the Symbolic Order*. Chicago: University of Chicago Press

– 1981b. 'Social Movements and Social Change: Perspectives of Linearity and Fluidity.' In L. Kriesberg, ed., *Research in Social Movements, Conflict and Change*. Greenwich: Jay Press

– 1984. 'On the Side: Practical Action and Social Constructivism in Social Problems Theory.' In Joseph W. Schneider and John I. Kitsuse, eds., *Studies in the Sociology of Social Problems*. Norwood, N.J.: Ablex Publishing Corporation

- 1989. 'Constructing the Ownership of Social Problems: Fun and Profit in the Welfare State.' 36(5) *Social Problems* 431–41

Hall, Peter. 1986. *Governing the Economy: The Politics of State Intervention in Britain and France*. New York: Oxford University Press

Hall, Stuart. 1979. 'The Great Moving Right Show.' 23(1) *Marxism Today* 14–20

Hall, Stuart, et al. 1978. *Policing the Crisis: Mugging, the State, and Law and Order*. London: Macmillan

Harker, Richard, C. Mahar, and C. Wilkes, eds. 1990. *An Introduction to the Work of Pierre Bourdieu: The Practice of Theory*. London: Macmillan

Hart, Herbert Lionel Adolphus. 1963. *Law, Liberty, and Morality*. Stanford: Stanford University Press

Hartley, Nina. 1987. 'Confessions of a Feminist Porno Star.' In F. Delacoste and P. Alexander, eds., *Sex Work: Writings by Women in the Sex Industry*. San Fransisco: Cleis Press

Hawkins, Gordon, and Franklin E. Zimring. 1988. *Pornography in a Free Society*. Cambridge: Cambridge University Press

Hébert, Jacques. 1970. *Obscénité et Liberté*. Montréal: Editions du Jour

Heller, T. 1984. 'Structuralism and Critique.' 36 *Stanford Law Review* 127–98

Hendrix, Gordon. 1972. *Origins of the American Film*. New York: Arno Press

Herman, Didi. 1993. 'Beyond the Rights Debate.' 2 *Social and Legal Studies* 25–43

Herrnstein Smith, Barbara. *Contingencies of Value: Alternative Perspectives for Critical Theory*. Cambridge: Harvard University Press

Hilsden, Hudson T. n.d.. 'Pornography: A Blight on Society and What We Can Do About It.' Statement from the Pentecostal Assemblies of Canada

Hoy, David Couzens. 1985. 'Interpreting the Law: Hermeneutical and Poststructuralist Perspectives,' 58 *Southern California Law Review* 135–76

- 1986a. 'Power, Repression, Progress: Foucault, Lukes and the Frankfurt School.' In D.C. Hoy, ed., *Foucault: A Critical Reader*. Oxford and New York: B. Blackwell

- 1986b. *Foucault: A Critical Reader*. Oxford and New York: B. Blackwell

Hughes, D.A. 1970. *Perspective on Pornography*. New York: St Martin's Press

Hunt, Alan. 1990. 'Rights and Social Movements: Counter-Hegemonic Strategies.' 17 *Journal of Law and Society* 309–28

Hunter, Ian A. 1976. 'Working Paper 10: Limits of the Criminal Law: Obscenity – A Test Case.' 8 *Ottawa Law Review* 299–321

Hyde, Montgomery H. 1964. *A History of Pornography*. London: Heinemann

Ignatieff, Michael. 1983. 'State, Civil Society and Total Institutions: A Critique of Recent Social Histories of Punishment.' In Stanley Cohen and Andrew T. Scull, eds., *Social Control and the State*. Oxford: Martin Robertson

Ince, Susan. 1982. 'Pornography – Good Questions, Wrong Answers.' 3(34) *Aegis* 66

Inglis, Dorothy. 1983. 'Pornography: Newfoundland Women Fight Back.' 8(3) *Status of Women News* 15–18

Interchurch Committee on Pornography. 1986a. 'Statement of Principle and Recommendations in Relation to Pornography: A Response to the Report of the Special Committee on Pornography and Prostitution.' March

– 1986b. 'A Response to the Report of the Special Committee on Pornography and Prostitution.' (February)

– 1987a. 'Pornography: Myths, Facts.' (leaflet) (March)

– 1987b. 'Liberty, Artistic Merit and "Dirty Pictures": A Critical Analysis of the New Pornography Bill.' Prepared by Robert D. Nadeau, 26 May

– n.d. 'Future Direction for ICCP.' (leaflet)

Iser, Wolfgang. 1978. *The Act of Reading: A Theory of Aesthetic Response*, Baltimore: Johns Hopkins University Press

Jaggar, Alison. 1983. *Feminist Politics and Human Nature*. Sussex: Harvester Press

Jeffreys, Sheila. 1982. 'Free from All Uninvited Touch of Man.' 5(6) *Women's Studies International Forum* 629–54

Jessop, Bob. 1982. *The Capitalist State*. Oxford: Martin Robertson

Kairys, David, ed. 1982. *The Politics of Law: A Progressive Critique*. New York: Pantheon Books

Kaplan, E. Ann. 1983. 'Is the Gaze Male?' In Ann Snitow et al., eds., *Powers of Desire: The Politics of Sexuality*. New York: Monthly Review Press

Katz, Michael. 1968. *The Ironies of Early School Reform*. Cambridge: Harvard University Press

Kealey, Linda, ed. 1979. *'A Not Unreasonable Claim': Women and Reform in Canada, 1880–1920*. Toronto: Women's Press

Keating, Charles H. Jr. 1971. 'Keating, Charles H. Jr.,' in *For or Against Censorship*. New York: Hart Publishing Company

Kellough, Gail. 1990. 'The Abortion Controversy: A Study of Law, Culture and Social Change.' PhD thesis, University of Toronto

Kelly, K. 1985. Testimony presented to the Houston hearings of the Attorney-General's Commission on Pornography, Houston, Texas (September)

Kendrick, Walter. 1987. *The Secret Museum: Pornography in Modern Culture*. New York: Viking

King, Lynn. 1985. 'Censorship and Law Reform: Will Changing the Laws Mean a Change for the Better?' In V. Burstyn, ed., *Women Against Censorship*. Vancouver: Douglas and McIntyre

King, Lynn, and Anna Gronau. 1984. 'Critique of Current and Proposed Censorship Legislation in Ontario.' Caro Publications (June)

Kinsey, Alfred Charles. 1948. *Sexual Behavior in the Human Male*. Philadelphia: W.B. Saunders

Kinsey (A.C.) Institute for Sex Research. 1953. *Sexual Behavior in the Human Female*. Philadelphia: Saunders

Kinsman, Gary. 1983. 'Porn Beyond the Impasse.' *Pink Ink* (August) 18–21

– 1985. 'Porn/Censor Wars and the Battlefields of Sex.' In A Space, *Issues of Censorship*. Toronto: Our Times Publishing

– 1987. *The Regulation of Desire: Sexuality in Canada*. Montreal: Black Rose Press

Kivisild, Emma. 1986. 'The Great Sex Debates.' *Kinesis* (October) 20–1

Kritzman, Lawrence D., ed. 1988. *Politics, Philosophy, Culture: Interviews and Other Writings 1977–1984*. (Michel Foucault). New York: Routledge Chapman and Hall

Kronhausen, Eberhard, and Phyllis Kronhausern. 1964. *Pornography and the Law: The Psychology of Erotic Realism and Pornography*, 2d ed. New York: Ballantine Books

Kuhn, A. 1982. *Women's Pictures*. London: Routledge and Kegan Paul

– 1985. *The Power of the Image*. London: Routledge and Kegan Paul

Lacan, Jacques. 1966. *Ecrits*. Paris: Editions du Seuil

Laclau, Ernesto, and Chantal Mouffe. 1985. *Hegemony and Socialist Strategy: Towards a Radical Democratic Politics*. London: Verso.

– 1987. 'Post-Marxism Without Apologies.' 166 *New Left Review* (November–December) 79–106

Lacombe, Dany. 1984. 'Two Views on the Oppression of Women: The Limitations of Marxist and Radical Feminist Perspectives.' 6(2) *Canadian Criminology Forum* 165–76

– 1988. *Ideology and Public Policy: The Case Against Pornography*. Toronto: Garamond Press

– 1990. '*Pornography and the Sex Crisis*, by Susan G. Cole' (book review). 17(2) *Critical Sociology* 123–8

– 1993. 'Un genre troublé: le féminisme, la pornographie, la réforme du droit et la thèse de la reproduction de l'ordre social.' 16(3) *Déviance et Société* 239–61

– 1993. 'Les liaisons dangereuses: Foucault et la Criminologie.' 26(1) *Criminologie* 51–72

Lahey, Kathleen A. 1984. 'The Canadian Charter of Rights and Pornography: Toward a Theory of Actual Gender Equality.' 20(4) *New England Law Review* 649–85

Lambert, J.L. 1981. 'Pornography – Censorship – Report on the Williams Committee.' 59 *Canadian Bar Review* 423–37

Landau, Reva. 1986. 'Pornography: Differences in Viewpoints, Differences in Strategies.' Paper prepared for the Ontario Status of Woman Council

Latour, Bruno. 1988. *The Pasteurization of France*. Cambridge: Harvard University Press

Latour, Bruno, and Steve Woolgar. 1979. *Laboratory Life: The Social Construction of Scientific Facts*. Beverly Hills: Sage Publications

Lauretis, Teresa de. 1984. *Alice Doesn't: Feminism, Semiotics, Cinema*. Bloomington: Indiana University Press

– 1987. *Technologies of Gender: Essays on Theory, Film and Fiction*. Bloomington: Indiana University Press

Law Reform Commission of Canada. 1975. *Limits of the Criminal Law: Obscenity – A Test Case*. Working Paper 10. Ottawa: LRCC

Lederer, Laura, ed. 1980. *Take Back the Night: Women on Pornography*. New York: Bantam Books

Lefort, Claude. 1986. *The Political Forms of Modern Society: Bureaucracy, Democracy, Totalitarianism*. John B. Thompson, ed. Cambridge: MIT Press

– 1988. *Democracy and Political Theory*. David Macey, trans. Minneapolis: University of Minnesota Press

Leiser, Burton M. 1979. *Liberty, Justice, and Morals: Contemporary Value Conflicts*. 2d ed. New York: Macmillan

Leong, Wai-Teng. 1991. 'The Pornography "Problem": Disciplining Women and Young Girls.' 13 *Media, Culture and Society* 91–117

Lesbock, Suzanne. 1984. *The Free Women of Petersburg: Status and Culture in a Southern Town, 1784–1860*. New York: Norton

Levinson, S. 1982. 'Law as Literature.' 60 *Texas Law Review* 373–404

Lloyd, Denis. 1956. 'Obscenity and the Law.' 9 *Current Legal Problems* 75–95

Lockhart, William B., and Robert C. McClure. 1954. 'Literature, the Law of Obscenity and the Constitution.' 38(4) *Minnesota Law Review* 295–395

Lowman, John. 1985. 'Vancouver Field Study of Prostitution, Research Notes.' 2 vols., Working Paper no. 8, Special Committee on Pornography and Prostitution. Ottawa: Ministry of Supply and Services

Lowman, John, et al., eds. 1987. *Regulating Sex*. Burnaby: School of Criminology, Simon Fraser University

Lutes, Robert. 1974. 'Obscenity Law in Canada.' 3 *University of New Brunswick Law Journal* 30–52

Lyotard, Jean-François. 1984. *The Postmodern Condition: A Report on Knowledge*. Minneapolis: University of Minnesota Press

McBarnett, D. 1981. *Conviction: Law, the State and the Construction of Justice*. London: Macmillan

McCormack, Thelma. 1978. 'A Critical Review of Research on Violence and Pornography.' 25 *Social Problems* 544–55

– 1985. 'Making Sense of the Research on Pornography.' In V. Burstyn, ed., *Women Against Censorship*. Vancouver: Douglas and McIntyre

Macdonald, Donald. 1985. 'Pornography.' *Current Issue Review*. Reviewed 22 May 1987. Ottawa: Library of Parliament, May

McDonald, Lynn. 1983. 'Censorship and the New Pornography.' *Canadian Forum* (May) 36–7

MacDowall, Cyndra. 1985. 'The Struggle Over Freedom of Expression.' in A Space, *Issues of Censorship*. Toronto: Our Times Publishing

MacKay, R.S. 1958. 'The Hicklin Rule and Judicial Censorship.' 36 *Canadian Bar Review* 1–24

MacKinnon, Catharine. 1987. *Feminism Unmodified*. Cambridge: Harvard University Press

- 1988. 'Desire and Power: A Feminist Perspective.' In Cary Nelson and Lawrence Grossberg. eds. *Marxism and the Interpretation of Culture.* Urbana: University of Illinois Press

McLaren, John. 1986. 'The Fraser Committee: The Politics and Process of a Special Committee.' In J. Lowman et al., eds., *Regulating Sex.* Burnaby: School of Criminology, Simon Fraser University

MacMillan, P.R. 1983. *Censorship and Public Morality.* Aldershot: Gower

Macpherson, C.B. 1962. *The Political Theory of Possessive Individualism: Hobbes to Locke.* Oxford: Oxford University Press

- 1977. *The Life and Times of Liberal Democracy.* Oxford: Oxford University Press

Mailloux, Steven. 1982. *Interpretive Conventions: The Reader in the Study of American Fiction.* Ithaca: Cornell University Press

Malamuth, Neil, and James V.P. Check. 1981. 'The Effects of Mass Media Exposure on Acceptance of Violence Against Women: A Field Experiment.' 15 *Journal of Research in Personality* 436–46

Malamuth, Neil, and Edward Donnerstein. 1983. 'The Effects of Aggressive Pornographic Mass Media Stimuli.' In L. Berkowitz, ed., *Advances in Experimental Social Psychology.* New York: Academic Press

Malamuth, Neil, and Edward Donnerstein, eds. 1984. *Pornography and Sexual Aggression.* Orlando: Academic Press

Mandel, Michael. 1989. *The Charter of Rights and the Legalization of Politics in Canada.* Toronto: Wall and Thompson

Manion, Eileen. 1985. 'We Objects Object: Pornography and the Women's Movement.' 9(1–2) *Canadian Journal of Political and Social Theory* 65–80

Marchiano, Linda, and Michael McGrady. 1980. *Ordeal.* Secaucus: L. Stuart

- 1986. *Out of Bondage.* Secaucus: L. Stuart

Marcuse, Herbert. 1962. *Eros and Civilization: A Philosophical Inquiry into Freud.* New York: Vintage Books

Masters, William H., and Virginia E. Johnson. 1966. *Human Sexual Response.* Boston: Little, Brown

Mayer, John A. 1983. 'Notes Towards a Working Definition of Social Control in Historical Analysis.' In Stanley Cohen and Andrew T. Scull, eds., *Social Control and the State.* Oxford: Martin Robertson

Mayne, Judith. 1985. 'Feminist Film Theory and Criticism.' 11(1) *Signs: A Journal of Women in Culture and Society* 81–93

Melossi, D., and M. Pavarini. 1981. *The Prison and the Factory: The Origins of the Penitentiary System.* London: Macmillan

Metro Action Committe on Public Violence Against Women and
  Children (METRAC).
– 1987. 'Thinking About Civil Remedies for Women Harmed Through
  Pornography.' Prepared by Susan G. Cole
Mill, John Stuart. 1947. *On Liberty*. New York: F.S. Crofts
Millett, Kate. 1969. *Sexual Politics*. Toronto: Random House
Mitchell, W.J.T., ed. 1983. *The Politics of Interpretation*. Chicago: Uni-
  versity of Chicago Press
Morgan, Robin. 1977. *Going Too Far: The Personal Chronicle of a Fem-
  inist*. New York: Random House
Mosher, D.L. 1985. 'Freedom of Inquiry and Scientific Consensus on
  Pornography.' Presented at the Houston hearings of the Attorney
  General's Commission on Pornography, Houston, Texas
– 1986. 'Misinformation on Pornography: A Lobby Disguised as an Educational Organization.' *Sex Information and Educational Council of
  the United States (SIECUS) Report*, vol. 14, 7–10
Mouffe, Chantal. 1988a. 'Hegemony and New Political Subjects: Toward
  a New Concept of Democracy.' In Casy Nelson and Laurence Grossberg, eds., *Marxism and the Interpretation of Culture*. Urbana: University of Illinois Press
– 1988b. 'Radical Democracy: Modern or Postmodern.' In Andrew Ross.
  ed., *Universal Abandon? The Politics of Postmodernism*. Minneapolis:
  University of Minnesota Press
Mouffe, Chantal, ed. 1992. *Dimensions of Radical Democracy: Pluralism, Citizenship, Community*. London: Verso

National Action Committee on the Status of Women (NAC). 1983a.
  'Discussion Paper on Pornography.' Prepared by Jillian Ridington
  (March)
– 1983b. Letter to Members of the Metropolitan Legislation and Licens-
  ing Committee. Toronto: NAC
– 1983c. Memo. Toronto: NAC
– 1984. 'Brief to The Special Committee on Pornography and Prostitution.' Prepared by the Executive (February)
– 1985. 'Presented to the Federal Government (Justice Department) in
  Response to the Discussion Paper and Consultations on the Fraser
  Committee Report and Recommendations on Pornography.' Prepared
  by Donna Stephania (October)
– 1987. 'NAC Policy Resolutions on Pornography, 1983–1987.'
– 1988. 'Brief to the House of Commons Justice Committee on Bill
  C–54.' Prepared by Kate Andrew and Debra J. Lewis (February)

– 1983–88. *Status of Women News*
Nobile, Philip. 1979. 'Pornography Tough to Define.' Interview with
  Susan Brownmiller in *Iowa City Press Citizen*, 15 January
Norris, Christopher. 1982. *Deconstruction: Theory and Practice*. London
  and New York: Methuen
– 1983. *The Deconstruction Turn: Essays on the Rhetoric of Philosophy*.
  London and New York: Methuen
– 1985. *The Contest of Faculties: Philosophies and Theory After Deconstruction*. London and New York: Methuen
– 1988b. *Deconstruction and the Interests of Theory*. London:
  Pinter

Oakeshott, Michael. 1967. *Rationalism in Politics*. London: Methuen
Ontario Advisory Council on the Status of Women. 1984. 'Pornography
  and Prostitution.' (April)
Ontario Film and Video Appreciation Society. 1984a. 'A Brief to the
  Special Committee on Pornography and Prostitution.' Caro Publica-
  tions (May)
– 1984b. 'Critique of Current and Proposed Censorship Legislation in
  Ontario.' Prepared by Lynn King and Anna Gronau
Ontario Status of Women Council. 1979. 'Pornography and Its Effects: A
  Survey of Recent Literature.' Prepared by Jennifer Robertson
Orlando, Lise. 1983. 'Power Plays: Coming to Terms with Lesbian S/M.'
  Village Voice, 26 July

Palys, T.S., and J. Lowman. 1984. 'Methodological Meta-Issues in Por-
  nography Research: Ecological Representativeness and Contextual
  Integrity.' Paper presented at the meeting of the Canadian Psychologi-
  cal Association, Ottawa
Pearson, Geoffrey. 1983. *Hooligan: A History of Respectable Fears*. Lon-
  don: Macmillan
Peller, G. 1985. 'The Metaphysics of American Law.' 73 *California Law
  Review* 1151–1290
Petchesky, Rosalind Pollack. 1984. *Abortion and Woman's Choice: The
  State, Sexuality, and Reproductive Freedom*. Boston: Northeastern
  University Press
Peterson, David R. 1984a. 'Conference on Pornography.' *Ontario Lib-
  erals Communique*, 3 February
– 1984b. 'Statement by David R. Peterson to the Special Committee on
  Pornography and Prostitution.' *Ontario Liberals Communique*, 8 Feb-
  ruary

Platt, Anthony M. 1969. *The Child Savers: The Invention of Delin-quency*. Chicago: University of Chicago Press

Posner, Judith. 1983. 'Advertising Pornography.' *Canadian Forum* (August–September) 12–16

Posner, Richard A. 1988. *Law and Literature: A Misunderstood Relation*. Cambridge: Cambridge University Press

Poster, R.M. 1985. 'Interpreting Texts: Some New Directions.' 58 *Southern California Law Review* 15–18

Prentice, Alison. 1975. 'The feminization of Teaching in British North America and Canada, 1845–1875.' 8 *Histoire Sociale* 5–20

Prentice, Alison, and Susan Trofimenkoff, eds. 1985. *The Neglected Majority: Essays in Canadian Women's History*. Toronto: Women's Press

Price, David. 1979. 'The Role of Choice in a Definition of Obscenity.' 57 *Canadian Bar Review* 301–4

Prince, Michael. 1987. 'How Ottawa Decides Social Policy: Recent Changes in Philosophy, Structure, and Process.' In J.S. Ismael, ed., *The Canadian Welfare State: Evolution and Transition*. Edmonton: University of Alberta Press

Rabinow, Paul, ed. 1984. *The Foucault Reader*. New York: Pantheon

Rabinow, Paul, and W.M. Sullivan, eds. 1979. *Interpretive Social Science: A Reader*. Berkeley: University of California Press

Ratner, R.S., and J.L. McMullan, eds. 1987. *State Control: Criminal Justice Politics in Canada*. Vancouver: University of British Columbia Press

Rawls, John. 1971. *A Theory of Justice*. Oxford: Oxford University Press

R.E.A.L. Women of Canada. 1984a. 'Submission of the R.E.A.L. Women of Canada to the Special Committee on Pornography and Prostitution.' (February)

– 1984b. 2(2) *Reality*

– 1985a. 'Brief to Members of Parliament.' (19 November)

– 1985b. 3(3) *Reality*

– 1985c. 'Easy Divorce?' (leaflet)

– 1985d. 'Feminism and Its Canadian Connection.' (leaflet)

– 1986. 'Brief to Members of Parliament.' (18 November)

– 1987. 5(1) *Reality*

– n.d.a. 'Pornography (Bill C–54).' Brief to the Standing Parliamentary Committee on Justice

– n.d.b. 'What Is Pornography?' (leaflet)

Reich, Wilhelm. 1961. *The Function of the Orgasm: Sex-Economic Problems of Biological Energy.* New York: Noonday Press

Rembar, Charles. 1969. *The End of Obscenity: The Trials of 'Lady Chatterley,' 'Tropic of Cancer,' and 'Fanny Hill.'* London: Deutsch

Resources Against Pornography. n.d.. 'The Facts About Bill C–54'

Ricoeur, Paul. 1981. *Hermeneutics and the Human Sciences: Essays on Language, Action, and Interpretation.* Cambridge: Cambridge University Press; Paris: Editions de la Maison des Sciences de l'Homme

Rist, Ray C., ed. 1975. *The Pornography Controversy: Changing Moral Standards in American Life.* New Brunswick: Transaction Books

Robertson, Clive. 1981. 'Less Screening, More Trouble.' Fuse (May–June) 120–1

Rock, Paul. 1986. *A View From the Shadows: The Ministry of the Solicitor General of Canada and the Making of the Justice for Victims of Crime Initiative.* Oxford: Clarendon Press; New York: Oxford University Press

– 1988. 'Governments, Victims and Policies in Two Countries.' 28(1) *British Journal of Criminology* 44–66

Rolph, C.H., ed. *Does Pornography Matter?* London: Routledge and Kegan Paul

Rosaldo, R. 1989. *Culture and Truth: The Remaking of Social Analysis.* Boston: Beacon Press

Ross, Andrew. 1989. *No Respect: Intellectuals and Popular Culture.* New York: Routledge

Ross, Andrew, ed. 1988. *Universal Abandon? The Politics of Postmodernism.* Minneapolis: University of Minnesota Press

Rothman, David J. 1983. 'Social Control: The Uses and Abuses of the Concept in the History of Incarceration.' In Stanley Cohen and Andrew T. Scull, eds., *Social Control and the State.* Oxford: Martin Robertson

Rubin, Gayle. 1984. 'Thinking Sex: Notes for a Radical Theory of the Politics of Sexuality.' In C.S. Vance, ed., *Pleasure and Danger: Exploring Female Sexuality.* Boston: Routledge and Kegan Paul

Russell, Diana E.H. 1980. 'Pornography and Violence: What Does the New Research Say?' In Laura Lederer, ed., *Take Back the Night: Women Against Pornography.* New York: Bantam Books

Russell, Diana E.H., and Nicole Van de Ven. 1976. *Crimes Against Women.* California: Les Femmes

Russell, John, ed. 1989. *Liberties.* Vancouver: New Star Books

Rutledge, Denys. 1961. 'Dom Denys Rutledge.' In C.H. Rolph, ed., *Does Pornography Matter?* London: Routledge and Kegan Paul

St John-Stevas, Norman. 1954. 'Obscenity and the Law.' *Criminal Law Review* 817–33
– 1964. *Law and Morals.* New York: Hawthorne Books
Samois. 1979. *What Color Is Your Handkerchief?* Berkeley: Samois
– 1982. *Coming to Power.* Boston: Alyson
Saussure, Ferdinand de. 1966. *Course in General Linguistics.* C. Bally and A. Sechehaye, eds. W. Baskin, trans. New York: McGraw-Hill
Scheppele, Kim Lane. 1987. 'The Re-Vision of Rape Law.' 54 *University of Chicago Law Review* 1095–1116
Schneider, Joseph W., and John I. Kitsuse, eds. 1984. *Studies in the Sociology of Social Problems.* Norwood, N.J.: Ablex Publishing Corporation
Scull, Andrew T. 1979. *Museums of Madness.* London: Allen Lane
Segal, Lynn. 1993. 'Does Pornography Cause Violence? The Search for Evidence.' In P. Church Gibson and R. Gibson, eds., *Dirty Looks: Women, Pornography, Power.* London: British Film Institute Publishing
Shearing, Clifford D., and Philip C. Stenning. 1984. 'From the Panopticon to Disney World: The Development of Discipline.' In A.N. Doob and E. Greenspan, eds., *Perspectives in Criminal Law: Essays in Honour of John Ll.J. Edwards.* Aurora: Canada Law Book
Sheridan, Alan. 1980. *Michel Foucault: The Will to Truth.* London and New York: Tavistock Publications
Six Days of Resistance Against the Censor Board. 1985. 'Action Kit.' Toronto
Small, Neil. 1988. 'AIDS and Social Policy.' 21 *Critical Social Policy* 9–29
Smart, Barry. 1983. *Foucault, Marxism and Critique.* London: Routledge and Kegan Paul
– 1986. 'The Politics of Truth and the Problem of Hegemony.' In David Couzens Hoy, ed., *Foucault: A Critical Reader.* Oxford: B. Blackwell
Smart, Carol. 1989. *Feminism and the Power of Law.* London: Routledge
Smith, Dorothy. 1987. *The Everyday World as Problematic: A Feminist Sociology.* Toronto: University of Toronto Press
– 1990. *Texts, Facts, and Femininity: Exploring the Relations of Ruling.* New York: Routledge
Smith, Paul. 1988. *Discerning the Subject.* Minneapolis: University of Minnesota Press

Snitow, Ann. 1979. 'Mass Market Romance: Pornography for Women is Different.' 20 *Radical History Review* 141–61

– 1983. 'Mass Market Romance: Pornography for Women Is Different.' In Ann Snitow, Christine Stansell, and Sharon Thompson, eds., *Powers of Desire: The Politics of Sexuality.* New York: Monthly Review Press

Snitow, A., C. Stansell, and S. Thompson. 1983. *Powers of Desire: The Politics of Sexuality.* New York: Monthly Review Press

Soble, Alan. 1986. *Pornography: Marxism, Feminism, and the Future of Sexuality.* New Haven: Yale University Press

Soper, Donald 1961. 'Rev Dr Donald Soper.' In C.H. Rolph, ed., *Does Pornography Matter?* London: Routledge and Kegan Paul

Steele, Lisa. 1981a. 'Feminist Research: Interview with Five Women Who Are Actively Constructing the Links Between Theory and Practice.' *Fuse* (May–June) 152–61

– 1981b. 'The Decline and Faults of Ontario's Empire.' *Fuse* (August–September) 191–2

– 1981c. 'Censored! Only in Canada.' *Fuse* (November–December) 274–5

– 1982. 'Pornography and Eroticism: Feminist Varda Burstyn Talks About Sexuality and the Representation of Women in Film.' *Fuse* (May–June) 19–24

– 1983a. 'Freedom, Sex and Power: Interview with Charlotte Bunch.' *Fuse* (January–February) 233–7

– 1983b. 'Freedom, Sex and Power: Interview with Gary Kinsman.' *Fuse* (January–February) 243–6

– 1983c. 'Freedom, Sex and Power: Interview with Susan G. Cole.' *Fuse* (January–February) 247–54

– 1983d. 'Freedom, Sex and Power: Interview with Varda Burstyn.' *Fuse* (January–February) 251–4

– 1983e. 'Snakes and Ladders: Feminism in the Media.' *Fuse* (September–October) 80–2

– 1985. 'A Capital Idea: Gendering in the Mass Media.' In V. Burstyn, ed., *Women Against Censorship.* Vancouver: Douglas and McIntyre

Stehr, N. 1992. 'The Culture and Power of Knowledge: Experts, Counsellors and Advisors.' In N. Stehr and R.V. Ericson, eds., *The Culture and Power of Knowledge.* Berlin and New York: de Gruyter

Steinem, Gloria. 1978. 'Erotica and Pornography: A Clear and Present Difference.' *Ms.* (November) 54–5

Sundahl, Debi. 1987. 'Stripper.' In F. Delacoste and P. Alexander, eds.,

Sex Work: Writings by Women in the Sex Industry. San Francisco: Cleis Press

Taylor, Barbara. 1981. 'Female Vice and Feminist Virtue.' *New Statesman* (23 January) 16–17

Taylor, Ian. 1980. 'The Law and Order Issue in the British General Election and the Canadian Federal Election of 1979: Crime, Populism and the State.' 5(3) *Canadian Journal of Sociology* 285–311

Thomas, Donald. 1969. *A Long Time Burning: The History of Literary Censorship in England.* London: Routledge and Kegan Paul

Toronto Public Library Board. 1988. 'Brief to the Legislative Committee on Bill C–54.'

Turner, Bryan S. 1990. 'Outline of a Theory of Citizenship.' 24(2) *Sociology* 189–217

United Church of Canada Committee on Pornography. 1986. 'A Response to the Report of the Special Committee on Pornography and Prostitution.' (February) Vancouver

United States. Commission on Obscenity and Pornography. 1970. *The Report.* New York: Bantam Books

United States. Attorney General's Commission on Pornography. 1986. *Attorney General's Commission on Pornography: Final Report.* Washington: Department of Justice

Valverde, Mariana. 1980. 'Feminism Meets Fist-Fucking: Getting Lost in Lesbian S & M.' *Body Politic* (February) 43

– 1985. *Sex, Power and Pleasure.* Toronto: Women's Press

– 1989. 'Beyond Gender Dangers and Private Pleasures: Theory and Ethics in the Sex Debates.' 15(2) *Feminist Studies* 237–55

Vance, Carole S. 1984. *Pleasure and Danger: Exploring Female Sexuality.* Boston: Routledge and Kegan Paul

Victoria Civil Liberties Association. 1987. 'A Brief Concerning Proposed Amendments to the Canadian Criminal Code Respecting Sexual Depictions.' Prepared by Tom Gore. (July)

Walkowitz, Judith R. 1980. *Prostitution and Victorian Society: Women, Class, and the State.* Cambridge: Cambridge University Press

– 1982. 'Male Vice and Feminist Virtue: Feminism and the Politics of Prostitution in Nineteeth Century Britain.' 13 *History Workshop* 77–93

Wallis, Brian, ed. 1984. *Art After Modernism: Rethinking Representation*. New York: New Museum of Contemporary Art

Waring, Nancy W. 1986. 'Coming to Terms with Pornography: Toward a Feminist Perspective on Sex, Censorship, and Hysteria.' 8 *Research in Law, Deviance and Social Control* 85–112

Wasserstrom, Richard A., ed. 1971. *Morality and the Law*. Belmont, Cal.: Wadsworth Publishing Co

Watney, Simon. 1987. *Policing Desire: Pornography, AIDS and the Media*. London: Methuen

Webster, Paula. 1981. 'Pornography and Pleasure.' 3(4) *Heresies* 48–51

Weeks, Jeffrey. 1977. *Coming Out: Homosexual Politics in Britain from the Nineteenth Century to the Present*. London: Quartet Books

– 1981. *Sex, Politics and Society: The Regulation of Sexuality since 1800*. New York: Longman

– 1985. *Sexuality and Its Discontents: Meanings, Myths and Modern Sexualities*. London: Routledge and Kegan Paul

– 1986. *Sexuality*. Chichester: Ellis Horwood

– 1991. *Against Nature: Essays on History, Sexuality and Identity*. London: Rivers Oram Press

Weiler, Joseph. 1971. 'Controlling Obscenity by Criminal Sanction.' 9 *Osgoode Hall Law Journal* 415–32

Weir, Lorna. 1987. 'Socialist Feminism and the Politics of Sexuality.' In H.J. Maroney and M. Luxton, eds., *Feminism and Political Economy: Women's Work, Women's Struggles*. Toronto: Methuen

Whitmore, Harry. 1963. 'Obscenity in Literature: Crime or Free Speech.' 4 *Sydney Law Review* 179–204

Williams, Linda. 1989. *Hard Core: Power, Pleasure, and the 'Frenzy of the Visible.'* Berkeley: University of California Press

Williams, P.J. 1987. 'Alchemical Notes: Reconstructing Ideals from Deconstructed Rights.' 22 *Harvard Civil Rights–Civil Liberties Law Review* 401–33

Williams, Raymond. 1973. *The Country and the City*. London: Chatto and Windus

– 1977. *Marxism and Literature*. Oxford: Oxford University Press

Willis, Ellen. 1983. 'Feminism, Moralism, and Pornography.' In A. Snitow et al., eds., *Powers of Desire: The Politics of Sexuality*. New York: Monthly Review Press

Wilson, Elizabeth. 1982. 'Interview with Andrea Dworkin.' 11 *Feminist Review* 23–9

- 1983. 'The Context of "Between Pleasure and Danger": The Barnard Conference on Sexuality.' 13 *Feminist Review* 35–41

Windsor Coalition Against Pornography. 1983. 'Letter to Minister of Justice Mark MacGuigan.'

Winship, Janice. 1982. 'Book Review of *Pornography: Men Possessing Women* by A. Dworkin and *Pornography and Silence: Culture's Revenge Against Nature* by S. Griffin.' 11 *Feminist Review* 97–100

Wittgenstein, Ludwig. 1953. *Philosophical Investigations*. G.E.M. Anscombe, trans. Oxford: Blackwell

Working Group on Sexual Violence (British Columbia). 1986. 'The Pornography Paper.' (August)

Writer's Union of Canada. 1984. 'Statement on Pornography'

Zillman, Dolf. 1971. 'Excitation Transfer in Communication-Mediated Aggressive Behavior.' 7 *Journal of Experimental Social Psychology* 419–34

Index